# SO BIG THE LAND

Sue Grocke

First Published in Australia by Aurora House
www.aurorahouse.com.au

This edition published 2018
Copyright © Sue Grocke 2018
Typesetting: Prepress Plus
Cover design: Simon Critchell

The right of Sue Grocke to be identified as author of the work has been asserted in accordance with the Copyright, Designs and Patents Act 1988.

ISBN number: 978-0-6483292-8-2

All rights reserved. No part of this publication may be reproduced, stored in a retrieval system, or transmitted, in any form or by any means without the prior written permission of the publisher, nor be otherwise circulated in any form of binding or cover other than that in which it is published and without a similar condition being imposed on the subsequent purchaser.

 A catalogue record for this book is available from the National Library of Australia

Distributed by:
Ingram Content:
https://www.ingramcontent.com/
Australia: phone +613 9765 4800 | email lsiaustralia@ingramcontent.com
Milton Keynes UK: phone +44 (0)845 121 4567 | email enquiries@ingramcontent.com
La Vergne, TN USA: phone 1-800-509-4156 | email inquiry@lightningsource.com

Gardners UK:
https://www.gardners.com/
phone +44 (0)1323 521555 | email: sales@gardners.com
Bertrams UK:
https://www.bertrams.com/BertWeb/index.jsp
phone +44 (0)1603 648400 | email sales@bertrams.com

*For Warren*

# ONE

The day was a scorcher. Dry and hard. Untidy mallee trees gleamed with heat extruded oils. The glare of the limestone assaulted my eyes. The summer of 'sixty-nine had come early.

We had driven that morning from home in the verdant Barossa Valley to the grey-green melange of the Murray Mallee. Warren had been working here, not constantly but as the seasons required. He was now considering converting a small limestone hut on the property into a home where he could bring his young wife and our soon-to-be-born first child, albeit periodically. He wanted the place to be fit for us.

Chattels of former owners had been left piled high in four shabby rooms – old four-poster beds, chairs, cupboards, boxes of trappings. Hessian hung at unglazed windows offering at least some darkness and relief from the heat.

Lagging with full blown pregnancy, I was tired when we arrived and flopped backwards onto a saggy bed. A cloud of dust filled the air.

Rammed earth floors had been good enough for settlers gone. Concrete would be nice, I said, pretty much to myself.

For hours we carried stuff out of the house and onto the truck, leaving only the things I considered necessary for the household – primitive as it would be.

~

Three years earlier I'd been invited on a day trip to inspect the property, which had then been for sale. Driving around the four thousand acres of mostly virgin scrub, my normally exuberant fiancé seemed tense with wondering what I'd think of the place. If I was to be his wife, how would I fare out here? I'd loved farm holidays as a child and most of my ancestors had been on the land. I told him and saw the tension dissipate.

His parents bought the spread for a pound an acre. It would be their asset but their son's proving ground.

Warren's dad was a Barossa winegrower – enterprising, deemed successful by the community. Drive of a rhinoceros. But Warren could find no heart for the vines, despite his father's hopes for him. His love lay in sheep farming and his passionate dream, even at the tender age of twenty-four, was to own three thousand acres of productive grazing land in one parcel. I knew he pictured it – himself at the helm, raising prime, contented stock – a lifestyle that would give him all he could imagine. He was now at the beginning of his endeavours towards that dream – a rich life out of an unknown landscape.

~

When the hut was all but emptied, Warren, his father and an assortment of mates with various building skills made trips to the property.

Warren had sown wheat here soon after his parents bought the block – the first time this land had been turned. Now with our son barely five weeks old, we packed ourselves and a couple of weeks' supplies into the ute and drove to the farm for a promising barley harvest. Before seatbelts, I carried my babe on my lap, filled to overflowing with love for him.

This pioneering lifestyle was new to me, but I was eager for it. Concrete floors had been poured, windows set in, walls white-washed. A kerosene fridge – till now a shelter for mice and spiders – was restored to working order. A thumping great water heater that set up a tribal drumming each time it was lit, was installed in the lean-to bathroom outside. My mother, who had experienced a rudimentary way of life as a child, came with us this time.

With my husband out all day, it was my job to collect mallee stumps for the wood stove. Normally a confident driver, I felt intimidated by the large Bedford truck I was given for the task.

"A slip of a girl behind my wheel? A baby in a basket on my seat?" it seemed to ask in this tough country for hard men. Lincoln was oblivious as his wee form rocked with the impact of rocks beneath the wheels.

The white, stony yard needed softening so my mum and I planted pelargoniums along the sun-washed northern wall of the hut. We rigged a clothes line between two trees and fashioned a strong pronged branch to lift it from the middle. I learned to manage the wood oven – how to know when it was hot enough and how to keep it that way. I discovered that gravy beef needs cooking for three hours, until it gives in.

From time to time there'd be the smell of kerosene burning – a warning that it was time to tweak the wick of the fridge. As night came in we'd fill and light the lanterns, with small reward. The flickering flames merely translated our shapes into looming shadows on the walls. The darkness outside was vast, the hush of the universe unnerving, the old-house smell evoked a time of others more adept than myself.

When Warren came in he'd light the hurricane lamp – a delicate task needing skill not to shatter the fragile mantle. As this proper lamp hissed into life, the room would expand with light and the ghosts retreat. After tea, I'd wash the dishes in a chipped enamel bowl that had been left by others, and then wonderful rest. In the absence of armchairs, we'd sit at the worn country table – chins in hands, listening to the radio, while kettles chirped over the dying fire. On nights Warren was out rabbit-shooting, Mum and I would sit like this, talking till our words grew weary. We'd had our differences, but they were behind us now. I appreciated having her with me this time.

Warren had cut down an old Chevrolet and converted it into a ute. When one of the farm implements broke down, I was asked to drive it the fifteen kilometres into town to pick up the parts needed for repairs. With baby in basket I stood beside the car, loath to get in. There were no seats, no back window. I kicked aside spanners, wrenches, farmer's tools, and placed Lincoln on the floor. I climbed in behind the wheel and sat on the seat – a kerosene drum – the fuel tank actually, ingeniously connected to the engine. I didn't know I'd signed up for this.

Before I got to the first gate we were unrecognisable with dust. I was terrified at the responsibility of being out in this labyrinth of scrub with my baby. There was a maze of tracks and I couldn't be sure I was on the right one. With several difficult gates to open and shut along the way, it was more than half an hour before I found my way out of the property and onto the road to town.

I introduced myself to the storekeeper. He'd met Warren and seemed happy now to slot us, as a couple, into the right compartment. People of the bush need to know where everyone fits. With so few of us in such a vast area, there's a sense of security in it. He had the parts Warren needed and after the five minute transaction I headed for home. I had never been so dirty.

My upbringing in town had been sheltered – predictable and secure with loving parents and siblings, and clean, pretty frocks. This isolation was a far cry. I'd begun to realise that to spend my life with this man, I'd have to find strength and courage unimagined.

Returning home to the Barossa after these stints in the bush was restorative. The comfort. The familiarity. I could breathe. I'd make a beeline for the stereogram and play the music of the hit artists of the time – Little Richard, Bill Haley, Buddy Holly.

There was a party somewhere nearly every Saturday night. I'd put on some make-up, a stunning mini-dress would replace jeans and shirt, and Warren and I would dance without restraint. Music nurtured me - my love of it kindled in earliest childhood.

~

Jazz and Swing had brought my parents together.

It had been wartime. My mother had gone out dancing with her brother and his mates – one of whom was my father, who asked her to dance. In the enchantingly lit hall rustling with gorgeous gowns, they fell for each other as they stepped to the romantic big band music. A year later they were married. Within months Dad was offered a job in an engineering business in Tanunda – one of the Barossa Valley's main towns and the town of my birth. In those early days after the end of the war, there was an atmosphere of euphoria in my world – laughter, gaiety and renewed love amongst families and friends. How people must have appreciated the simple pleasures of life again after the scarcities, terror and grief of war.

In the evenings before my bedtime, I would snuggle between my parents on a moquette-covered club lounge while Dad played the saxophone and Mum sang jazz standards. During winter, a constant fire burned in the open fireplace of this small, charming room, which was both my parents' bedroom and our sitting room.

*'I'm in the mood for love
Simply because you're near me...'*

My mother's lilting voice made me drowsy-eyed as I watched the fire spray spit and fizz. Even then, the music like sweet syrup to me.

~

With opening rains, it was time to begin sowing crops at the farm. Workers had been employed – their meals my responsibility. Each morning I'd turn a loaf of bread into hearty sandwiches and pack them into a Tupperware container. Before lunch Warren would return to pick them up, sparing me the risk of getting lost out there. Having run out of bread one day, I cooked a curry. By now I had some idea of where the men were ploughing, and after loading baby and food into the Chevy I set out, leaving the warmth and security of my kitchen behind. A blizzard of wind snapped at my face as we bounced over the scant, rocky track. On reaching the place of industry, I marvelled at the huge area of work already completed and drew in the rich smell of freshly turned earth. I placed Lincoln in a cluster of bushes and lit a fire. On stones I'd laid around the edge, I heated my pan full of beef and vegetables. The men came in. It was so cold even lunch couldn't coax them out of their great coats.

> In the shelter of the bushes round the fire we squatted
> four work-browned men and I
> too cold to talk
> and eating from enamel plates in a pioneering way.

We'd kept three iron beds with flock mattresses that were now lined up dormitory style in the back room – the workmen's quarters. Beside each bed lay a jute bag mat. An iron washstand with bowl stood neatly in the corner. Before the men came in each evening, I'd light a kerosene heater to warm their room. I was thankful for the one in our room too – a priceless luxury through the cold Mallee nights.

There were shooting expeditions. I'd lie in bed alone, listening to the crack of rifle shots in the distance, the creaking of mallee branches rubbing together, the shrieking bark of a vixen calling her cubs. Only the gentle breathing of my sleeping baby comforted me. He lay in his basket on two chairs beside me, a net over him – not to protect him from mosquitoes but mice.

The spoils of the night – to be used for dog food – were brought back to the hut where, right beside our bedroom window, the gutting and skinning took place. With adrenalin still pumping, the hunters re-lived the night's action in high, excited tones while I lay wide-eyed and rattled until the telling was done.

Each night before bed, I'd set the table for breakfast and fling a net over all. At first light, the men, having washed and sometimes shaved in a basin of water from the still warm kettles, would, with respectful and now sober quietness, stoke the fire. Thick slices of bread would be toasted over coals set aside while eggs and bacon spat and sizzled on the stove top. Being in my small kitchen with three or four rugged workmen was daunting for me, so I was pleased with the morning arrangement of having them fend for themselves. I feared any attempt I might make at conversation about their work would fail dismally. Thankfully, they seemed to understand that my knowledge of farming was still in its infancy.

I grew accustomed to the squeeching sound of corks being prised from flagons of wine as, in their quarters, the workmen primed themselves for days of lashing winter. Hard-working, salt-of-the-earth blokes, they were from the wine-growing Barossa Valley and the sweet fortified bracer like mother's milk to them.

With Warren, then, they'd set out for work and I'd get up to deal with the aftermath. I'd restore my kitchen and have breakfast. Later, in the enamel bowl, in a shaft of morning sunlight on the table, I'd splash warm water over my beautiful baby boy. I was breastfeeding and grateful to have him so content. In this man's world, I took this thin corner of motherhood delightfully for myself.

Preparing food for all was a constant task – sandwiches, cakes fresh from my wood-fired oven, and in the evenings, roasts or great pots of hearty stew or soup.

At the end of one of our stints there, I was travelling home with one of the workmen. Warren and the others had a little more to do and were coming later. Lincoln was asleep on my lap. Allan shouldn't have been driving. He'd had more than a couple of sherries. Fortunately, I knew this dirt road well and realised we were travelling much too fast to take a sharp bend just before coming into a small settlement on the River Murray.

'Allan, there's a bend,' I yelled.

He hit the brakes and yanked the steering wheel. The ute went into a slide as we took the corner two feet from the edge of a sheer thirty metre cliff with no guard rail. Faint with the knowledge of how close we'd come to death, I quietly thanked God for our lives.

# TWO

The harvest of 'seventy was a good one for the area and the proceeds were used to reduce the overdraft that had been incurred in paying for seed, fertiliser, labour, sheep and some second-hand equipment – namely two quite elderly tractors. These weren't easily started, especially the Field Marshall. A cartridge filled with gunpowder would do the trick but at a dollar a pop it was expensive, so towing it until it swung over was the preferred option. If there were no other men in camp, this was my job. My husband would hook the obstinate brute up to the Chevy and I'd take up the slack of the towing chain. He'd climb aboard the tractor, give me the signal to go and I'd give the Chevy heaps. If after several attempts he still hadn't got the thing going, there'd be hell to pay. I hadn't driven fast enough and the barrage of expletives to follow would pepper my still young and fragile ego. I believed the farmer had some calming down to do, but in hindsight I equally had some toughening up to do.

From our earliest days together, there'd been times when Warren had been dispirited and withdrawn – a far cry from his usual exuberant self. These moods confused me. It would feel as though he was angry with me but I had no idea what I'd done to upset him. When I asked, he'd tell me he didn't know and just needed to be left alone. I knew nothing of depression then but was aware of some traumatic events that had struck him in his childhood.

~

Two days before his eleventh birthday, he'd been excited about the air gun he hoped to receive. Unlike kids who dawdled home from school, Warren couldn't wait to get to his farm where there was scope for a new project every day.

On this day, he left his bike at the garden gate and ran to the house for his usual jam sandwich and change of clothes. His mother, who was always there to greet him, wasn't to be seen. He found her in bed. Warren had sensed that his mum had been under par for some time but with a household to run and family to care for, she'd soldiered on.

'What's up, Mum?' he asked.

'The doctor's been to see me, Love,' she replied. 'I have to go to hospital. It might be for a long time.'

The prospect terrified him. He loved his mother and the comfort she provided in his life.

Later that night, as they sat at the kitchen table eating their evening meal, the family talked at length about the doctor's suspicions – tuberculosis.

Lin was admitted to the Royal Adelaide Hospital next day and a little later underwent radical lung surgery. She would be confined to a city rehabilitation centre for an indefinite period.

Warren's father took his two children – scrubbed and polished – to visit their mother once a fortnight, on a Sunday evening. Through that summer and another five seasons, the children endured the hour long fortnightly trip as they tried to contain their excitement at seeing their mother who, from her hospital bed, would swathe them in the love they so desperately needed and missed.

Although Warren's fifteen year old sister assumed a motherly role towards her brother, the two of them were deeply traumatised by this loss. There were to be substitutes – a strict grandmother in their home and later, for Warren, living in the city with a dour though kindly aunt. He hated his new city school and became so unhappy and rebellious he was soon returned home. But still he missed his mother, and life would never be the same.

His cousin Jack – an only child who lived just down the road – spotted the gap in Warren's life and leapt at the chance to occupy a space in it. The two boys embarked on a life of mischief and unfettered adventure. But a world without boundaries was an often wide and lonely place for Warren.

Lin did return home to her joyful family, and despite being told she would never be strong enough to lead the life she once had, her powerful will proved this to be a fallacy. Within a year she had regained much of her old vitality. But even so, the spectre of loss was deeply embedded in her son.

~

It was always going to be supremely important for me to be at my husband's side. I understood where the need came from, and also that there was a significant place for me in the working partnership.

It was almost shearing time, but a shed would have to be built. Several helpers were employed for this and after four weeks of sawing, hammering and drilling, a sturdy two-stand shearing shed stood impressively a hundred metres from the hut. For first shearing, Warren went down a couple of days earlier than me to muster the four thousand acres with motorbike and dogs. His old mate Schmaaly would help with this job and also the shearing. Cooking for the men would again be my job. Lin offered to look after Lincoln for the few days I'd be away. 'You'll be busy,' she told me. The separation from my babe would be a wrenching for me, I knew.

A retired farmer associate of Warren's would class the wool. He and his wife called for me at four in the morning in their ute. It was strange travelling to the farm sitting shoulder to shoulder between two people I'd never met before. And the absence of my wee, warm babe who'd been a part of me for ten months, left me feeling strangely hollow.

The morning was frosty and the car had no heating. The genteel lady had brought a travelling rug for our laps, and sandwiches, and as we drove, the pink gold day yawned and lit the landscape.

The routine of a shearing day is set in concrete. Unchanged for decades. Four two-hour runs. At seven-thirty the motor groans into action and hand-pieces are pulled into gear. At nine-thirty the last sheep of the first run is dragged from its pen and smoko must be in the shed. For the men, the energy expended during the day is equivalent to running a marathon and they're hungry. They eat, rest for twenty minutes, and on the stroke of ten are back on the board.

Shearers are a cheerful mob. Above the din of the motor, they joke and jest to keep the demon, pain, from their minds. At noon tools are downed and again they must eat. The meal that has taken me hours to prepare is consumed in minutes, in the house. They return to the shed where they rest in the piles of wool. Another two-hour run to three o'clock, more food, then back on the board at three-thirty. Seconds before five-thirty the last sheep is dragged. Maintenance to tools is done, then, greasy and sweaty, the toilers seek comfort for their aching bodies and beer for their raging thirsts.

~

Warren had been a shearer in our early courting days. There'd been mornings I'd gone with him to the shed he was working in, if it wasn't too far away. I'd drive his eye-catching S-series Valiant then, back to my work. There was a tenet amongst our group that if a girl was seen driving her boyfriend's car, it could be presumed a serious relationship was underway. The lads prized their cars.

At the end of my workday I'd return to the shed to pick him up. This had been a new environment for me but there was something homespun about it and I drank it in. I discovered shearing was a profession unto itself – steeped in tradition. There were words and terms one would hear only around sheep – "runs", "ringers" (head shearers), "yoes" (ewes), "crossies" (cross-breds), "cut-outs" (finish of shearing on a property).

Still in my snazzy work clothes, I'd sit on a bale of wool watching my guy at work. His good looks were breathtaking. He was strong and fit, a good talker and had a wonderfully uncomplicated sense of humour. I was madly in love and felt loved in return.

~

Now, marriage and the pressures of work had clouded our love, but I had to remind myself that the stuff of our courtship would always be there, albeit sometimes buried. We had sung and danced, laughed and talked. Warren had been an open book and it hadn't taken me long to see a man of passion, generosity, spontaneity and dreams. All this I had to remember.

~

We hadn't been together long when I turned eighteen. Warren had planned to take me ice-skating but when he called for me at seven, he told me his horse Rio had cut his leg and the vet was attending him.

'I just need to go down the river to see if the vet's finished before we leave,' he said. 'A few of the fellas are down there helping out.'

When we arrived at the place, I was surprised to see how many cars were there. I got out of the Valiant and twenty or so of our friends emerged from the trees. 'Happy birthday, Sue,' they shouted.

Warren laughed when I asked him where Rio was. He'd chosen a beautiful spot beside the river.

> The grass was still green with the tailings of spring
> A huge campfire roared at the fading light
> Late ducks rattled off the water towards sunset
> and reeds rustled with waterfowl
> Giant red gums towered over us

Chops and sausages were soon sizzling. A keg of beer kept the night cheery and someone's transistor radio, reliably full of Saturday night rock 'n' roll, was turned up flat out.

Later in the night, our mate Dean brought out his guitar and we sang every hit song we could think of, until one by one couples lay back on their rugs and became quiet.

I was blissfully happy. It still seemed amazing to me that we were together. We often talked about the night we met.

~

Rosemary was one of my closest friends and had been going out with Warren's cousin Jack. One evening, she phoned to tell me Jack wasn't coming to see her that night and suggested we catch up. Later, with cushions, coffee and our favourite records, we nestled in on her lounge room floor, ready for an evening of girl talk. I hadn't been there fifteen minutes when Jack arrived. So much for our girls' night. And within half an hour Warren, who'd been looking for Jack, called in too.

Warren and I had seen each other at sport and a few social functions over the years and I must say he had certainly attracted my attention – driving around town in his MG sports car, usually with a beautiful girl at his side.

The boys stayed, so the four of us sat talking and drinking coffee as we fed the record player with vinyl – mostly albums of our favourite singer, Little Richard. We couldn't sit still. The boys began to teach us how to rock 'n' roll. They were good at it. I found myself being thrown around like a rag doll by Warren as we danced till we dropped. Not the kind of evening any of us had expected.

A few nights later Warren phoned me.

'Rose and Jack and myself are going to the drive-in,' he said. 'Would you like to come?'

'I don't think that would be right,' I said. 'You know I'm going steady. What's Rosslyn doing?'

Everyone knew that he and Rosslyn were a couple.

'Sue, I've got to talk to you about something.'

'What about?' I asked, as all sorts of possibilities raced through my mind, none of them anywhere near the mark.

'It's important,' he said. 'Can I pick you up in half an hour?'

It sounded serious and so, malleable with curiosity, I agreed.

He drove us to the end of my street where the vineyards began. There was no small talk.

'Sue,' he said, 'I've got a strong feeling we're going to spend our lives together.'

'*What?*'

It was pitch dark except for the dim light of his car radio. I couldn't see his face and he couldn't hear the pandemonium in my head. Within moments I had a flash back to a primary school concert. I was eight years old. Grade Seven kids were performing the operetta *Hiawatha*. I was riveted, when onto the stage crept Black Otter, an Indian brave, dressed in fringed leather pants, open vest, a feather stuck in a headband round his shiny dark hair. He and his singing were so hauntingly beautiful that it was weeks before I could get that boy or his songs out of my head. He'd left the school soon after the concert – his primary school days over – but the memory of that night never left me. It would be years before I'd see him again, but something portentous had occurred. Warren was that boy.

Now I was almost eighteen and he almost twenty-two. But his belief about us couldn't possibly come to pass. There were other people in our lives. It was complicated.

# THREE

For almost two years I'd been going out with Leon, and for some months Warren had been dating Rosslyn.

Leon and I had met in high school. No longer totally focussed on academics, I'd been champing at the bit to be out in the world, grown up. But I had one more year of study ahead and wanted to pass my Leaving exams. A privilege reserved for upper school students were off-lessons. These were spent in the library where we were supposed to be mature enough to swot for upcoming tests or begin homework assignments. If Rosemary was in there with me though, or Jill or Marion, my other best buddies, there'd be little work done. Instead there'd be a constant writing and passing of notes – about current boyfriends or how we might spend the weekend.

There without my girlfriends one day, I was studying when something made me look up. One of the boys had his chin in his hand and was looking at me. A shy smile crossed his face before he looked back to his work.

I'd been longing to make use of the freedom of being allowed out on dates since I'd turned sixteen, four months earlier, and on the Saturday after the library incident, the boy who had smiled phoned me. He referred to the study period and introduced himself as Leon Friend. With little preliminary he asked if I'd like to go to the drive-in with him that night. I was elated – a rite of passage.

One of Leon's mates and the girl he had invited came with us. We all sat properly apart, each in our own quarter of the car for the first film, but shortly after the beginning of the feature, the boys slid simultaneously across the bench seats and put their arms around our shoulders. I was feeling more grown up by the minute and had always imagined that my first kiss would be as sensual as anything from the movies, but in reality it was awkward, and I forgot to breathe.

Three weeks later, when it was Leon's turn to borrow the family car, he invited me to the drive-in again. This time we went by ourselves. He was polite and attentive, and with the benefit of hindsight I remembered to breathe when he kissed me.

I was playing tennis for our town and the club had organised a barbecue in winter. I invited Leon. Held in the stately old family home of one of our players, it was a classy party, but even the open fire, soft lights and romantic scatting of The Ray Conniff Singers on the radiogram as we danced, didn't stir in me anything more than a liking for the young man. Tucked under his protecting arm, I was happy and content.

He began to phone me, just to talk. Looking for privacy and escape from the friendly teasing of his family, he'd walk some distance to a public phone where, often through freezing winter nights, he'd stand for hours in the booth as we talked. I was the chatterbox. He was quiet – his words always just enough.

Tall and lean with short dark hair, Leon wore a confident posture that masked an underlying shyness. His reticence didn't matter. He was popular at school, manifested by his election to deputy head prefect. I liked and respected him, but I sensed by now that his feelings for me had grown a little deeper.

About this time we had our mid-year school social. I loved these wonderful nights of music and dancing. And it usually meant a new dress – designed by me and sewed by my mother. Leon was there that night but so too was Butch, a boy I'd been keen on for years and who had been my dance partner at previous balls and dances. Out of the blue, here he was asking me to dance and sweeping me off my feet again. Son of a local butcher and belying his nickname, Butch was handsome and refined. And a glorious dancer. Being in his arms in the dimly lit hall while the orchestra played the sultry minor key standards that we loved, had me in a state of bliss.

I had a few dances with Leon but most with Butch, and at the end of the evening, while the band played *God Save The Queen* Leon came up to Butch and me and asked to take me home. With the same feeling I'd have for a protecting big brother, I left the hall with Leon. He continued to phone, and despite my long-term infatuation with Butch, the friendship between us grew.

Debutante balls were held from time to time and one of my girlfriends was to "come out". She invited me and a friend of my choice to her pre-ball dinner in their rambling country homestead, and so I asked Butch. He was a year younger than I was and not driving, so my dad drove us there. Amidst much pomp and ceremony, we danced to the music of a big band in the lavishly decorated hall afterwards. Leon had been invited by another girl, but as he danced with her and several others, he kept close to Butch and me all night – a strategy that succeeded in dampening any romantic mood between us.

For the following few weeks there were no dates, but Leon continued to phone me and we talked long and well. I guessed that after the ball he was unsure of where he stood with me. Eventually however he must have felt reassured enough to start visiting me at home where he began to grow comfortable with my family.

He lived in a small country town and was part of the close-knit community there. At various parties he gradually introduced me to his clan. They were a fun-loving bunch and welcomed me into the fold.

Leon was a talented baseball player and sometimes took me to watch night matches in Adelaide. Going to the city with a boy was so "of the world".

Despite the fact that we were together a lot, I wasn't in love. Every now and then sparks for past boyfriends would flare up.

During my first year of high school I had enrolled in a ballroom dancing class where I'd met Eddie. I hadn't noticed him at our large school, but in this small hall on a Friday night, I discovered he was the loveliest boy I knew. Tall for thirteen, he had a mop of soft curly brown hair and a gorgeous smile. After our first dance we were love-birds. There were nights he'd ride his bike the six kilometres from his home to be at the class. Sometimes he'd be late and I'd fear he wasn't coming, but when he walked through the door and our eyes met, angels sang. He was my boyfriend, which at that age meant having our friends tease us whenever we passed each other in the school yard.

The romance had languished with the new attention of Butch, but every now and then, the old torch I carried for Eddie would be rekindled – often in spring with a warm wind blowing away winter, and the smell of blossom in the air. School blazers off. Shirt sleeves rolled up. Bodies developing. Hormones running riot.

Although these spikes of passion still cropped up, they typically lasted just a few days. Leon was my rock, and despite my belief that I was not in love, I felt cared for and safe with him. And I was aware of his unfailing patience with me.

But over the next few months something began to stir. It was love – exquisite and vastly different from the infatuations of the past. In quiet moments and places, our talking changed. We became comfortable, near.

In our last week of high school, we had our customary end-of-year social and although Butch and Eddie were there, Leon and I danced only with each other. Now, rather than it being about music, dancing and infatuation, it was about first true love.

A week or two later, Leon took me to a special party. Dignitaries of the Barossa – Sir Condor and Lady Laucke – had been hosting a Rotary Exchange student – a friend of Leon's. Their Art Deco two-storey mansion was like something from a movie set. Built into the side of a hill, it overlooked town. In the magnificent lounge room whose French doors opened onto an extensive balcony – exotic with palms and wrought iron – we were served hors d'oeuvres and punch in crystal glasses. I wondered if I could ever live in a home as splendid as this. The clear vinyl voices of Buddy Holly and The Crickets filled the night air through strategic speakers, inside and out. Leaning on the ornate railing, we looked out over the breathtakingly lit grounds and onto the bespoke dance floor below. It wasn't long before we all needed to be on that floor. Every song made us want to dance. Buddy had taken the world by storm and although he'd been tragically killed in a plane crash, he was still alive to us through his music.

Nineteen sixty-three. The Beatles had hit the world stage. My friends and I were crazy over them. Light headed with mania, groups of us would burst into song anywhere and at any time – often in the schoolyard. On top of the charts and driving us insane were *Love Me Do, I Wanna Hold Your Hand, It's Been a Hard Day's Night*. Our boy buddies began to dress like them – slim-legged black trousers, black pointy-toed boots, mop-top haircuts. Not Leon though. Although always impeccably dressed, he was conservative.

Some homes were havens for me and my friends on weekends. We loved music and we danced. Talk was becoming important to us. We were developing views on world affairs. There was no alcohol. We felt quite grown up enough to be drinking coffee. Although small, our home was modern and unique and always open to my friends. I was proud of my intelligent and open-hearted parents.

As Leon lived a few kilometres from the hub of the action, we didn't spend as much time at his place as others, but when we did, it was just as genial. In his cosy community, if someone had a special birthday or celebration, the whole town turned out. There was alcohol at these parties and it was in this environment that I first dared to try it. I found the taste of beer horrible and so someone offered me vermouth and lemon. I sipped it gingerly. The "coffee only" weekends had come to an end.

With a perpetual twinkle in her eye, Leon's mother was the pianist with a wide repertoire at all the parties in their town and was treated with great affection by her husband, sons, and all who knew her.

Leon's older brother Chris was in many ways the inverse of his brother – outgoing, gregarious, flirtatious. Lots of girlfriends.

In December of 'sixty-three, I walked out of my high school gates for the last time. Excited about my future, I was also sad at the possibility of losing touch with dear friends. It was time for us all to disperse into adulthood and the most diverse directions.

Leon gave me his prefect's badge as a symbol of his love and we spent Christmas, New Year and the next few weeks in a euphoria of freedom and happiness. We worked together during vintage

– backbreaking work as we stooped all day to pick grapes from the old bush vines that bore their crops so close to the ground. But there was no room for romance in the vineyard. Leon was not prepared to expose us to the jibes, albeit friendly, of fellow pickers. This hurt me a little. I would have happily leant against him as we sat on the ground to eat our lunch but he was not one for demonstration and sat apart.

One night at a baseball match in the city, we bumped into Leon's brother and his girlfriend of the week. After the match, Chris, by now au fait with the "in" places in Adelaide as a medical student at uni, took us to The Catacombs coffee lounge. We descended a creaky wooden staircase into a smoky, dimly lit series of underground rooms. Rush matting covered the floors. Large posters of folk singers loomed from the black walls. The smell of incense wafted through the place. When my eyes grew accustomed to the dark, I noticed a live performer. I was over the moon. I'd presumed the music was recorded.

Dressed in tight black slacks, sloppy joe jumper, pale pink lipstick, heavy eye make-up and black-rimmed glasses, I felt wholly and solely in my place. Stephen Foster was singing that night. Doug Ashdown and Tina Lawton, renowned folk musicians of the sixties, were regular performers. For me, a portal had been opened to the bohemian world. I began to discover how thoughts and ideas can become art.

Leon and I were constantly together in these weeks after the end of school. There were picnics on the river, tennis parties, impromptu gatherings at our house where on weekends friends would pass by, and seeing us sitting on the lawn, park their cars and join us. With our transistor radios emitting the thin mono sounds of our beloved pop songs, we'd lie on rugs and sing and talk and laugh. We discovered Chinese food, ten-pin bowling. There were progressive dinners and cabarets.

But apart from all this, Leon and I loved to be quiet together – to go to the drive-in, to sit in the sanctum of the car as we talked, to cuddle into the wee hours. In the light of day though, there were careers for us to think of and the holiday bubble had to burst.

I bought myself a navy blue linen suit – Chanel style with white trim, a pair of white stiletto heels and white gloves, and began catching the train to the city to seek employment. I applied for ticket-writing jobs, copywriting, cadetships in journalism, and although I was sometimes called back, the prize I was after eluded me. Oddly, it hadn't occurred to me that to get a job like this I would need to type. After submitting a few pieces of copywriting for John Martins, the personnel officer told me he'd have a position for me as soon as I learned to type.

In the meantime, a new phenomenon had hit town – the Kiwis! Three boys from New Zealand had come to the Barossa to work a vintage – Kiwi, Byrnesy and Blue. They'd taken rooms at The Tanunda Hotel.

Just as lions treat a strange male lion trying to infiltrate their pride, our local lads lowered their heads, looked at them through narrowed eyes, silently warning them to keep away from "their girls". But they joined our tennis club and it wasn't long before they were in – accepted by all, even our lads. They were fun – newcomers with strange accents and a long repertoire of traditional songs. Larger than life, charismatic and full of joie de vivre, they captured our hearts. My girlfriend Jill and Kiwi fell in love. I became so caught up in the excitement and whirlwind of outings that revolved around them, that for a few weeks Leon and I struggled to sustain the quality time we'd grown to enjoy as a couple. It couldn't have been easy having me for a girlfriend. Often our dates and phone calls would end with me in tears as Leon found obscure ways to show me how it felt to be hurt. But as the tennis season drew to a close, vintage finished and the dust settled, I came to my senses and the two of us grew closer still.

I continued to look for work and Leon applied to join the Air Force. He was accepted and in the weeks leading to his posting at Laverton RAAF base in Victoria, even though we were only seventeen and eighteen, we began to talk of marriage. Practically inseparable, we spent nights at each other's houses. There was no sleeping together, though there were times of intimacy – exciting as a child's night before Christmas. Pleasure sharpened by restraint. The night we'd been cuddling in the car and Leon's hand dropped, for the first time, inside my blouse, I felt every fibre of my sexual being awaken. But he was an honourable young man.

'We can't go all the way, Tiger,' he said. 'A girl at school got a baby that way.'

Condoms? I had no idea what they were and Leon would have been too embarrassed to buy them from the local chemist who knew everyone. Besides, sex before marriage was taboo.

One of my buddies, Joey, had joined the navy and I remember being floored when he told me it was a six year commitment. Now Leon was about to go for six years as well, and it might as well have been a lifetime.

I got a job in retail at David Jones, and thankfully was due to start the day after Leon's departure. With our remaining time together diminishing, we found words to say to each other that were without restraint. I was deeply afraid of not having him near. I knew there would be letters and the odd phone call but the thought of seeing him only once every three months was unbearable.

On the day of his departure I went with the rest of his family to the railway station to see him off. We'd been hand in hand for half an hour but just before boarding, he held me and kissed me.

'We'll be alright, Tiger,' he whispered.

*Will we*, I thought.

He turned away and boarded the train that was beginning to move. In an elongated Paramount movie moment, he waved until out of sight. The emptiness I felt as I walked back along the platform without him was a physical pain beating at my chest.

# FOUR

Starting work that week could not have come at a better time. The girls in my department were lovely and soon invited me to join them for lunch, to their family homes for tea, and to The Princeton Club – the newest and hippest dance venue in town. The meal invitations I accepted but the dances were on the weekends when I was happy to go back to my family and friends in the Barossa – an hour away.

My girlfriend Jill had got a job at David Jones as well and her parents had arranged for us to board at a girls' hostel, quite near the city and what's more, The Catacombs. Having this den of music so near our lodgings was perfect. Like a butterfly leaving its cocoon, my artistic wings were beginning to unfurl.

We were given our quarters – a comfortable dormitory type bedroom and study which we were to share with two other girls. The bathroom was down the hall and there was a communal lounge room at the front of the gracious old stone home where we were allowed to entertain male friends until eleven pm.

The head of the house – Matron Minge (I'm not kidding) – was a small, severe spinster with sharp features. Dressed in sensible billowing skirts and brown cardigans clutched firmly to her breast, she ran a tight ship. There were house rules and curfews. Between twelve and sixteen of us lived there – most studying to be teachers or nurses. Jill and I were the only ones with jobs and the freedom to spend the evenings as we pleased. We'd go to The Catacombs, or Sigalis coffee lounge downstairs in the city where we'd order non-alcoholic cocktails and sit for hours listening to live music played by dedicated jazzmen. The eloquence of the piano, the swish of the top hat, the heartbeat of the bass – music nectar for me. One of the band sometimes sang, as jazz musicians often do – not spectacularly but simply to describe the music.

> '*A tinkling piano in the next apartment*
> *Those stumbling words that told you what my heart meant*
> *A fairground's painted swings*
> *These foolish things remind me of you..*'

Sigalis was swank – red plush carpet, white table linen, silver service, mood lighting, ambience of velvet. Without the luxury of our parents' cars, as we'd had in the Barossa, Jill and I would walk or catch a bus into the CBD. We had to be in by eleven but were allowed a midnight once a week. It was rare though for us to be in on time. We'd be met at the door by a tired and tart Miss Minge, delivering yet another lecture on the importance of obeying the rules.

We ran amok daily – falling about with laughter, sneaking into the kitchen after lights out to steal leftover desserts, undoing the stoppers in each other's hot water bottles and flooding the beds, jumping out of wardrobes to scare each other. High on freedom, I dyed my hair cherry red, which broke my father's heart.

We were always hungry. Meals were meagre, plain, predictable. Mondays – Irish stew. Thursdays – liver and bacon. Fridays – English cod with cauliflower. Ugh. There were prayers and Bible reading at breakfast each morning. Jill and I dreaded this, as a near inaudible snort or snicker from the other would render us nearly bursting with laughter and incapable of taking our turn at reading. The task would then be handed to a more sensible girl.

Leon and I had spoken about going out with others while we were apart, but deep down I hoped he would not, and I'm sure he felt the same about me. Several times a week I'd find myself a quiet corner where I'd write to my boy. While penning these love letters, the pain of missing him disappeared. He usually wrote once a week. I longed for more but hadn't considered he was probably also writing to his parents, his brother, and even Joey – his friend and mine, from time to time. Some of his letters were topical and others romantic. The ones about life on the base were interesting but read once, the beautiful love letters worn ragged with reading.

One Friday night I accepted an invitation from a girlfriend at work to go with her to a dance in the city – a formal affair, boys on one side of the hall, girls on the other. As each dance was announced, we'd brace ourselves for the sea of males sweeping across the floor towards us.

After two or three waltzes with unremarkable boys, a particularly nice-looking, well-dressed one invited me up. He was chatty. We had the next dance together and the next. He asked to take me home. We talked in his car for half an hour before I went in.

I had begun a typing course at night school and one evening found him waiting for me in the car park. I appreciated not having to catch the bus home that night.

We started to go out, but they weren't the usual dates. Tony liked to talk and so he'd park at the beach or overlooking the city and we'd chat. After three or four weeks of this, he invited me home for tea to meet his family.

I was acutely aware of how upset I'd be if Leon went out with another girl but I justified my time spent with Tony by telling myself it was simply a friendship. And I hated staying in while all my friends were out with their boyfriends. Even so, it was a double standard I know. I had told Tony from the outset that I was in a serious relationship with Leon, but despite this, he'd started to visit me in the Barossa on the weekends. I was in love with Leon. I would wait for him, and I would be his wife. Any boy I went out with while he was away was always only a friend to me. The boys however, sometimes had other ideas. Tony was soon calling at the hostel nearly every night. I had to tell him I couldn't go out with him anymore. I wanted desperately for him not to be hurt but as sensitively as I tried to terminate the relationship, he took it badly. After he'd left the hostel guest room in tears, Jill berated me sternly for leading him on. This triggered a flood of tears of my own – mainly in self-pity over having my boy so far away. I resolved to clip my wings and wait single-mindedly for Leon to return. Although we were geographically so far apart, I felt a new peace about us.

How life never allows us to become complacent. A few days later, Leon's brother Chris phoned. He asked if I was sitting down. I thought he was going to tell me Leon was coming home early and a surge of excitement rushed through me. The news he delivered however could not have been further from this speculation. Leon was in intensive care, in a critical condition. He had fallen onto a steel spike and been impaled on it. It was a miracle he hadn't died instantly. He was in the Wagga Base hospital.

The news of this accident threw us all into shock. His parents flew to Wagga immediately. Chris went over next day. It was three days before I could get a week's compassionate leave from work. Through these days of fearing for his life and longing to be with him, I cried in waves. My mum and dad wrapped me in nurturing love and offered me their car to drive to Wagga. It would be a ten-hour trip, but as I was still only seventeen, Mum felt a need to come with me. However it was my mission and I drove all the way.

To not have a moment alone with Leon when I arrived at the hospital was another grief, but I understood his family's need to spend as much time with him as possible. After a couple of days, we were given the time alone we were longing for. Despite Leon's frail state, I lay gently in his arms on his hospital bed as we whispered about how we couldn't wait to be together always. The week flew. Leon was to spend at least another two months in hospital there to undergo several operations. If all went well he would be out of danger, and then be transferred home to recuperate. His parents and Chris, and Mum and I, drove back together in two cars. To break the long trip we stayed overnight in an imposing old pub overlooking the lake in Daylesford. The small group of us had a meal together and talked of the week past. Longing to be in Leon's arms and with my world feeling suddenly surreal, I had a little too much to drink. I needed to be alone now. Wandering along the dim passageways to my room, I came across a pair of glass doors with the word "Ballroom" etched into them. Although the large chamber was in darkness, I went in. Walking over to a magnificent picture-window, I caught sight of the moon rising over the lake and cried the tears that needed to be shed.

I was unable to get any more leave from work and feel sad even now to think of how Leon might have hoped each day for the surprise of seeing me walk through the door of his hospital room.

We continued to write, but something changed in him after this accident. Some of his letters were as lovely as ever, but some were cold. I wondered what could have happened between our saying goodbye and these strange brief missives. I longed to talk to him about it face to face but was unable to get any more time off work.

In June that year, The Beatles hit Adelaide. The city lost its mind. They called it Beatle-mania. Traffic stopped on North Terrace as three hundred thousand people gathered outside the South Australia Hotel where, it had been announced, the group would appear on the balcony. The energy was electrifying as we screamed at every movement from the windows – frightening and euphoric at the same time. When they finally appeared, a mass scream went up like Adelaide had never heard before, and probably never since.

That night, the City closed all CBD streets and organised free buses to Centennial Hall where the boys from Liverpool would be singing. Tens of thousands who'd not been able to get tickets, thronged outside to hear the concert. I was among them. It was difficult to hear anything above the mass voice

> but sublime
> to be in the eye of the storm
> and to walk home afterwards
> in a crowd of one accord
> through a city where only untidy buses full of screams
> were crawling through the swarming streets.

Perhaps it could only be compared with the day the Second World War ended.

When I got home that weekend, Mum told me a boy had called to ask me out. 'Who was it?' I asked.

'Warren Grocke.'

I looked at Mum in disbelief. Warren Grocke? The enchanting Indian brave from the Grade Seven play? Bizarre. We had never spoken to each other. Mum had told him I was at The Beatles concert and so he took Rosslyn out, for the first time.

Leon's homecoming was constantly on my mind. I didn't want to think about the years of being apart while he trained. His warm letters repaired me after each cold one and on the weekends, through my waiting, I was sustained by the companionship of my friends. Like similar cells grouping together in a sea of others, our crowd, without planning, would gradually find each other – at Rosemary's, or our place, or at an open-house party, a dance or the drive-in. Or all of the above on the same night.

Warren's cousin Jack was part of this crowd. His reputation preceded him. Slight of build, highly strung and short of fuse, he was "the wild one", the daredevil to beat all. An anomaly was his amazing singing voice and he idolised the then-famous tenor Mario Lanza. From time to time there'd be talent quests in our town and this year he entered, singing one of Mario's songs. The winner would be established by way of penny votes from the audience. Jack spent the week before the show canvassing – handing out dozens of pennies to his friends. He didn't need to. He was going to win anyway.

Jack invited me out. I'd made my decision about going out with others. He knew I was going steady with Leon. However, we'd bump into each other on the weekends, at a party or the drive-in where he'd ask me out again. The answer was always the same. One weeknight he phoned me at the hostel and asked what I was doing. I told him I'd planned an early night. The conversation was short. About forty minutes later, Matron knocked on my door to tell me there was someone in the front room to see me. It was Jack – Tanunda's fastest driver. The trip normally took an hour. He had Warren with him! I was relieved as I knew this would make the situation lighter. The three of us sat in the car and talked. *The House of the Rising Sun* – my favourite song and a huge hit of the time – came on the radio. Conversation stopped as we all listened, and when it was over our chatter turned to music – a common passion for us all. After about an hour I said I had to go in. Jack leaned over to kiss me goodnight, but I dodged that bullet! Leon would be home soon.

Eventually, Jack struck up a friendship with Rosemary and the day he came home from the city with an MGA sports car, Rosemary was won over. She was soon allowed to get behind the wheel – a sign that the relationship was now a romance. With her rare beauty, my friend cut a million-dollar figure in that car.

In the middle of that year I was offered a secretarial job at Kaiser Stuhl Wines. The offer and pay was too good to refuse so I returned to the Barossa to live with my family.

Leon loved to surprise me and one Saturday morning, without word, he knocked on our door. His cheeky smile and protecting arms wrapped lovingly around me soothed the wounds of all the lonely days and nights without him. We held each other as if it was the last time.

He was to have two more weeks' recuperation at home, followed by ten weeks' training at Edinburgh, South Australia, and then would have to return to Laverton Air Base in Victoria.

We saw each other nearly every day for a week – a luxury I'd dreamed of, but this new beginning for Leon and I was fraught with danger. He'd had a near death experience and would look at life differently now. Any thought of the soul searching he might have done while in hospital for eight weeks, had not entered my mind. Although I was still only seventeen and he almost nineteen, I would have married him in a blink. He, on the other hand, was now ready for a life well-lived, which is what I'd been doing while he was away. Fishing, football trips, time with his brother and his mates. We didn't talk about it. It just happened. This male-bonding or whatever it was, began soon after his first week back, and before long I felt I'd been put away for later. Perhaps he'd contemplated this before coming home, but I couldn't guess how long it would take.

After two months of confusion and aching sadness, I feared our relationship was in its death throes. Then, just as suddenly as he'd gone AWOL, Leon returned. But there was a different dimension to us now and I wasn't sure what it was. Knocked out by it all, we just talked of how we felt older and wiser. But still I wondered what had jolted this sublime first love off its axis.

Since Rosemary had been going out with Jack, my time with her had been limited. We'd been looking forward to our girls' night at her house. Girlfriends can have volumes of wisdom for each other in times of crisis, and I certainly felt I'd just come through one. But instead of the expected heart to heart with my friend, I danced with Warren Grocke – one of life's strange interventions. Sitting up in bed later that night, I wrote in my diary about the joy of making up with Leon.

Three nights later Warren phoned to say he needed to talk to me. I knew he'd been seeing Rosslyn for several months, and he was well aware of my relationship with Leon. I couldn't imagine what he wanted to talk to me about. But what he had to say knocked me for six.

Spend our lives together?

~

'Do you love Leon?' he'd asked.

'Yes. I do.' My emotional reply startled me.

Silence for a little while. Then, 'Sue, I've been thinking about this for days. I know you and Leon are serious, but I have such a strong feeling about us. I've never felt like this about anyone before.'

As he took my hand, I was stunned with the gravity of what was happening. He seemed so convinced.

'I think we're meant for each other. And I believe if you want something badly enough, you'll get it.'

There was something enormous in those words but I was at a loss, and could now only think of the need to be alone to digest what was happening.

'I'd better go in.'

I touched him on the knee and got out of the car. The next night Leon came home from the base and we spent the evening at home with my family. He must have wondered at my unusual introversion. In the quiet time we had together before he went home, our talking was suddenly different.

A party at Rosemary's had been planned, to farewell Jill who was about to begin training as a nurse. Leon picked me up that following night and we went together. Warren and Rosslyn were there. The music and people were soundless and shapeless for me that night. In the dim light there were only Warren's eyes, illuminated now and then by the glow of his cigarette. I couldn't stay.

Leon took me home and thinking I was unwell, treated me tenderly. We lay in each other's arms with only our thoughts between us, for an hour or so. I was accustomed to his economy of words but on this night he didn't know what to do with mine. Without resolve, he kissed me goodnight and left.

Next morning, he phoned to ask if I'd come with him to see his grandfather who was unwell. I said I would, but little bits of us were beginning to fly off. We were breaking up. I lost my appetite, couldn't concentrate at work, sat on my bed for hours talking to Mum, hoping she would make it easy for me and tell me what to do. She didn't.

'You must do what's in your heart,' is all she offered wisely.

Leon went back to the base. Warren and I talked for the next three nights. I felt shattered over the imminent break up but could also feel a groundswell of happiness. Warren went to see Rosslyn and told her it was over for them. She gave him his birthday present – six weeks early. He came to see me afterwards. He was solemn and contemplative.

'It wasn't easy,' he said.

Something astonishing was waking in me. Something telling me my life *would* be with this man.

The following weekend Leon couldn't come to visit as their car was out of action, so he invited me to his place for Sunday lunch. At once I knew this would be our goodbye day. Courage didn't come naturally to me, but I had to find it now, to step away from all that was comfortable and familiar into the unknown with Warren.

Leon's mother had prepared a wonderful meal. Three weeks earlier it would have been the happiest of days but now, as Leon's family and I sat around their kitchen table, I felt as though my bones had dissolved. Everyone sensed there was something wrong. This would be the last time I'd be with them all. With eyes brimming with tears, I took Leon's hand and asked if we could be excused. As we walked out to my car, Leon's eyes told me he knew what was about to unfold. We sat in the car, and with my heart pounding I tried to explain what had happened. Every now and then I'd pause, hoping for access to his thoughts, but there was none. I could feel his pain, and mine was all-consuming. With my words finally exhausted, he looked away. We sat like that, holding hands, for a long time. It could have been ten minutes or thirty. We were wrapped together for the last time in bewildering, wordless, heartbreaking emotion. When he finally turned and looked at me, I kissed his tear-stained face and we held each other – a warm and timeless hug. He got out of the car. As I drove away, I looked in the mirror and through my own tears, saw him diminishing like a small vessel cut loose on a calm sea.

In his stoic way, there was no fuss. The fact that we parted this way seemed almost inconceivable to me. It had all happened so quickly. How had I found the courage to leave the person I'd grown to love so much, for the unknown?

I believe our subconscious can know our destiny, and when the Indian brave stood on that stage all those years before, I must have had an inkling.

Warren and I saw each other or spoke on the phone daily. There was so much to talk about. It was a dramatic time. We started to go out. Our friends were amazed at the turn of events. Although I felt a coming home with Warren, there was a deep sadness too as I gradually let go of my time with Leon, but not the memory.

Longer than always.

# FIVE

Within three weeks of our first talk, Warren and I had slipped into sweet chatter about where we would live, how many children we'd like to have, and how we had never loved like this before. For months though I had a recurring dream – that I was driving interminably to see Leon. I had loved him for so long and needed to know if he was okay. But in the dream, I could never reach him.

It was time now to close that heavy door.

Warren and I met each other's families. On our first Christmas Eve together, he took me to his church – St John's Lutheran. Compared with the humble Methodist celebrations I'd been accustomed to, this was an extravaganza. A huge tree, ablaze with lights and spectacular decorations, stood majestically in the corner. Dozens of angelic children dressed in the clothes of the Nativity, sang straggly carols, and recited and giggled with the excitement of the season.

After the service, the congregation spilled into the churchyard, and in the balmy night air, beneath two giant Norfolk pines, we chatted with people we knew. Warren was president of the church's Young People's Association and many of the members welcomed me warmly. Apparently, he'd never taken a girlfriend to his church before.

It was religion that had brought our ancestors to the Barossa as they'd fled religious persecution in their homeland, Silesia. It was joy in their new-found freedom that had led them to build the magnificent churches that now adorned the Valley. Church-going was still tantamount to the memory of those pioneers.

Heady days followed – days of incredible freedom, with enough money in our pockets to do whatever we wanted.

At work, I was made to feel a valued member of the team. I felt privileged, even though my office was above a fermenting tank whose fumes, at times, were almost unbearable. To be sitting at a desk with my own typewriter satisfied something fundamental in me. In my lunch hours I began to write a novel.

Warren's work with his father was largely without pay. It was understood that in return he'd ultimately inherit the property. So, to earn the money his dreams and plans required, he went shearing for several months of the year, and bred and raised pigs. His uncommon ambition was something I could already sense.

Warren and Jack, with one of their closest mates, Darryl (a friend since primary school), bought an old Essex car. Canvas hood, leather seats, chrome and Bakelite fittings. It seated nine comfortably – still no seat belts required, no maximum number of passengers. A great novelty, it was taken out on nights of large gatherings – its first, the Friday night before Christmas.

The town's shops were all open – colourfully lit and decorated – and hundreds of townsfolk lined the street. Bouncing children were waiting for Santa, adults happy to be out, exchanging banter. Without planning, we suddenly found ourselves in the procession, relishing the amused attention drawn by the stately old car.

A demolition derby was held annually at Rowley Park Speedway in the city. A few local lads, including Warren, planned to compete. Cars were sourced, chopped and channelled. A week of preparing the machines after work and into the wee hours saw the sleek old Chevys, Oldsmobiles and Fords kitted out and painted with numbers and nicknames (Otto for Warren), ready for the event. There were nights we girls joined them. Sitting on drums in the oily, dim corners of Mickan and May's garage, we watched the long shadows of our guys at work by trouble light. Half listening to them speak the language of cars, we talked about what we would wear on the night our boys would be stars.

On the evening of the event, a buzz of excitement was in the air. The winner would be the last driver still mobile – his task to render as many cars stationary as possible. The starter held up a red flag. My heart was thumping. I was about to see my boyfriend in multiple car crashes. The green flag went up. There was a roar of engines and a cloud of smoke that made it nearly impossible to see. Then came the sound of cracking collisions, and as the smoke subsided, the sight of dozens of cars reversing into each other, until one by one they became motionless.

Warren's car was one of the last still limping amongst the carnage, but finally it too ceased to move. When I saw him climb out of his wreck unharmed, I sat back with enormous relief. But he was charged with adrenalin and wanted to do it all again somewhere else. In the real world, however, there was work to be done. Vintage was just around the corner and the hot rod passion put on the back burner.

The Grocke team of sixteen or more grape pickers took ten weeks to harvest around a hundred acres. Besides the home vineyard of sixty acres, there were various smaller ones to be picked under contract. On days the team was picking on the Kaiser Stuhl estate, Warren would call into my office and invite me out into his Bedford truck where we'd have lunch together. He was known and respected by many of the staff here and I felt proud to have him call for me. I'd be dressed to the nines and he'd be sporting the grape stains of vintage. I loved the purple hands that picked the fruit that made the noble wine.

I was happier than I had ever been. Warren was brimming with enthusiasm for life and work and I had a profound sense of peace about the prospect of spending the rest of my life with him in our valley.

Along with the earliest settlers, my mother's ancestors had arrived here in the early eighteen hundreds, bringing with them traditions of food, worship, music and winemaking – all still very much alive and abounding in the sixties. Century old vineyards were everywhere – on small blocks within the towns, on larger holdings around the edges, and out into the countryside. Old tractors with implements crawled up and down rows. Hats bobbed above the vines as vignerons and their workfolk pruned, tied canes to the wires, shifted soaker hoses in summer, and finally picked the grapes. So much of our community was under those hats. Life revolved around the making of wine and food, worship, work, and merry-making – reward for labour. The Lutherans knew how to celebrate and give thanks.

> Here spreads a valley where history lies
> slumbering passively midst sagacious old vines
> where it creeps among casks and ages the wine
> A valley that filters tradition through streets
> steeped in old secrets
> A valley of peace

Warren's mate Darryl was studying chiropractic in Adelaide, but we'd often catch up with him on the weekends. He'd call in to our place looking for Warren and on one occasion asked if my sister could come out to the drive-in with us. But Darryl was twenty-three and my sister not quite sixteen so naturally it was not allowed. Nevertheless, there were some daytime outings snuck in. Erica and I had always been the best of friends and it was lovely to have her with me again. While I'd been living in Adelaide and going out with Leon, our time together had been scarce. But it had only been a few short years since our lives had revolved around each other completely.

~

Through our childhood we'd been adventurers to the bone. There'd been routine chores for us to do at home on the weekends but once we'd completed those we'd jump on our bikes and head off. Discovering new places was usually the quest – somewhere near water, with soft grass to lie back on and watch clouds go by. Trees to befriend. Rocks to climb. A bridge under which to write our initials in charcoal, with those of our boyfriends.

We'd pad or ride, barefooted in summer, the kilometre through the vineyard that began at the end of our street – the soft green vine tendrils fingering our sun-kissed legs as we passed. Before reaching our beloved creek, we'd have to tiptoe through Lance Panach's fruit orchard. Not a whisper between us, hardly breathing. In summer the man would keep a constant vigil – the loss of fruit by passing children apparently enough to warrant it. If he spotted us, he'd deliver a tirade to make us bolt. He was a tall, handsome man but his anger made no sense to us. An apricot or two, what harm? Perhaps it had something to do with the war.

Old Alfie Fuhrbach, a remnant of the First World War, lived on the edge of town in an iron shack next to the creek – a Dalmatian dog his only companion. He was a spindly man with long grey hair and a week's worth of whiskers. The war had ruined him. He worked in the vineyards intermittently but only until he had enough money to buy a side of mutton, some tea, sugar, flour and a jar or two of plonk. His shotgun was always at hand but the consensus was that he was harmless – unless he was experiencing the frightening hallucinations of Delirium Tremens.

During one winter, the creek had come up and after a couple of days a neighbour thought he should check on Alfie. He called out to him from across the river and was greeted with a burst of shotgun fire. With water halfway up the walls of his hut, the veteran had been sitting on his kitchen table for forty-eight hours with his dog, gun and (now empty) jars of wine.

'Hands up,' he'd said to his faithful dog one day, thinking it was an enemy soldier. When the dog didn't obey, he shot it. Poor thing. No-one would have been more distraught than Alfie when he realised what he'd done.

On days we were looking for high adventure, Erica and I would head for his place. While still fifty metres away and making sure we were concealed in the undergrowth, we'd wait and watch. If we saw him in his yard or heard him talking to himself, we'd turn for home. We dared not risk being spotted. But if all was quiet, we'd run like rabbits past his house until out of shotgun range. I don't know how we gauged how far that was.

The creek was our favourite route to anywhere. Some days we'd wander along the healthy water course through king brown snake country to the park. Here we'd sit under the bunya pines, eating our Vegemite sandwiches embellished with the fallen pine nuts we'd gleaned – imagining we were princesses or mothers.

On Sundays we went to Sunday School in the tiny corrugated iron Methodist church. My father was of Cornish descent and had been brought up a Methodist. There were four grand Lutheran Churches in our town.

The family who ran our little Sunday School were kind, selfless people. Their faith made a deep impression on me. I loved the children's hymns and sang with a joyful heart. The Bible stories held me spellbound. I dreamed of becoming a Sunday School teacher when I was old enough and would tell these stories with passion.

Our walks home from there were unhurried and we'd take different routes each week to keep in touch with what was happening in our town. We needed to see what flowers the three spinsters Ottens had on show in their front garden – poppies, stocks, maybe sweet peas – the fragrances wafting heavenly. Were the grapes in the vineyards ready to eat? How much water was still in the creek, and how did the oval and bunya pines look from the top row of the grandstand? Bonded by a love of the earth beneath our feet, my sister and I led a healthy, free and adventurous life.

~

I knew Erica had grieved a little as I'd gradually become more interested in boys and our halcyon days of play had come to an end, but now she too was almost a young woman, and we would be together again.

Warren and Darryl were mad on surfing – a new rage. On rare occasions Erica and I were invited to go with them. It was an austere life – surfing. Several other local lads went with them and if the surf was up, they'd strap their boards to their cars and head for the coast. They never thought of taking spare clothes or much food, and often there'd be no shop within fifty kilometres of where the waves were. Almonds, a loaf of wholemeal bread and a block of cheese were usually sustenance enough. If there was good surf, they might sleep on the beach or in their cars to be ready for the fight at first light to get out into the sea that only ever wanted to put them back on land.

The boys would return home tired, salty and sunburned, charged with countless tales of mindless risks and dangers.

Over the next few months, not only did Warren and I see each other in the evenings but we'd spend weekend daytime hours together as Warren went about his work and I helped. I was preparing for a farming life with him, and to leave my family home forever.

I'd loved my childhood, but now, with an awareness probably brought on by my maturing, I began to sense something amiss with my parents – pain, tension, a noticeable distance between them. My mum and dad, with their beauty, romantic music and dancing had seemed a fairytale to me. But things were changing.

Dad had been working for some years as foreman at an aluminium fabrication works and was unfulfilled by it. Mum, with a gift for communicating with children, had begun work as an assistant kindergarten teacher. She'd established close ties with some of the kindy mums and also loved the idea of being able to contribute financially to the home. Money decisions had always been, and still were, made by my father. Gregarious by nature, Mum was happier than I'd seen her since I was very young, but her high spirits were short-lived as my father was less than pleased with having his wife in the workforce. It was humiliating for a man to be perceived as not being able to provide sufficiently for his family. But it was not about that. My mum just wanted to be out in the world, and although it came at the price of Dad's disapproval, she stayed with the job she loved. She joined a ladies' tennis group. Dad played golf on the weekends. Erica spent hours with her horse. I played tennis and went out with Warren. What had once been a close-knit family now seemed to be unravelling.

Our parents had been determined to give us a happy childhood, their own having been less than ideal.

~

Dad had grown up on his family farm near Snowtown in South Australia's mid-north. His mother had died when he was only thirteen – a tragedy that would burden him for life. Within a year of her death, his father had re-married. His new stepmother was a concert pianist and music teacher from the city. At fifty and never having been married before, she'd been abruptly confronted with the rigours of farm life and caring for six grieving children. It was a disaster and must have been a time of little comfort for them all. Within two years, all the children had dispersed to various jobs and relatives, in spite of which they all remained extremely close throughout their lives – bonded by this joint childhood trauma. Leaving his beloved farm – the place where memories of his mother were strongest, my dad was sent to live with an aunt in Adelaide where he began an apprenticeship in boiler-making. He was fifteen.

My mother grew up in Adelaide. Her parents had separated when she too was thirteen, but unlike Dad who had become melancholy and withdrawn, Mum had become a Pollyanna. Life for her was a beautiful garden of love, laughter and song. Her father had manufactured and sold homoeopathic medicines. I never met him, even though he lived until I was about thirty. Mum rarely spoke of him. During the Depression, feeling helpless in the face of unemployment and the inability to provide adequately for his family, he began drinking. Of course this had only exacerbated the hardship on them all. Life must have become intolerable for my grandma. One day her two sisters walked into their house and told my grandfather he needed to leave. He did. There was no custody battle.

Grandma worked as a florist and housekeeper to support herself and her three children. Only recently, a relative who'd known my grandfather told me he'd been sober for the last seventeen years of his life. I felt an overwhelming sadness. Over time, Mum has shared a little about him when pressed, recalling the nice things for us – that he loved classical music, especially the tenors of the twenties and thirties, and that he wrote poetry. I have a deep remorse that I never sought him out. When I let myself think about it, it is a physical ache.

~

Mum and Dad never quarrelled in front of us but we discovered later that this had happened in hushed tones after we'd gone to bed. I'd become aware though of their underlying pain. Eventually both were prescribed large doses of Valium – the new wonder drug – and we wondered where the parents we once knew had gone. I wasn't unhappy. I had Warren. I simply created a world for myself in which there was no time to think about what was happening to my precious mum and dad.

When Erica was sixteen, she started going out with a boy her own age. A car enthusiast, Wayne spent countless hours fastidiously maintaining his first car. It wasn't unusual for him to arrive at ten pm to take Erica to the drive-in. She'd be impeccably and stunningly ready for him at seven but by nine would be in tears and wrecked on her bed. He'd arrive in his Ford Prefect – face aglow with the excitement of getting stuck in the mud out in the back blocks somewhere between his place and ours – only to become naively bewildered by Erica's forlorn state. He'd pacify her tenderly and she'd forgive him in an instant.

We were often a foursome – at the beach, out dancing, or at the drive-in. And there were many nights, especially through the winter of 'sixty-five, that we'd all sit in our lounge room by the fire – talking, laughing and drinking coffee. I think we delayed the demise of our mum and dad's marriage with our youthful joie de vivre.

With our bond re-established, Erica and I had romances to talk about now and the love of modern music to share. The pop and rock stars we'd been listening to on the radio and seeing on television for the past few years had seemed larger than life – almost fictitious. Now they were beginning to come to our country, even our city Adelaide.

# SIX

The Rolling Stones had hit the world stage – their songs constantly on the airwaves. On the night of their first concert in Adelaide, we were there. When the lights went up and Mick burst onto the stage, his energy had every seat in the house vacated in seconds. As the crowd surged we were carried forward, and with every other girl there, I held my head and screamed.

The Barossa had been parochial and steeped in European traditions for more than a century. Now our generation was inviting in the rest of the world. The Beatles, Rolling Stones, American pop stars. Cabarets were new, dinner parties, fondue, tuna mornay and pottery-making. I joined a pottery class. The feel of the clay in my hands and taking a finished piece from the kiln was pure joy. My love of unique pottery has endured decades of fads.

Jill's parents were the first to throw a dinner party. It was certainly a more elegant way to enjoy the wines of our region than the "men only" schluck in the vineyard or the back shed. In the sixties, the only red wine was claret and rarely drunk by women, who were only just dipping their toes into the water of wine appreciation. They might drink a Moselle, a Riesling or perhaps a wee sherry as an aperitif. Port after a meal was still a "men only" rite.

Jill's parents invited Rosemary and Jack, Jill and her boyfriend Dean, and Warren and me to a dinner party. Jill and Kiwi were no longer together. The Clarkson home, built of local stone, was charming – the dining room cosy with antique cedar table, bentwood chairs and an early Barossa chiffonier, all lovingly restored by Jill's father. The craftsmanship of our ancestors was beginning to be appreciated, and discarded pieces were being rescued from farmyard barns and outhouses. In this gracious room, kerosene lamps had been converted to electricity. Original paintings and etchings hung on the walls. Fresh flowers and candlelight added to the ambience.

We girls hadn't yet acquired a taste for wine so while the boys drank beer, we sipped cocktails in fine glasses with sugar-coated rims and cherries on toothpicks. With the Ray Connif Singers and Buddy Holly on the turntable, we normally would have danced, but this was our first dinner party and we felt more inclined to stay at the table, enjoying the home-cooked modern food served by Mr and Mrs Clarkson. Feeling posh and of the world, we discussed world affairs, social issues and our own burgeoning philosophies.

My parents did the same for the six of us a few weeks later. In our small but tastefully appointed modern home, they prepared and served a wonderful meal with love and panache. The open fire, soft lights, and music of The Glen Miller Band, created the intimate atmosphere on which my romantic soul thrived.

This new in-home dining was something that appealed to my mum and dad and it wasn't long before they and their friends too were entertaining in this way. Prior to this, the only communal eating we'd known was the greater family Sunday lunch, church teas or chop picnics.

~

Sunday roasts with extended family had been a tradition in my early childhood. All food had been grown locally. Mr Lindner called once a week selling vegetables and eggs from a large wicker basket balanced skilfully on the handlebars of his bicycle. Mum usually offered him a cup of tea which he always accepted as he tipped his felt hat and removed it. He was a slight, polite man in a tweed coat with patches at the elbows. I was fascinated by him. He looked like a character from one of my story books – a visual image stored away in my writer's mental treasure trove.

At our small stone settlers' cottage – my first home – on those Sundays of the roasts, the men would gather in the shed to survey Dad's projects, while the women cooked. Stealing crunchy morsels of meat before it was served was an activity that caused much laughter and smacking of offending hands with various utensils. Perhaps the ladies had enjoyed a sherry or two.

Having come from the cooler climates of Europe, our ancestral grandmothers had upheld the tradition of the Sunday roast cooked in their wood-fired ovens – no matter that our Barossa summer days were often above forty degrees Celsius.

In winter there were chop picnics. With several other families, we'd drive down to the Murray River flats where the men would chop out mallee stumps for our fires.

After the slow creeping about of cars through the bush in search of the best picnic spot, we'd clear an area and lay out the family rugs. Never a chair. I was interested in the fire lighting process as the countryside was usually damp on these days and there was a skill to the task. Dad had taught me how to find dry grass and leaves under stumps or logs and I'd run off to collect enough to get the fire started. The scent of smoke rising from first gum leaves was divine to me. Before long, the flames, fanned by the gentle Mallee breezes, would be dancing with self-importance. I'd be happy then to leave it.

We kids would disappear into the bush and begin building huts out of tree branches. We'd fashion small stone walls around them, and if there were wild flowers, we'd pick them to decorate the finished build. All through my childhood one of my favourite games was erecting huts.

At these picnics, chops and sausages were cooked in wire holders over the coals, and on the side, nothing more exotic than potatoes and onions. The fresh eucalyptus-scented air gave us raging appetites and there were always home-made cakes afterwards – lamingtons, butterfly cakes or cream lilies – and billy tea for the adults. No tea or coffee for kids until we were fourteen. A family rule.

After lunch, the men would take their axes into the bush, and we'd resume our games. When the fathers had chopped enough wood to fill the car boots, they'd return to the picnic spot for a beer. Traditionally then the portable record player would be brought out, wound up, and Victor Borge records played. Victor was a German pianist and comedian who made the adults crack up, and although the same two records were played at every picnic, they always laughed as if they'd never heard the jokes before. I loved to see my dad happy. He was a serious man but these were his mates and he loved these outings with them. Their wives and Mum were friends too, but not close. Mum had not yet found a friend to suit her free spirit.

One Sunday we had the car packed ready for one of these excursions when it began to rain. After some conferring amongst the adults, the picnic was cancelled. We kids were bitterly disappointed but, undaunted, Mum set about creating one for us anyway – indoors. She spread our rug on the kitchen floor, and as we ate the chops that Dad had cooked on a fire outside (long before the modern backyard barbecue), she helped us imagine the sounds of the bush, the smell of the soft damp earth and the smoke. And whenever we sat still with Mum long enough, we'd sing. Perhaps it was *Dark Town Strutters' Ball* that day.

> *'I'll be down to get you in a taxi honey*
> *You'd better be ready about half past eight*
> *Now dearie don't be late*
> *I wanna be there when the band starts playing...'*

No cutesie nursery rhymes for us. We were raised on jazz, and I loved that.

Sometimes we went to visit my grandfather. I can't imagine how difficult it must have been for him, while still in his fifties to have sold his farm at Snowtown and retire to the city. The tenet within the family was that his second wife, Myrtle, had not been able to adapt to life on the land.

Before we had a phone, we'd arrive at their house unannounced, at around ten on a Sunday morning. Myrtle would answer the door – more than often in her dressing gown.

'Oh hello,' she'd say politely. 'We're not dressed yet. Will you wait?'

She'd close the door and for the next twenty minutes we'd mill in the garden, waiting until they were ready to receive us. Grandfather would come to the door then, dressed in a nice shirt and tie, tailored pants, polished shoes. Myrtle would be in her best frock and shoes and rich lady's jewellery.

Their home was filled with antique furniture, not the least of which was a magnificent grand piano. We'd always ask Myrtle to play. Erica and I knew she was a virtuoso but our main motive for asking was to experience the sweet agony of impermissible laughter.

She'd take several requests for it before going to sit on her stool – facing us, not the piano. For the next five minutes she'd engage in the conversation whilst warming her slightly arthritic hands. The suspense would be killing us.

'Please will you play?' we'd beg.

She'd turn to the piano then and flick her dark bobbed hair. Hands raised, she'd stall them a foot above the keys, flick her hair again and finally attack the keys with Rachmaninovian gusto. We knew that laughter wasn't allowed but we'd be nearly bursting with it as the wild music erupted. But more than the delight of naughty giggling was my absolute awe of the divine sound emanating from the instrument's recesses. I often wonder if there are any recordings of her recitals. I'd love to hear them now.

Grandfather was a nice man. Formal. Remnants of his English heritage. When I was older I learned to take any rings off my right hand before greeting him – his handshake was so painfully firm. He always seemed happy to see us, and I know Dad enjoyed the short visits to see his Pop. After a cup of tea and a biscuit at the oak pie-crust-edged dining table, Grandfather would take Dad out to show him his backyard. For decades this man had risen before dawn to feed his horses and prepare them for work. He'd cleared his land with axes. He'd ploughed the earth, sowed his crops – unprotected against the rigours of winter. He'd reaped grain and stooked hay, built miles of fencing from posts he'd cut by hand. Now he had a square of lawn, a lemon tree, a plum, and a board-edged patch of beans.

~

Family outings like these were all behind us now, and old traditions dying – picnics, eating customs, entertainment.

Earliest restaurants were opening. Warren and I discovered The Havana in Adelaide. A large sweep of curved floor-to-ceiling windows offered a glorious view to the city and her lights. The place was chic with white tablecloths, silver cutlery glittering with candlelight, a live band with the rakish, roving tenor, Giovanni, playing and singing Italian love songs. The food was good but at our age the least important feature. More importantly it was downtown, modern, and a far cry from the Sunday roast.

Some of our local lads formed a band – The Chosen Few. Their music, even in those early days, was urbane. They'd been runners up in The Australian Battle of The Sounds. One night they were playing in our town. A few of us poked our heads in at about ten and the band was in a capsule of creativity. The hall was dark, the stage well-lit. The crew and girlfriends of the musicians were standing around – indistinct in the darkness other than for the glow of their cigarettes. The boys were playing something moody, slow – The Shadows perhaps, in a state of Miles Davis-like introspection. Someone said, 'This is a bit dead. Let's go.'

'No,' I said, 'let's stay.'

The music was good. Really good.

'Come on, let's dance,' I said to Warren.

I didn't care that we were the only ones. We loved dancing and I closed my eyes as the improvised music did its work on me. Soon others joined us, and within an hour, the band had upped the tempo, and decibels, and there were a hundred or more on the dance floor. Now they were playing Ray Charles's *What'd I Say*. Dancers and band were totally connected – everyone singing. The place was rocking. We didn't need drugs. We were high on music, freedom, love.

A whirlwind of cabarets, barbecues, sherry parties and balls followed. Our friend Dean, winemaker and sherry-party host extraordinaire, organised a table of thirty-six for a Rotary Club cabaret and invited us all to his parents' home for a party before the function.

As a child, I'd watched my mum and dad and their friends gather in our home before balls and had been in awe of the women in their gorgeous evening wear. I loved dressing up and was chuffed with the curves my body had developed. Now here I was in my own gold-on-white satin, sleeveless, princess-line gown – crystal sherry glass in one gloved hand, cigarette in a holder in the other, while expounding intellectual views on world affairs. At the end of the evening however, the group of thirty-six would have been unsophisticated, unreservedly chummy and some sick.

Rosemary and Jack had married and were living in a rented house in town. Here we played grown-ups. To see the girlfriend I'd begun primary school with, now a wife in her own home – preparing meals, keeping house, entertaining – seemed almost surreal.

The four of us spent long evenings together. Sipping alcoholic drinks in their candlelit unit, we listened to non-stop music on the radiogram, sang, danced and talked. Idyllic. If this was what marriage was all about, I couldn't wait for our day. Ha! Living in a hut in the bush with rough-hewn men was not what I'd pictured.

In December of nineteen sixty-five, Warren and I became engaged and celebrated with a quiet, romantic dinner together at The Havana. The announcement appeared in *The Advertiser* the following day. A lot of our friends must have been expecting it as there was a deluge of congratulations that very morning – phone calls, telegrams, people stopping us in the street, calling out from passing cars. We'd told our gang there was to be a party at my home that night for Warren's birthday. Forty friends came bearing engagement gifts.

A week or two later I had a special visit. Leon and his brother Chris called in. Although Leon was his usual quiet self, I felt no animosity from him. The small talk between us drew us together and kept us apart. I wasn't sure what the visit was about. My engagement to Warren wasn't mentioned. A year had passed since I'd seen Leon. I sensed he was happily entrenched in the Air Force. Whatever had prompted them, it was lovely to see them again.

My young brother thought the world of Warren and didn't need to be asked twice to accompany him on various farming tasks. This meant a lot to me. The joy of Dale's birth, and how lucky we were to have him, was still a vivid memory.

~

Dad had desperately wanted a son. I was six years old when my brother, Dale, was born. The hot early summer had brought on sudden sun frocks when my parents brought their wee babe home and placed him on a bed of soft white cotton in the plywood crib that Dad had built for him. In my parents' cool, darkened bedroom, Erica and I peeped quietly in at him – tiny and sweet-smelling in his snowy white singlet and nappy. He was a special gift and cherished by us all.

A couple of years later, Allan, a friend of Dad's, called in to our place one Saturday morning. He was a tall, cheerful bloke who whistled like a bird. To me, it was as delightful as listening to a beautifully played jazz flute. Allan had a habit of reversing out of our driveway at high speed and this morning, as he was about to leave, my mother ran to the window to search for Dale. She saw him playing in the driveway directly behind Allan's car. Her scream was deafening as she saw the vehicle back over her child.

We rushed out to find Dad with our precious little brother in his arms. There'd been tons of sand spread in our driveway the day before, ready for concrete to be laid. Dale must have sunk into it when the wheels went over him as he was still alive. I remember the chill as, standing at a distance, I watched my parents in terrifying panic. Mum ran inside to phone the doctor who pulled into our driveway within minutes. He took Dale from my mother's cradling arms, laid him gently on our kitchen table and began to examine him. The dread in the room was overpowering. My sister and I had moved to an out of the way corner of the room and huddled there together. Everyone was silent, waiting – for the doctor to speak.

'I think he'll be okay,' we heard.

It was a miracle. The bruises across his chest told us that had it not been for the sand, the outcome would have been bleak. If it was possible to cherish him more, we did.

~

Now he was twelve, and at Warren's side at every opportunity.

I'd met and bonded instantly with Warren's sister, Jenny, and her husband-to-be, Evan, both of whom were living and working at a missionary training college in Tasmania.

It was about this time that I was taken to the property at Copeville for first inspection. Warren had been relieved then elated at my enthusiasm, his father quietly chuffed.

In the summer following our engagement, my family and I took Warren to meet my father's sister and her husband – farmers at Corny Point on South Australia's Yorke Peninsula. As a child, I'd spent two weeks there during harvest.

~

The Corny Point farmhouse was built of limestone. Its gracious rooms seemed opulent to me as a thirteen year old. The dry, harsh summer that only crows and flies shrugged off, couldn't touch us in the cool dark house. In the grand lounge room was a pianola, where I'd spend as much time as my aunt would allow, pedalling away with gusto as the roll's intricate little pin-pricks scrolled down to produce Beethoven's exquisite, soul-stirring *Moonlight Sonata.*

On the day I went out to help Uncle Vern it was more than forty degrees as we climbed into his Jeep and drove out to one of the paddocks. There was a stand of barley in bags that hadn't yet been stitched. This was my job. When I'd finished, Uncle Vern loaded them onto his truck via an elevator. We headed for Edithburgh where the grain was to be unloaded. Aunty Roma had packed cucumber sandwiches for our lunch but by the time we got to eat them, they were near steaming and I was in pain with hunger. I was glad to return to the consoling house at the end of the day and ease into the Art Deco bath filled with warm water from the wood stove.

There was no electricity. A generator supplied enough power for lights, but Uncle Vern was the only one who could start it. So, in the evenings Aunty Roma and I would sit at the lantern-lit kitchen table – she silently smoking, and me with a mull of creative thoughts as we waited for the commanding farmer to come in from reaping. A room is quiet without electricity. I'd be past hungry and so tired I'd fall asleep with my head on my arms. It was rare for us to have our evening meal before ten.

Aunty Roma was a petite, intelligent woman. Daughter of a farmer. Wife of a farmer. Refined. She had recognised my artistic bent and one morning offered me her set of watercolour paints of the most vibrant colours. I packed up a folding chair, an easel, paper and the paints, and set out for the sea – more than a two kilometre walk along a sandy track through a tunnel of tea trees. In a shady spot at the beach's edge where I could see the dazzling water through the trees, I began to paint. I was delighted with the way the picture took shape – my first plein air painting. For years afterwards, whenever I came across this picture in my cupboard, the memory of that lovely day would be rekindled.

Aunty Roma had books – classics. I'd curl up in an enormous club lounge chair in the big, silent sitting room and read voraciously – blissfully free of interruption.

The homestead stood in the middle of an almost treeless stony paddock. A few pot plants on the verandah and a mulberry tree in the backyard were like diamonds on a plain girl. Aunty Roma was destined to live in arid environments. A few years later they were to sell this farm and buy a huge sheep station in Western Australia.

After my week at Corny Point I was ready to go home. The last day dragged as I longed for my family to come and retrieve me. In the eerie twilight, I went to a lonely hide where a litter of kelpie pups lolled in the sand. Their mother was out with Uncle Vern. The wind sighed and wailed about the corners of the house as I thought wistfully of home. But then the pups rallied, and I was comforted as they began to play and romp all over me. Sitting on a frayed bag in the sandy hollow, acutely aware of the remoteness of this farm, I imagined my family at their evening meal, excitedly anticipating their trip to collect me next day.

Being re-united with my parents and siblings was as lovely as warm socks on a cold day. Our meal together that evening was enjoyed at a reasonable hour as Uncle Vern had almost finished harvest, and the room came alive with the chatter of all that had happened during our time apart. I hadn't been altogether happy about being sent here without my sister, but as I talked of all that I'd seen and done that week, I began to recognise it as a privilege.

Next day was New Year's Eve. Uncle Vern's parents had invited us to one of their renowned parties. They owned a beach resort at Corny Point. Sea-Acres was a lively place in the fifties and sixties. A row of modern beach units – each one painted a different colour as trend required – was strung along the shore.

The Hills were extraordinary hosts and during summer holidays, in the spacious front room of their gracious home, they provided nightly entertainment for their guests. The whole family was talented musically, and with sing-alongs around the piano, there'd be an atmosphere of fun and merriment. On each holiday here, there'd be new friends to be made, a different boy to "fall in love" with, nights around beach campfires watching the moon come up and singing country songs. Uncle Vern played the piano accordion and my dad the harmonica. The evening's catch – whiting or garfish – would be cooked over coals, incited now and then by a sea breeze, then served on enamel plates and eaten with sounds of satisfaction. When the final swim had been swum, and all the kids were too cold and too tired to talk, we'd curl up on the Onkaparinga rugs and, wrapped in our mothers' cardigans, we'd drift towards sleep, smiling with the music and the sighing of the sea.

~

Uncle Vern – a dyed-in-the-wool farmer – liked Warren instantly, and so the first thing he needed to do was take him out 'roo shooting. The 'roos were in plague proportion that year and so the Jeep was made ready for the hunt. After tea, Dad, Warren and I climbed into the vehicle with quiet instructions from Dad, 'Just remember, when Vern says "Hold on", he means *Hold on!*'

I watched my uncle throw a bag of wheat into the back for ballast and prepared myself for action. Warren was operating the spotlight, and Dad and Vern had rifles.

The first 'roo was sighted.

'Hold on!' the anticipated command.

Vern dodged and wove through the bush at breakneck speed. Every now and then, he'd hit a fox-hole and we'd be thrown from our seats or were heaped onto each other as he'd take a sudden swerve to avoid a fence. The couple of 'roos shot were brought home to feed the dogs. No tinned pet food in those days. My uncle tied one to a shed rafter and lowered it a little each day as the dogs ate their way through it – an inglorious end for such a magnificent creature. Intellectually, I understood that this was about life in the bush.

After the hunt, we sat around the kitchen table drinking coffee. The men smoked and talked – of rainfall, yields, and sheep. I was the only female still up. I listened, and learned.

# SEVEN

Nineteen sixty-six. The Vietnam War. US and Australian troops were entrenched. Youth were protesting passionately. Music was changing. While previously we'd been singing along to uninspired songs like *Rubber Ball* and *Ahab the Arab*, we were now listening to *A Hard Rain, The Times They Are a-Changin, Blowin' in the Wind*. Discontent, ideas, philosophies were being expressed. Warren and I were mad on Bob Dylan – enigmatic poet/ singer/ songwriter.

On the radio one Sunday morning I learned of an arthouse documentary to be shown that day in the city – Dylan's *Don't Look Back*. We had to be there. Directions to the venue were sketchy and it took us a while to find the small warehouse tucked away in one of Adelaide's small lanes. Only a poster on the doorway indicated we were in the right place. We entered the intimate blacked-out space and found ourselves amongst others of our kind – a small gathering of about fifty – Adelaide's earliest devotees. Lights were dim. Large black and white posters of Dylan covered the walls and his music fuelled our fever.

> 'Johnny's in the basement, mixin' up the medicine,
> I'm on the pavement, thinkin' 'bout the government...'

Kindred souls, we all sat haphazardly on an eclectic scattering of chairs, speaking in hushed tones, listening and waiting for almost an hour. I was mad with anticipation. When the film finally began, it was all I'd hoped it would be. A crew had followed Dylan on a concert tour of Britain, filming him and his band as they rehearsed, talked with agents and fellow musicians, and performed. It was the poet about him that had me enthralled – the storytelling, the art, the delicious ambiguity.

Jimi Hendrix too had me on a lead. Guitar playing genius – wild, expressive, experimental. Being in a room exploding with his unbridled riffs stirred my creative juices irrepressibly. The poet within me was beginning to stir.

>HENDRIX
>Infringement of fear
>Billowing breath
>Ant language merges in a glass case
>louder and higher
>Seeds drop
>are picked up
>thrown high
>Leader laughs too late
>too loud
>over and over and under
>the thunder ends it

# EIGHT

Ian Schmaal was an old school mate of Warren's, and a farmer. He and his fiancée, Nat, had planned a short holiday and invited us to go with them. Although we hadn't met Nat before and I hardly knew Ian, we were to spend a week with them in Port Lincoln.

On the day we left, despite my being nineteen years old, a sense of impropriety wrestled with my excitement. A weekend away before we were married – quite risqué.

Ian's car radio emitted quiet classical music. For me, the prospect of having to listen to the ABC for the entire trip felt akin to standing in the corner at school. Nat was a piano teacher and in those days reserved – as I too could have been perceived. And so, to the quiet strains of Mozart, Bach, Beethoven, et al, we drove for hours while the boys talked farming. It would be another six years or so before I'd rediscover the classical music I'd loved as a child.

~

A close friend of my mother had played classical piano. Mum had taken me, as a three or four year old, to listen to her practice. I'd been mesmerised by the haunting melodies of Chopin and

Debussy that filled her front room. There were visual delights for me too. Exquisite vases, clocks, figurines, ancestral photographs. And aromas – sweet peas in a vase, ambrosial cedar furniture, the mustiness of heavy drapes.

~

The four of us booked in to the grand old Boston Hotel on Port Lincoln's esplanade. Nat and I were wearing engagement rings but without wedding rings we dared not book in as couples. Nat and I were shown to our twin share room and the boys to theirs. We dressed for the evening and went down to the graciously furnished dining room for dinner where, over a couple of drinks, we became better acquainted. There'd been innuendos over dinner about room arrangements and so later that night when the hotel had become quiet, I gathered up my belongings (with nod from Nat) and tiptoed down the corridor to the boys' room. I knocked on their door.

'Nat's waiting for you,' I said to Ian as he opened it. He made some cheeky remark, gathered his luggage and left the room.

That night Warren and I had a festival of what our young bodies craved – tempered a little for me by a feeling of having my hand in the cookie jar. I felt sure that in the morning there would be people tut-tutting about us.

*Tunarama* was the other festival on in Port Lincoln that week and each day we revelled in the town's party atmosphere, played tennis, went to the beach which was just a few metres from our hotel, or did day trips in the car. I'd never experienced such luxury.

Warren and I began to plan our honeymoon. We'd set a wedding date – after grain harvest and before the vintage of 'sixty-seven.

Through part-time study my dad had become a draughtsman – a lifelong ambition realised. So with his help, Warren's parents began to design a new home whose mortgage payments would be our responsibility in return for possession of the Grocke homestead in which Warren's father had lived all his life. For years his mother had dreamt of building a light-filled home on the hill, with views across the vineyards to the ranges. I was now brimming with ideas for the one that would be ours – the eighty year old stone home overlooking vineyards, farmyard, thatch-roofed barns, Gomersal Bridge and the creek of my childhood. What a privilege it would be to care for this wonderful old holding.

Our courtship was not without challenges. Warren was prone to mood swings that mystified me, and I tended to be possessive of his time. He was my world and I missed him terribly when he was working away. Men's own country, Copeville at this time, was still considered too rough for women. Most of the time though we were blissfully happy and I believed these small issues would be easily resolved once we were married.

In the final months before our wedding, there were still afternoons with my girlfriends. We'd sit on our beds and share our deepest feelings as we'd always done. Not for a moment did I contemplate that once we were all married, these precious times would be gone forever.

~

Jill and I had been friends since primary school – our friendship cemented one Arbour Day. The folly of having cleared too much bush in South Australia had been realised, and on this day of each year, kids planted trees around the town in the morning and had the rest of the day off.

We were in Grade Seven, and on the day before this particular holiday I'd been handed a note by one of the boys in our class – "Jill and Susan. Meet us down at Gomersal Bridge. One o'clock tomorrow – PK and RB."

Pete Kraehenbuhl was one of our pals, and Robert Bouquey, a new kid at school, the son of publicans. He had a little of the toughness of pub life about him, an aloofness – perhaps something contrived in wisdom as a way of escaping boys' initiation rites. All the girls thought he was "keen", and to be invited out by him was no less than winning a ribbon in the Legion of Honour.

Jill and I were sure our parents would not allow this rendezvous and so, that night, I asked Mum if I could go around to Jill's next afternoon and Jill asked her mother if she could come to my place. Crafty rascals. The mothers were happy with it.

When school broke up next day, we headed out of town for the bridge. The boys were waiting. We all smiled. I felt a little wayward. Well? Here we are, was our body language. With a small sideways toss of his head, Pete said, 'Come on. We've got something to show you.'

We followed them through the grass, under low tree branches, up a steep embankment at the river's edge, down again, through some reeds until they stopped and pointed at a boy-built wooden raft sitting proudly on the water and tied to a tree. It was as if they were showing us no less than the tomb and treasure of Tutankhamen.

They jumped on board and offered us their hands by way of an invitation to adventure. Pete reached out to Jill, and Robert took my hand. A rush of something lovely rippled through me.

Tied to the raft were two poles cut from tree trimmings. Using these, the boys pushed us away from the bank. I don't know how far down stream we travelled – a kilometre perhaps. It was so pristine there was little need for conversation, and besides, the boys needed all the strength their eleven year old bodies could muster to steer the heavy craft around logs, tricky bends and down small waterfalls. Jill and I sat like princesses on the Nile. I wasn't scared. It was too exhilarating. We reached a clear landing where the boys helped us ashore. I don't think they had the strength to take us back upstream to where we had embarked, so they secured the raft to a tree and we headed back on foot. We didn't ask whose raft it was. Years later though, I learned it had been built and was highly valued by Warren and Jack. They'd been furious at having to search the river for their craft after it had been borrowed by us and left on the wrong side for them.

As we neared the bridge on our return, Jill said 'Well, we'd better go now. Thanks for inviting us.' And we cantered off like frisky foals. We hadn't gone far when a loud '*Oi*' stopped us in our tracks.

The boys were beckoning to us from where we'd left them. We ran back, feeling safe at the sight of their cheeky schoolboy smiles. They stepped towards us. Pete kissed Jill, and Robert kissed me. Kissed by Robert Bouquey and able to tell no-one! Excruciating. Off we pranced again, giggling and skittish. It was two kilometres to Jill's house and another three to mine. I arrived home with my secret at five. Years passed before I told Mum about that day.

Rosemary's mother grew roses. Her father was a distinguished and contemplative man who played the trombone. In winter he'd sit by the fire in their kitchen, playing the melancholy instrument or smoking his pipe and thinking thoughts we could never guess. Mrs Traeger cooked or arranged flowers. It was a happy home. Religious verses on the walls. As teenagers, Rosemary and I would sit on the floor of their lounge room talking about boys, clothes and music as we slipped our cherished vinyl discs out of their covers and onto the family's modern HMV radiogram. We had sport in common too – particularly tennis. And we loved athletics.

Marion – sunny, loving and confident – had become a friend in our final year of high school. We four were bonded by non-conformity, laughter and pranks, each of us always desperately involved in some romance, the essence of which needed constant scrutiny by the "enlightened council of four".

~

My girlfriends had been with me through the gamut of my relationship with Leon. They'd seen me through the intense time of breaking up with him and into the birth of my relationship with Warren. We'd grown up together but we were women now.

It was time to begin wedding plans. My bridesmaids would be Erica, Jill and Rosemary. Marion had left to teach in New Guinea. Warren's groomsmen would be his three cousins – Jack, Rob and John. Another book could be written about what these three lads got up to as kids.

During lunch breaks in my office, I pored over bridal magazines. I turned a page one day to see my dream wedding gown. It was breathtaking. I would ask the gifted seamstress who was now making most of my self-designed clothes, to create it. It would be of French ribbon lace and cost me a fortune, but I didn't care. I'd save for it. If I could look half as beautiful as my mother did on her wedding day, I'd be happy.

Warren and I bought travel magazines and planned our honeymoon. We would have three weeks in Surfers Paradise.

Stan Arnold's bicycle repair shop had been an icon of our main street but when Stan died, it had been bulldozed. In its place now stood a new hall, built by the Country Women's Association – the absolute bees' knees in wedding venues – so we booked it for our reception.

I was ready to leave my parents' nest, and Mum and I were having the not uncommon mother-daughter fights. Mum's inherent happiness had been sorely tested by her failing marriage and a still raw grief over her mother's early death. The laughter was gone, the sparkle faded.

My grandma had suffered a coronary occlusion when I was about thirteen and recovered. Two years later though she had died of a heart attack – just sitting in her armchair one evening. She was only sixty-two. Mum was devastated.

Grandma had been a sunny person who'd developed a sense of fun – to compensate perhaps for the loss of her husband to alcoholism during The Depression. After her three children had grown up and left home, she'd worked as a nanny and housekeeper for a wealthy family. From then, she'd not had a home of her own, so we had never been able to visit her. On rare occasions she came to stay with us. I loved her pretty face, her silky skin soft against my cheek when she kissed me, and her laughter. Her name was Dorothea but most called her Dolly, and all who knew her loved her. I was sad when she passed away, but not as traumatised as when my cat died a year later and I cried for two days.

About eighteen months after Grandma died, there'd been a phone call in the night. I can't forget the sound of my mother's terrible weeping. Her only brother, John, had died of a heart attack at the age of thirty-six. He and Mum had always been the best of mates.

I think the trauma of those two early deaths made its mark on my mum. Apart from grieving for her loved ones, she feared it was a genetic thing that might take her down as well.

After each of our conflicts, she'd remind me of Grandma and Uncle John, and tell me to think about how I'd feel if she should die. I hated that. I was champing at the bit for independence. Ready to set sail on my own life's journey. I'm not sure what the fights were about. There must be a time when the dynamics between mother and daughter change, when a daughter knows she is no longer a child and the mother is still seeing her as one. Perhaps it was that.

On the eve of my wedding, gowns hung from wardrobe doors, designer shoes peeped out of tissue-lined boxes and new make-up lay enticingly on my dressing table.

It was customary in the Valley to have a "tin kettling" on this night, and ours was a corker. Beer and wine, cheese and mettwurst, German cake and coffee were served to the dozens of wellwishers who called. Neighbours brought gifts. Jack brought gelignite! He'd planted it in the vineyard behind our house and at about ten that night a deafening explosion rattled our unique curved plate-glass windows. Within minutes the local constable arrived. He told Dad he'd been watching the Lionel Rose world title fight when his TV flickered off and on. We all knew by then who'd set the five sticks, but Dad pleaded ignorance. With a barely discernible twinkle in his eye, the officer issued a warning.

We later heard that the neighbour who lived nearest the "bomb" site, and who'd been thinking of cutting a doorway through his dining room wall, didn't need to now. There was a crack wide enough to walk through. Our Jack.

Next morning I woke at five – too excited to think about how this would be the last day of my living in this house. Dad was the one reflecting on that. At sixes and sevens with all the to-do, he was trying to find a space for himself in his small house full of females. He and Dale busied themselves with organising drinks for the reception. Mum prepared a delicious champagne and chicken lunch – the champagne just enough to fill the house with silliness and laughter. Mid-afternoon my girlfriends and I applied our make-up and stepped into our gorgeous gowns – bridesmaids in apple-blossom strewn pink silk and me in my French ribbon lace. It was time – the biggest of all days for a girl in the sixties. I thought I could picture my life as a married woman. I knew it would be nothing like my mother's. More like what I'd seen of my mother-in-law's. But most alluringly I could see companionship – being in a so far conjectural partnership with the man I loved.

The church was alive and brimming with flowers and friends as I walked down the aisle on my father's arm. My husband greeted me at the altar with a look of tenderness that said he would love me forever. I had no doubt he would.

I'd dreamed of our reception being the wonderful party that it was. At the piano, a friend of mine from high school, played the romantic jazz standards that were his passion, and mine.

At around ten my husband and I slipped back to my family home and changed into our travelling clothes – sixties tradition. We returned then to farewell our guests and attempt a getaway in the Valiant that we'd entrusted to Jenny and Evan to keep safe from mischief. They'd done this well but when they arrived with our car, Jack and his cohorts sprang into action with ready-made strings of empty cans which they tied to the rear bumper bar. Despite a super quick "pit stop", we rattled off down the highway sounding like rubbish tins in a wind storm.

We drove to Waikerie, an hour away, where we'd booked into the "honeymoon suite" of the no-frills country hotel. For months we'd been preparing for this day and now it was almost over. We were married, and finally and absolutely free to spend the night alone together. The intimacy of undressing in front of each other in a room with the light on was something we'd experienced only once before – on our holiday to Port Lincoln. We'd been accustomed only to the confines of the car. We slept all night in each other's arms.

Our destination, Surfers Paradise, was the new Australian "Riviera". We'd planned to take a week to get there. We dallied in towns, got up late, had long breakfasts and candlelit dinners in swanky restaurants. We'd bought new clothes for our holiday and each morning I'd put on a carefully chosen dress, make-up, best perfume, new wedding ring shining brilliantly. The whole experience had me feeling like royalty.

In Surfers we stayed in a new resort, complete with pool and restaurant – standard today but luxury then.

Early in the week, Warren discovered a slot car racing track where we spent an hour or so. Next morning he suggested we go again. After another hour of watching these crazy little cars buzzing around a track, I asked if he'd like to come to the shops. He said he'd stay, so I went alone. We met for lunch, went back to the resort for a swim and then Warren ducked up to the slot cars again for "a spot of racing". Over the next two or three days that were a repeat of this, we became increasingly cranky with each other. Begrudgingly, Warren came to the shops with me one morning and, picking up a Hawaiian grass skirt and lei, asked me if I'd like it. No, I said. He bought it anyway.

In fact, this farm boy and country girl had become bored after two or three days of the ritzy life in one place, and in all probability would have been happier camped by a cheery creek in the bush.

We returned home to the prospect of living with Warren's parents for four long months.

# NINE

Lin and Otto's new house was still being built so Warren's bedroom became our very cosy marital space. Here we slept each night in his single bed. Not what I'd dreamed of, but as Lin reminded me, she'd lived with her in-laws for years.

I'd left my job to become a housewife – protocol of the sixties – and I was not yet a strong-minded person. I helped Lin with the running of the household and she schooled me in the "art" of being Mrs Grocke. There were dozens of eggs to be collected every morning. Monday was washing day. Tuesday – ironing. On Wednesdays eggs had to be washed and prepared for sale. Thursday – cleaning and gardening. Friday – shopping and going to the hairdresser! Saturday – baking. And Sunday – going to church and visiting or being visited. The evenings were spent mending or knitting while watching TV.

The men's boots and shoes were cleaned weekly and men were always served first at the table. If Lin and I were having a cup of tea when Otto or Warren walked into the house, she'd jump up, make them a hot drink and not sit down again until they'd left the room – a custom she'd learned, I presumed, from her mother-in-law. I was truly amazed at, and not at all enamoured by the daily routine. I would have to wait until I could establish my own. There was nothing gradual about leaving the way of life I'd been accustomed to.

~

Although there'd been an element of structure in our home life before my marriage, my mother had been a far more random housekeeper. She'd just seemed to have put one foot in front of the other each day to deal with whatever was priority. Her philosophy was and still is "Live in the moment."

Our meals though had been reasonably predictable. Once a week the butcher turned into our street, tooting the horn of his van to herald his arrival. The housewives would emerge from their homes carrying large tea towel covered plates. Greeting each other formally, they'd gather at the rear of the vehicle where they'd choose the cuts of meat that would feed their families for a week.

The butcher carried a leafy bough and for as long as the back doors of his van were open, he would switch at flies – real or imagined. Mum usually bought a piece of fritz for our school sandwiches, some rump steak, minced beef and six lamb chops – two for Dad and one each for the rest of us. If we were expecting visitors on a Sunday, she might buy a leg of lamb, or a chicken from the local poultry farmer. Everything was served with three veg. No choices for kids. Although Mum was a good cook, I complained one evening about the chops. Dad sent me straight to bed. I was so hungry by breakfast I never complained again.

By five-fifteen each evening, Dad would be home from work. While Mum cooked tea, he'd have a beer and read the newspaper. Erica and I would set the table and shell the peas or slice the beans in the blue bean cutter screwed to the edge of the table.

I loved our conversations around the table each night as we shared the events of the day and listened to our dad, who was normally a quiet man, telling us of world affairs, amazing facts about the universe and stories of his childhood. He had a wide general knowledge due to the fact that he listened a lot and read the newspaper daily. I remember the night he taught us about the difference between fission and fusion. I was already fascinated with words, and my mouth dropped open at the magnitude of the word antidisestablishmentarianism – the longest word in the English dictionary, he told us. Typical discourse. In talk of his childhood, his mother was rarely mentioned. We knew she'd been dearly loved by her family but I think for Dad it was still, even then, too painful for him to speak of her. He'd just toughed out his loss and kept his grief to himself. More often, his boyhood stories were of the strange sudden stepmother and the harshness of life on the land as the son of a farmer whose heartbreak had consumed him.

Each night after tea, Erica and I had to tidy the kitchen and do the dishes – a task I hated with a passion. Mum is still famous for the state of her kitchen after she's been cooking. It's terrifying by her own admission. The kitchen work was always our job, no matter how tired we were, and we were often spent by the physicality of our play.

After the dishes, we'd adjourn to the lounge room where we were allowed to listen to Bob Dyer's *Pick-a-box* on the radio. I loved testing myself with the quiz questions. Adding to my stash of general knowledge, I believed, would hold me in good stead for life. Homework was to be done after that, but on weekends or during holidays we were allowed to stay up and listen to *Harry Dearth's Playhouse* or the evening serial. These programmes stimulated my imagination almost as much as reading. English was already my favourite subject at school and writing a joy.

Sometimes, after these broadcasts, Dad would take his *Hohner* harmonica out of its ornate cardboard box, warm the wee instrument in his hands and begin to play the jazz standards that I love to this day – *Autumn Leaves, September Song, Stardust,* et al. We'd go to bed then with the comforting and familiar sounds of the mouth organ and Mum's dreamy songs lulling us to sleep.

Each Saturday my sister and I would clean the house while Mum dealt with the laundering and repair of clothes, gardening or baking. Whatever was imminent.

~

Very soon I would be my own kind of housekeeper. That I would one day be a farmer and not just a farmer's wife, could not have been a more distant notion.

I loved the farm and often imagined its olden workings – the drawing of water from the well, the lighting of the fire under the copper on washing days, the constant stoking of the wood stove in the kitchen to keep it hot for cooking, the milking of cows, plucking of poultry, a year's worth of preserves and smallgoods made and stored in the cellar. Most of those activities gone now – all but the preserving of food.

Four months after we were married, Lin and Otto moved into their new home and we were at last alone in our own. Although I'd had a moment of panic when I realised I'd have to do dishes every day for the rest of my life, the freedom of having my own home was almost intoxicating. With a strong interest in interior design, I began to decorate. We bought a fabulous T H Brown dining suite – solid teak and of stunning Scandinavian design. Around this table our family and friends have gathered for more than forty years. As modern today as it was then, the timber has only improved with age, and the furniture still draws admiring comments from visitors.

I'd done some abstract paintings that now hung on our walls – sixties stuff – paisley-esque and geometric shapes, hard edges. Posters were in. Hippies had them hanging in their pads. So did I. I designed and made my own. Loving the bold, patterned fabrics of the time, the explosion of colour, the realms within a paisley design, I pored over my *Vanity Fair* magazines and went to my canvasses at night with my own abstractions.

The old Grocke family radiogram stayed with the house and we began to build our own collection of LP's – Patsy Cline, Buddy Holly, Elvis Presley, Chuck Berry, Little Richard.

We threw parties. I loved getting the house ready, creating a bohemian atmosphere with candles, kinky bric-a-brac, posters of Dylan and Hendrix. Our music was always loud and we'd dance all night. In winter a fire burned constantly in the open fireplace. We drank alcohol, but there was no anger, there were no fights, we just got happier and funnier. There were still endless cabarets, balls and parties where we stayed out till all hours. This was just how I'd imagined married life to be. Ha!

Warren accepted an invitation to join the local Apex Club. By now he was also secretary of his church and a member of the Emergency Fire Service. It hadn't taken long for me to realise my husband loved to be involved in his community.

One of my first jobs on the farm was to help inject pigs against tetanus. I was to hold the babies by the back legs while Warren did the needle work. The first piglet made such an enormous noise – far greater than warranted – that I nearly dropped it with fright.

As we now had a mortgage, we needed more money than Warren could earn from pigs and shearing, so he bought a hammer mill, built a shed for it and began to produce stock feed for sale. Enterprising to the core. His main work, however, was still with his father – helping in the vineyard, running sheep in the hills, share-farming, and working the property at Copeville.

Warren was passionate about livestock and animal husbandry. His dream and plan was to build a flock of sheep big enough to provide us with a good livelihood. But he was constantly frustrated at having to work in the vineyard to the exclusion of his own ambitions. About twelve months into our marriage, he arranged a meeting with his father. He would propound setting up our own business, our independence.

Otto was not an easy man to communicate with, especially on matters such as these, but Warren had prepared his case. He told his father he believed he could make a good income from running sheep and pigs, doing a little shearing and some share-farming. Taking care of the Copeville property for his father was also something he was happy to continue with, all of which should leave Otto free to manage the vineyards. His father nodded and listened. *His* dream was for his son to be a vigneron, but Warren did not want to surrender his own unique life, imagined and amorphous as it still was, to a life-term of work he had no heart for.

In his head, but not his heart, his father agreed, and so began the business partnership of WJ and SN Grocke. We had to succeed or we would sink.

September was shearing time. It was always an arduous, day-long exercise bringing the sheep down from the hills, past properties with broken fences or no fences at all, to be shorn in the primitive shearing shed at home. The mob would straggle and eat its way down for hours. Because of the inconvenience of all this, Warren considered buying some land closer to the Grocke grazing country on which to build a new facility. He approached a neighbour with the prospect of buying a small piece of his land. Graciously, PT Falkenberg agreed to sell us twenty acres. The bank lent us the money and Warren was elated.

Soon after this property purchase, a community decision was made to demolish our town's original show hall and build a new one. Tenders were called for to remove the hall, and Otto won the project. He and Warren employed about fifteen local men to help put down the huge corrugated iron edifice. The salvaged materials were brought home – aged Oregon timbers, tons of iron sheets, windows, doors, louvres – all to be used for farm and shearing sheds of the future. For nights Warren worked on a design for his shearing shed. Finally, he was satisfied and, with the help of his father, began the build. It was a magnificent thing when completed. Built of the old materials, it already had an air of age about it.

Our business had got off to a good start. With money in the bank, I proposed a new kitchen. The yellow and blue painted cupboards and grey speckled rubber floor had graced the room for decades. Parties usually spread into kitchens and ours was too small for a decent sized shindig. We knocked out a wall. A local master-builder/ cabinet-maker built our new cupboards. Blackwood. Featureless. Forever modern – thanks to my dad's gift for design. Quarry tiles on the floor. Everything else white except for the red papered wall. I still have this kitchen and love it today as much as I did then.

I was twenty-three. Erica had married Wayne and was living in the city. Dale at seventeen was on a Commercial Art path. Mum and Dad's marriage was hanging by a thread. I often dreamt of still being at home with them when we had all been so happy. It was a sad place now.

Rosemary and Jack's relationship had deteriorated. Nobody had heard of bi-polar disorder back then, but Jack would fly into rages, become inflated with grandiose schemes, spend money like a sailor, drink well into the night, verbally abuse Rosemary or any who got in his way, apologise deeply next day, then do it all again.

On a day his car had broken down, he phoned Rosemary to tell her to bring their other one to tow him home. She did so, and after a rope had been tied between the two, she was told to steer the car being towed. Jack set out at high speed. My friend, by now in a fragile state through emotional trauma, was terrified. She started flashing her lights hoping he would stop. He did. She told him she was scared and asked him to slow down, but in a rage about the car breaking down, he began to drive even faster. Rosemary flashed again and tooted the horn until he stopped a second time. There was no calming him. She shot out of the car and fled to a nearby house.

'My husband's trying to kill me,' she sobbed as the startled homeowner opened his front door.

The compassionate man took Rosemary to the doctors' clinic where she was diagnosed with having had a nervous breakdown. She was sedated and confined to a hospital bed for two weeks.

Jack was deeply remorseful, but his wife would never return home. She moved to Sydney where she could assume the anonymity she needed just then. It may just as well have been the other side of the world as far as I was concerned. I missed her terribly.

Jill had left the Valley too. She and Kiwi had parted three or four years earlier. While they'd still been deeply in love, Kiwi had gone to Great Western in Victoria to work a vintage. One day his letters had stopped and he could not be contacted. Jill was distraught. A few months later, as I was driving back from visiting Leon in hospital, I spotted Kiwi walking down the main street of the town of Great Western, hand in hand with another girl. His good clothes still hung in a wardrobe in Jill's family home.

Over time, Jill recovered from her loss and began going out with Graeme – a veterinary surgeon. Kiwi must have got word of this and, out of the blue, phoned Jill to ask if he could see her. Jill was floored and deeply relieved to hear from him. With a need for closure, she agreed to see him.

Kiwi picked Jill up from work next day and while driving through the streets of Adelaide, told her he still loved her. Too late, she told him. He became incoherent with an outburst of emotion that frightened Jill so much that she jumped out of the car as they slowed for a red light. She never heard from him again.

Decades later, one of her daughters who'd become a winemaker, was working in New Zealand. On her travels she met someone who'd lived next door to Kiwi's family. She mentioned to this person that her mother had gone out with him years earlier. Jill's daughter was then told that in nineteen sixty-eight – at about the time of the incident in the car with Jill, Kiwi had disappeared. He is still missing without a trace.

I was married to a farmer. Rosemary was on the mend and working in Sydney. Jill had married Graeme and joined the horse racing fraternity. Marion, who'd married Allan, an agricultural advisor, was living and working in New Guinea. The four of us were worlds apart and our cherished years of sorority over. It would be thirty-eight years before we'd find ourselves all together again.

~

My life now revolved around my husband and baby. Although Warren and I had been ready to start a family within a year of getting married, it had been almost three years before Lincoln was conceived. We'd now celebrated his first birthday.

My stints at Copeville had become fewer as Jack, trawling his way through grief over Rosemary's leaving, often accompanied Warren there. The two of them would work together in the mornings but as Jack became less responsible with alcohol, he'd be relegated to the hut for "domestic duties" in the afternoon. He was a reasonably good cook and knew how to keep house.

In nineteen seventy-one I gave birth to our beautiful daughter Marlo. She was a contented baby just as Lincoln, now twenty-one months old, had been. The love I had for my husband and two little ones warranted a soundtrack.

Although life was becoming busier, I found a new pleasure in gardening. My attempts however were thwarted on numerous occasions by sheep that had been put out to graze the "long paddock". The problem was, there were no fences between this track and my garden, and I'd frequently be overwrought to find my flowers and shrubs eaten to the ground.

I'd been asked to trim vine rootlings ready for planting. Sitting on a kerosene drum in a sunny spot in the winter warm shed, I snipped repetitively at the seemingly lifeless sticks while Marlo slept in her basket beside me and Lincoln tinkered with his father's tools. I'd offered to care for an orphaned lamb and was feeding the helpless little creature with a bottle. In high mothering mode I was shattered when it died.

We finished paying for our shearing shed block and within months a property adjoining Otto's grazing country came up for sale – rolling lofty hills strewn with moss rocks, yakkas, she-oaks, banksias, acacias. The damp gully floors oozed with spring water that quenched the thirst of towering red gums. We took on the challenge of another mortgage and felt like the owners of a rare jewel. We named the property "Lance's" after the vendor.

Warren joined the local archery club. He'd given up football when it had become impossible for him to get home from shearing in time for training. He was a gifted instinctive archer.

We'd been married five years and life had become hectic. Often Warren came home after a long day's work, had a shower, a quick meal, then rushed off to a meeting – Apex, Country Fire Service, Church, archery.

I was playing A grade tennis for our town in summer and teaching Sunday School. As a couple, we had little time together. There were still parties and the wonderful Barossa events we went to on many weekends – thanks to our parents looking after the children – but these nights were usually spent catching up with everyone but each other.

We were out with close friends Sue and David Fechner one night when we began to bandy about the idea of a weekend away – just the four of us. Melbourne. A shopping excursion. How ritzy, I thought.

About twelve months earlier, while I'd been pregnant with Marlo, Warren, Lincoln and I had enjoyed a short holiday at the beach. Warren had seen a *Triumph* TR5 sports car for sale and fallen in love with it. I'd thought it totally impractical for a family of four, but Warren's motto? "*If you want something badly enough, you'll get it*". So, we swapped our six-seater S-series

*Valiant* for a two-seater sports car. It took me about two weeks to take a shine to it. Sue and David had a TR5 as well.

The Melbourne trip was planned.

The four of us spent the first night in a rustic cabin in Portland, Victoria. Next morning, I took rare time with my hair and make-up, put on my loveliest mini dress and wore Madame Rochas perfume. Most of my days now were spent in farm clothes and boots.

That day we conquered the Great Ocean Road and although I'm not proud of the speeds we reached, we found out how fast the Triumphs would go. With hoods down, hair blowing in the wind, we took in great draughts of freedom.

We booked into a comfortable apartment in the city and hit the shops. The House of Merivale was known nationwide – an exclusive house of fashion for guys and girls. This was our prime port of call. We walked through the door into something like a theatre space – black walls, spotlights, throbbing music. The clothes were outrageous. After two hours of shopping bliss, we walked out of the place with large designer bags full of extreme flares, wild platform shoes and stunning tops. We were on a high.

I didn't have to wear what was in fashion, although these clothes were, but I loved to express myself in what I wore. I designed most of my outfits – an art form for me.

The short four day holiday refreshed us, but soon after our return Warren began to grow restless.

Earlier that year, a young man had knocked on our door and asked if we'd have a place for him in our team of grape pickers. He'd been travelling Australia doing seasonal work. Otto employed him. Warren had been inspired by the stories of John's adventurous travels and was now beginning to make noises about doing the same. With two small children? Impossible I told him. Impossible? Not in his vocabulary.

Twelve months passed as the desire swelled and ebbed in him. It frightened me each time he brought it up because I knew if he wanted it badly enough, it would happen. And it would not be small. It would be for years.

He wanted it badly enough.

# TEN

The only communication we'd have with any of our friends or family for the next two years would be by letter.

Pine Creek in the Flinders Ranges was our first night's destination. We'd planned to meet Sue and David there but none of us had any idea of the vastness of the place, so despite searching, we failed to find each other. Long before mobile phones or laptops, this was another sadness – to have to leave home without saying goodbye to two of our dearest friends. That night we camped, utterly alone in wilderness – a precursor to our life to come.

Next day we drove to Marree where we'd planned to put our caravan on the train to Alice Springs. We'd heard that the road north was rough. Clear from the outset was that Linc and Marlo would be intrepid little travellers. Not once did they ask how long before we get there. They must have understood there was no specific destination and that this was to be a new way of life for us.

Having set camp for the night near the railway station at Marree, I found a tap and filled a bucket with water. In it I washed the clothes and nappies of the past two days, and draped them over bushes to dry. I'd had periodic moments of panic about water and prayed that we'd always have enough – for drinking at least. Actually there'd be more than enough for a while. A big rain had flooded the country ahead.

As the Ghan train pulled into the station at daylight next morning, the driver blew the whistle. An eerie echo filled the air. We were in the middle of Australia, on flat featureless ground, with thousands of kilometres of desert all around us. How could this echo? I wondered how many more mysteries there would be to marvel at in this ancient, rugged land we were about to explore.

Loading the caravan onto the train required the precision of a watchmaker. With me guiding him, Warren backed our twenty foot van up and along a narrow, hundred foot ramp, then onto a rail trailer with no sides and only inches wider than the van. It took nearly an hour, and at any point, with the smallest error, our home could have fallen over the edge.

As we headed north without it, water lay across the landscape. With no fences to guide us, there were times we lost the track. Driving at walking speed, Warren concentrated hard to feel the road beneath the wheels. Then the car stalled and wouldn't start. Standing in water up to his ankles, Warren dried the distributor with a cloth and we continued. But the water was relentless and it happened again, and again. Finally, he found a piece of plastic, wrapped the distributor in it and we were able to continue without impediment.

That evening we reached Oodnadatta where we'd planned to stay at the town's Transcontinental Hotel. The luxury the name conjured up had us anticipating a night of comfort, until we were shown to our room – a lean-to out the back. Red dust covered everything, including the beds and pillows. Curtains, rotted from the assault of the sun, hung in shreds, and cockroaches lay on their backs under the beds. The price was equivalent to that of accommodation in a five-star hotel in the city. It wasn't long before we realised that every material thing one needs from the Outback comes at a larger than life cost.

What we were doing was unorthodox. Those living out here considered us hippies, and some expressed their disapproval of our taking two young children into this untamed landscape. One was an acerbic woman who ran the Kulgera Station roadhouse and cabins. We'd booked into one of the huts. There were sprinklers going on small patches of grass beside each cabin. I stripped Linc and Marlo down to their undies. It had been so hot and they'd been confined and uncomplaining for so long that I was delighted to see them frolicking in the water. But within minutes the dragon lady came storming over, glared at me, and without comment turned the tap off – hard.

Next morning as we were getting up, I accidentally stepped on my glasses that, in the absence of a table, I'd put on the floor beside the bed. They broke beyond repair and I hadn't brought another pair with me. Being short-sighted, I could see little without them and there was nothing I could do about it until we got to Alice Springs.

Days were searing, nights freezing. Air-conditioning in cars was unheard of. The Outback was a stranger to me. I hadn't realised there'd be no fresh food to be bought anywhere along the track. Thankfully I'd packed cracker biscuits and Vegemite, bananas, dried fruit and nuts, and we lived on those for the next three days. However, a few hours after leaving Kulgera, we came across a small group of people standing beside a stationary vehicle – a man in his forties and two women, one of them a nun. They'd hit a brumby and wrecked their radiator. We stopped to see if we could help. A tow into the Alice – about a hundred kilometres, would be appreciated they told us, but first we'd have to eat the large amount of prawns they had on melting ice. The prawns were divine – sweet and succulent, and as we stood there feasting and talking, we learned that this bloke was the brother-in-law of our old friend Tony Juttner who we'd be seeing in a few days. Tony and his wife, Helen, lived and worked on an Aboriginal settlement – two hundred and eighty kilometres north-west of Alice Springs, in the Tanami Desert. We would be there with them for three months.

~

It had been vintage time when we left home. Warren had broken his ankle and was on crutches – unable to do the bucket-carrying his father had counted on. The job needed someone strong enough to carry four large buckets of grapes at a time, climb a ladder (no hands) and tip them onto the truck. Old mate Pete, of my childhood raft adventure, fitted the bill and got the job. Warren managed to hop along on his one good leg and pick grapes with the rest of the team. Otto was testy with the stress of the season, and Warren on edge anticipating his father's customary vintage blow-up which came one Saturday morning. An altercation of serious proportions erupted between them.

    Otto's vineyard was his passion, but also his burden. In his home, all conversation revolved around it. Frosts, severe heat events, dismal prices, hail, and even lack of respect from winemakers – some aspect of all of this was expressed extensively and often. Instilled in Warren were childhood memories of times when a pall would settle over the household as they listened to the outpourings of a disillusioned man. But not only was there this reprehension in Otto, but the aftershock of a traumatic event, indelible in his memory.

~

A year or two before Warren and I started seeing each other, there'd been an accident on the farm.

One late afternoon Warren had come home from shearing to find the house in disarray. No-one about. Lights on. Blankets pulled from the linen press and lying on the floor. Radio still going. The scene filled him with dread. He feared something perilous. His parents arrived home a little later – grim-faced and disconsolate.

That afternoon, a local couple employed by Otto had been pruning the vineyard. It was school holidays and they'd brought their eleven year old son with them for the day.

Otto had been hoeing around the vines with a specially designed implement attached to the side of his tractor. The job took great concentration in avoiding contact with and hence shock to the vines. Simultaneously, a rear-attached rotary hoe was tilling between the rows. Barry, the child, was fascinated with the machinery and asked his parents if he could sit on the open tractor with Otto for a while. They gave their permission and told him to hold on tight. He stood on a step at the back of the tractor, watching the implements at work. A sudden bump made Otto look around. Barry wasn't on the tractor. He threw the machinery out of gear and turned to see the boy covered in dirt. The plough had gone over him. Otto yelled from his depths to the parents working a few hundred metres away. It was a voice of dire urgency.

'Barry's hurt,' he bawled through his cupped hands.

The boy's parents ran to where the tractor was stopped. Otto was already on his way to the house three hundred metres away to phone for a doctor. He burst through the back door, alarming his wife with the horror on his face. As he dialled the doctor's number, he related to her in breathless sentences what had happened. Lin ran to get blankets and towels and together they rushed back down to where Barry's father had his son in his arms. The mother took the blankets from Otto and wrapped and tucked and cradled and sobbed.

The doctor arrived within ten minutes but there was nothing he could do to save the precious boy.

After this tragedy Otto struggled with feelings of deep despair. Mostly he kept them to himself but the stress would wax and wane, building to exploding point when those dearest to him would have to take the brunt, and then subsiding until the next wave. The accident had happened just before Otto's birthday and for many years afterwards, Barry's parents would visit him on that day. While there was no blame laid for what had happened, these visits would re-ignite the terrible memory, and the darkness of post-traumatic stress would descend upon Warren's family again.

~

Otto's unremitting expectations of his son and the consequent divisiveness between them had worn Warren ragged. Warren's passion was for animals – sheep, horses, pigs, his dogs. The inanimate vineyard held no allure for him, only the certainty of heartache and disappointment. Standing in the harsh, bleak, frost-biting elements of winter, pruning vine after vine, row upon row, acre upon acre, week after week was without challenge for him. Without soul. Without reward.

Although Otto knew Warren's love lay in farming and grazing, and that we had some land and a business of our own now, he could still only see it as secondary to his vineyard. His and his son's purposes were irreconcilable.

On the day of the argument we were to go to a wedding but Warren was racked by the fracas and I went alone. When I got home that night, he told me we were leaving.

'What do you mean leaving?' I asked, realising in that instant that the time had come.

'I have to get away for a while. See some of the rest of the world, think about our future.' He was overwrought.

I sank into a chair. I loved my comfortable home, my family, my friends, and I knew what an ordeal it would be to take two small children into the Outback. Lincoln was three years old, Marlo twenty-one months. But even though Warren knew I was more than reluctant, he believed that to strike out at this time would be best for all of us.

While I'd been at the wedding, he'd made his plans. We were to buy a four-wheel drive vehicle and a caravan. Our first port of call would be the Aboriginal settlement in the Tanami Desert. He'd phoned Tony who told Warren there'd be a job for him when he arrived. The plan was to travel until it was time for Lincoln to start school, and in that time to see as much of Australia as possible.

Today, as a grandmother, I can imagine how devastating this must have been for our parents. To not see my grandchildren for two years would be painful beyond words.

Warren had put incalculable time and effort into breeding his herd of pigs and so it was with a heavy heart that he took them all to market. We advertised our house for rent, sold our Triumph TR5 and with the proceeds bought a Toyota tray-top ute with canopy, and a twenty foot caravan.

It took an intensive three weeks to organise the leaving. I was mostly too busy to contemplate the reality but every now and then I'd find myself in a state of terrible sadness. One of the hardest things I've had to do was to walk out of my home as strangers moved in. I was to have a recurring nightmare about it for years – a dream in which I'd weep bitterly.

Late in April, nineteen seventy-three, we drove away from our home, our roots, our security. There was pain as we said goodbye to Warren's parents. Tears from Lin. Silence from Otto. We went to my parents' house for our final farewells. Mum and Dad, Erica and Wayne, Dale and his girlfriend, Heather, were all there to see us off. As we were about to pull away, my brother opened the door of the Toyota and threw in an old horseshoe with a cheery 'Good luck'. He was twenty now and buoyed at the thought of the adventure that lay ahead for us. But tears welled in me and as we set out along the highway heading north I sobbed inconsolably.

Warren shared with me years later that for days he was filled with his own terrifying feelings of doubt and anxiety. It was no small thing to take his family into the Outback and to meet even our basic needs. After the three months' work he had lined up on the settlement, there was no guarantee of any more. We were about to embark on the trip of a lifetime.

# ELEVEN

Four days after leaving home, we arrived in Alice Springs. The road had been rough, the travelling slow. We collected our van from the railway yard and took it to the caravan park where we'd planned to stay for a few days. We were happy to be back in what was to be our little home for the next two years.

Linc and Marlo had brought their favourite toys and books, art and craft materials – special gifts from grandparents and friends. What we were to discover though, was that they would spend a lot of time playing outdoors with other kids. This would be an invaluable social experience for them.

On our second day in the park, a stranger knocked on our caravan door. He'd noticed our four-wheel drive vehicle. Warren listened and nodded as he asked my husband if he'd be interested in taking him out to Chamber's Pillar – a huge sandstone monolith – in the Simpson Desert. This is a famous landmark now but in nineteen seventy-three it was remote, mysterious and rarely visited. The chap told Warren he knew an old Aborigine who would go with them. There was no road out to it, only hundreds and hundreds of sand dunes. The twenty-five dollars he offered in payment was more than enough incentive for Warren to accept the charter. It would be a great adventure, he told me, and the money would be handy. The two hundred dollars we'd left home with had dwindled considerably. The fact that he was about to drive a hundred and fifty kilometres into a desert with strangers didn't deter him for a minute.

I felt weak at the imagined peril and at the thought of being abandoned so early in our trip – left in a strange place with our very dependent children. And even more vulnerable without my glasses that I had to send off to Darwin for repair. Be tough, I chided myself. I knew it would always be called for in my life with Warren.

They left early next morning, estimating that if all went well they'd be back by nightfall. That day Lincoln went missing.

He'd made a friend and they'd been playing just outside our van. I'd been looking out every couple of minutes to check on them but in an instant they were gone. With Marlo's hand firmly in mine, I began searching the large caravan park, but being at a terrible disadvantage without my glasses, I was unable to see anything more than featureless shapes. I came across the other boy's mother, as frantic as I was. At least she could see distances. Our boys were not in the park. Adrenalin coursed through me. My mouth was dry, heart thumping. We ran across the road to the Todd River bed, dotted with Aboriginal families sitting about. As we went from group to group asking if they'd seen two little boys, they shook their heads gravely. We dashed back to the park. By now several of the residents were aware of our search and one of them offered that she'd seen them heading towards an exit on the western side. I picked Marlo up and we ran in that direction. On the street we met people who'd spotted them. The other boy's mother remembered a kindergarten with a playground. She'd taken her child there to play a couple of times. As we neared the school we caught sight of two little figures in the playground – our sons – happy, oblivious, and unperturbed. We'd been searching for nearly half an hour. Marlo trotted off to join her brother while I crumbled onto a swing, waiting for my heart rate, legs and brain to return to normal.

Warren returned safely that night, brimming with stories of his adventure. Indeed there'd been no road and they'd driven for hours over enormous dunes, trusting the old black fella and the vehicle with their lives. Warren said the pillar was amazing and that I'd be able to see it when we had our Super 8 film developed.

It was time to head for Yuendumu – the Aboriginal settlement where our friends Tony and Helen were expecting us. We called them from a public phone to tell them we were on our way.

'You should be here in time for tea,' Tony told us. 'The road's a bit rough. Drive carefully. It's three hundred kilometres. Should take you about six hours.'

The track was horrendous. Corrugations rattled the car, the van and our bodies. Speaking was useless. After about four hours of this, we drove over a cattle grid. The vehicle jolted and lurched.

'We've lost a wheel,' said Warren, battling the steering to bring us safely to a stop. We all got out of the car while he inspected the damage. One of the axle's locking tabs had broken. Simply changing the wheel would not get us going. Warren searched the road and found bits of the tab, but it was beyond repair. His arms hung in limp submission as we all stood looking at the empty wheel arch. I was afraid of the isolation, of having my children in danger. We hadn't seen another car since leaving Alice Springs. I'd packed a few snacks and we had enough water for probably two days, but what after that? I had already seen a little of my husband's resourcefulness when he'd fixed the distributor with plastic. I dared to hope he would keep us safe again. He was deep in thought but his body language offered me no assurance. Then we heard a faint distant sound.

'Is it a car?'

'I think so,' said Warren.

Within five minutes a Toyota four-wheel drive pulled up beside ours. A couple of road workers got out to see if we needed help.

'Not unless you've got a spare Toyota locking tab,' said Warren with little hope.

They'd have a look, they said, but were doubtful. There was an enthusiastic search through tool boxes but no tab was to be found. Then Warren spotted a piece of copper pipe on the back of their vehicle.

'I might be able to use this,' he said. We all stood back and watched as he cut, pounded and fabricated a tab. 'I think this should do the job,' he said. He replaced the wheel, securely. Trust, marvel and gratitude welled in me.

We thanked the road guys who then drove behind us for a few kilometres to make sure we were okay. The wellbeing of our vehicle was our lifeline out here.

We arrived at Yuendumu at eleven – dead tired and with every nerve on edge from the deep corrugations we'd endured the entire way. Despite the hour, Tony and Helen greeted us joyfully and slapped some big juicy steaks on the barbecue. Linc and Marlo had snacked on fruit and were sound asleep, so we put them into their dusty beds before enjoying a meal and confab with our friends. There were already stories to be told, and we couldn't wait to hear about this place and what lay ahead for us.

At about one-thirty, as we were about to go to bed, a haunting sound drifted out of the bush. A primitive singing. Tony had told some of the black fellas that one of his "brothers" was coming to stay for a while. They'd been waiting for us to arrive and for our chatter to be done. To the clacking of rhythm sticks, they sang for us as we went to sleep. With an air of the deeply spiritual, this guttural chanting was one of the most beautiful gifts I have ever received.

These were the Pintubi and Warlpiri people from the surrounding Tanami Desert lands. Some of them had been in from there no more than fifteen years. The settlement had been established by the Native Affairs Branch in the nineteen forties for the purpose of their welfare, and later Baptist missionaries had come from the south to help run the place. Now, in nineteen seventy-three, it was still government run.

We set up our van in Tony and Helen's backyard. Their generosity touched us deeply. For three months they would share their bathroom and laundry, their garden, their home with us. Their two boys, Juan and Christopher, were about the same ages as Linc and Marlo, and the four chummed up in a blink.

The Juttner home was basic – Besser brick, comfortable, arty with posters. It hardly ever rained here but Tony and Helen had a good patch of hand-watered lawn, two or three fruit trees, a grapevine and a bougainvillaea.

Tony was head mechanic and responsible for running the bore that supplied the community with water. He also refuelled the Royal Flying Doctor and mail planes. Helen was a trained teacher and worked at the school, ever prepared to give any kids who turned up a good education.

A couple of days after we arrived, Tony invited Warren to a cricket match at the oval. The two of them had been gone an hour when I became aware of an escalating commotion outside. A frenzied muster of Aboriginal men, whipped up about something, were running past our caravan towards the sports ground. The pitch of their voices frightened me. Lincoln and Marlo were playing in the van and wanted to go out to see what was happening. Not now, I told them.

When Warren got back, he told me how two or three young blacks had broken into a car, in fact, ripped the door off to get to a carton of beer. Alcohol was prohibited for the Aboriginal people here. A large crowd had gathered then, to see an old woman, grandmother of one of the boys, beating them about their heads with an iron dropper.

We learned quickly that they had their own way of dealing with transgressions. If a man slept with another man's wife and her husband found out, he would "sing" the adulterer, torment him with accusations, curse him until he could no longer stand the persecution. The adulterer would then admit to the offence and submit to a public meting out of punishment. Hundreds would gather to witness the husband driving a spear into the perpetrator's thigh. The sight of young men limping about with heavily bandaged thighs was not uncommon.

Linc and Marlo had contracted "bung eye" from the flies. I'd bought them fly nets but they wouldn't keep them on, so I'd just administer ointment daily until it cleared up. I sent home photographs of them with their eyes black with flies. Not a good idea. Both grandmothers were appalled.

There was a hospital on the settlement, a couple of nursing sisters, no doctors. If anyone became seriously ill, they'd be flown by Royal Flying Doctor to the Alice.

The mail went out and came in by light plane once a week, and the "Meat Truck" delivered meat and groceries, weekly also, for the whole community – weather permitting. We'd send our orders back with the driver each trip. During one of his runs the track had become impassable with rain. The truck full of groceries remained stuck in the mud for almost a week. By the time our food arrived, the perishables were unrecognisable. We lived on tinned and dried foods bought from the settlement's only shop until next delivery.

On pay day, the community folk would be in and around the store all day. Generally, they had little understanding of the value of money. Many would spend their entire welfare payment in one day. For thousands of years, their food and commodities had been from nature, and when they'd finished with them, the discards had disappeared into the landscape. White man's refuse was a different matter. Now tins, bottles, packaging of all kinds littered the precinct.

The Warlpiri and Pintubi people however were still skilled in hunting and gathering, and when all the processed food they'd bought had been consumed and all money spent, they'd return to the bush.

We'd met an anthropologist who was doing a twelve month study here. She often took the women out in her Land Rover to gather bush tucker. They relished the idea of not having to walk. Chris would invite as many as her vehicle would accommodate and set out quietly. Others would quickly spot the intended excursion and jump aboard. It was not uncommon to see her driving down the road with twenty or more women in and on her vehicle. Others, including dogs, would be running behind, trying to catch up. The Land Rover would gradually pull away from the loud and brightly coloured mob. Out on Country they'd gather yams, wild tomato and other bush foods in season, all of which they'd eat on the spot. Chris told me it always broke her heart not to be able to take them all.

One of Warren's first jobs in Yuendumu was to erect fences around a handful of new homes that were being built for some of the nine hundred Aboriginal people who lived here.

It seemed an odd, unnecessary job to me. Fences? For families so affiliated? Another alien concept for them. Many of the previously built homes stood empty and derelict – their doors, windows and furnishings having all been used for campfire fuel. And if anyone died in a house, it would never be used again, in fear and respect of the spirits.

The government had given the building project to a contractor from Adelaide. After a week of erecting fences, Warren was called in to his office.

'I'm making you leading hand on construction,' the boss informed him.

Warren, although skilled in many things, was not a builder, but the contractor had spotted leadership qualities. Over the next week, my husband studied the work of his peers and asked countless questions. The homes they were erecting were of simple design and my husband quickly learned the ropes. He communicated often with the boss and led the team in getting the homes built quickly and satisfactorily.

This contractor was a force to be reckoned with though. The fuel he ran on was adrenalin, coupled with rum from a large Thermos flask he carried with him at all times. After consuming the contents, he'd become adept at driving around the precinct at speed, towing one trailer whilst pushing another. He'd been warned that he could run over a child this way. His response? If he did, he'd keep driving and never return!

Before we arrived at Yuendumu there'd been two electrocutions on this job. Safety packs for the electric drills had not been provided, and a network of extension cords had been constantly strewn all over the site. With an investigation under way, the contractor had buried the offending drills, bought new ones and asked the workmen to testify in his favour. They would not.

By the end of our first two weeks, we were looking forward to Warren's first pay as there was little left in our kitty. On pay day the boss called the men into his office. The outcome of the investigation into the deaths was still pending and all funds were now frozen. There was no money in *his* kitty. It would be a while, the men were informed, before they'd see their wages. The contractor was sacked and a new one engaged.

Tony and Helen came to our rescue with a loan. We were so grateful. It was a month before Warren was paid, and thankfully paid well.

Our tenants were paying enough rent to cover our home mortgage. We'd paid off the loan for the shearing shed block but had taken out another one to buy the hills property. Warren had to earn enough for us to eat, travel and make these land payments. No wonder he'd scared himself on setting out.

One evening Warren invited me out for a ride to the main camp on the back of his motorbike. He'd got to know quite a few of the community by now. There was a bewitching light that sometimes lingers after sunset, and the glow of campfires. The air was smoky. Kangaroos lay charred and bloated over beds of coals. Skinny camp dogs ranged without intent. Some snapped at my heels. Naked children played and laughed. Some ran beside us laughing with delight. A cryptic sound of hushed contentment lingered in the air. I found no squalor there.

The Aboriginal children were fascinated with Linc and Marlo. They'd throw their heads back with laughter at their blonde hair and want to touch it constantly. Marlo had brought a small pusher from home and Linc, a plastic horse on wheels. These would often go missing and we'd find them later, abandoned somewhere on the settlement. Whatever possessions the Aborigines had, were shared. Their only toys were "graders" they'd crafted themselves from high tensile fencing wire attached to discarded brake drums. Making appropriate noises, they'd push these around by long wire handles, stopping periodically to scrutinise the tracks they'd made. Playing with stones too amused them for hours. The adults played gambling games with stones. Many a teapot and welfare payment were lost this way.

Tony and Helen had planned a two week trip south and so, during our evenings together, we'd ask them questions about what to expect of our time here without them. They'd been nurturing a small crop of grapes on a vine in their backyard and were looking forward to the eating once they returned. It was common for houses to be broken into while the white fellas were away – not maliciously but in all probability because of a lack of understanding of the purpose of fences and the concept of ownership. We asked what we could do for them while they were away. To look after their garden and discourage intruders were the priorities, they told us.

 They left early one morning and had not been gone an hour when I heard Marlo talking to someone outside. I went out to find her with an old black fella in the yard. Word must have already gone out that Tony and Helen had left. I was a little nervous and trying to hide it, asked, 'What's your name?'

 'Romeo,' he rasped.

 'What are you doing here, Romeo?'

 He giggled guiltily. Missing several teeth and grandiose of belly, he looked a sight. Standing knee high to him, Marlo was jabbing at his stomach with her finger. Romeo laughed with delight. I too was amused at my little princess's lack of inhibition.

 'Better not come in here, Romeo,' I said as he turned and wandered off without protest.

Warren was enjoying his work and camaraderie with his fellow builders, all of whom were single and living in quarters provided especially for the job. At the end of each day he'd have a drink with his new mates. After a few weeks, I was despairing that Linc and Marlo were most often in bed by the time their father got home. I talked to him about it one night. Bad timing. Having had a few beers with the boys, it didn't go down well. I left the caravan and went out into the chill of the Outback night. A caravan is a tiny space to have an argument in. I sat in Tony and Helen's backyard until the caravan lights went out, and then returned – teeth chattering. I crawled into bed with my husband. There was nothing else to do. But next day and from then on, he was home in time to eat with us. He was that kind of man.

His workmates invited us both over for a barbecue the following Saturday night. Tony and Helen were back from their trip and offered to look after Linc and Marlo. The guys were all about our age, affable and fun loving. When we walked into their hut, they asked if I'd like a drink.

'Yes thank you,' I said.

'What would you like?' asked Russell, camp cook.

'What have you got?'

'Beer or rum!' with a mischievous twinkle in his eye. He saw my face. 'I'm not kidding,' he said.

I chose the beer – lesser of two evils, I thought – and he handed me a can. I asked for a glass.

'A glass? Sorry, we don't have glasses. Carn luv,' said Russell. 'You can do it.'

So I struggled with the pull ring, opened it, and took an ungainly sip, feeling decidedly unfeminine.

Russell was a superb cook. His barbecue was something out of the box, and to reciprocate we invited the gang back to our camp the following weekend. Friendships were forged with

Chris The Pom, Russell Day and his brother Doogie who had one of the most infectious laughs I have ever heard. A room full of people would catch it whenever he started. The brothers Day were tuna fishermen from Port Lincoln. They, like Warren, had felt a need to break from what had been prescribed for them in their father's business.

There was no alcohol to be bought on the settlement and on one of the weeks the meat truck had been delayed, the boys ran out of beer. Russell and Doogie left early on the Saturday to drive into town to buy some – almost three hundred kilometres one way.

About nine am Chris The Pom knocked on our door. This was unusual. He looked bleak. He was a bleeding heart at the best of times but, wringing his hands, he began to tell us how a new carpenter had arrived in camp the previous night after lights out. He'd let himself in and bedded down quietly in the bunk above Chris's. There'd been unusual noises in the wee hours. Snoring, Chris thought, but when this new tradesman failed to stir at the sound of the morning's proceedings, Chris had become concerned. He tried to wake him but discovered he wasn't asleep but dead. An autopsy revealed he'd died of a heart attack. This job was gaining a high incidence of mortality.

One day a young Aboriginal boy died in the hospital. Warren was working nearby and became an accidental witness to the terrible sorrow that followed. Several adults emerged from the hospital. Oblivious to everything around them, they began to throw off their clothes and pound their heads with large rocks picked up from the garden. Their wailing cut Warren to the bone. It was ghastly, he said, to see blood seeping through their hair and down their grief-torn faces – a gut-wrenching outpouring he'll never forget.

That afternoon and for several days afterwards, family members, with eyes to the ground, walked around the settlement sweeping the dirt with leafy boughs in order to erase the footprints of the deceased child. How they could tell which footprints were his was beyond my comprehension.

On a day that Warren had finished work early he called in to the garage to see Tony. One of the black fellas told Warren that Tony was away refuelling a plane. He was fascinated with Warren's motorbike and asked if he could take it for a run. After satisfying Warren he could ride well enough, he headed out on it. Tony returned a little later and when Warren told him about the bike, he roared with laughter.

'It looks like you'll be walkin' home, mate.'

'Why?' asked Warren.

'Because he'll ride it till it runs out of fuel and leave it out there somewhere.'

Warren didn't see his bike or the rider for the rest of the day. The following lunchtime he called for the fallen-from-grace rider at the garage, and in our Toyota the two of them set out with a jerry can of fuel to find the poor forsaken thing which, sure enough, had been abandoned a long way from home.

One Saturday morning Tony told us he was going out bush to help some of his "brothers" get ready for a corroboree. He asked Warren if he'd like to come and help. That afternoon Warren bundled me and the kids into the Toyota and we set out to find the place. As we drove towards the site which was a few kilometres from the settlement, we saw, through a haze of campfire smoke, a figure running towards us. It was Tony, waving his arms wildly. We stopped. He was almost out of breath when he reached us.

'Get Sue and the kids out of here. It's men's business.'

There was so much to learn about their ways, and much they didn't want us to. These men loved and respected Tony and had accepted Warren as Tony's "brother", but this was no place for women or children. Warren did a quick U-turn, took us back to the caravan and went back to help.

That night, with utter reverence, he witnessed an ancient traditional initiation ceremony. This is how he related it to me.

During the afternoon they dug a large pit and at each end erected a totem pole cut from mulga trees and intricately carved with legends. Fires were lit and by nightfall were substantial enough to provide all the vital, symbolic smoke necessary. Eight young boys – fifteen year olds – had been living in the bush with some of the elders for three months as they were taught the Dreaming, songs and dances, how to hunt. It was time for them to come in as initiated adults. After the corroboree they would spend this last night in their mothers' huts, and in the morning leave as men – each to build his own shelter and prepare to take a wife.

When all was ready, Warren and Tony sat cross-legged on the ground at some distance. Small groups painted in colours picked up from the land, sat in huddles – talking intermittently in language like sounds from Nature. Strong silences passed in waves.

Then a wailing voice came out of the darkness, cutting the smoky air. Another echoed from the gathering. Four or five more elders joined the welcoming chant. Then a homecoming cacophony erupted as the boys came in.

On the rim of the ceremony, Warren's eyes were smarting as the ritualists, indeterminate through the smoke, danced and sang as if in trance. Green mulga limbs were torn from nearby trees and laid in the fires. When they were well alight the mesmerised men took them up, and walking backwards through the pit in single file, they beat the burning branches on the ground – barefooted and unflinching through red hot embers.

There were those among them whom Warren had known by day and now, this night, he saw their standing, their dignity.

At two in the morning he returned to me, reeking of smoke and in a state of utter wonderment.

'How was it?' I asked sleepily, sensing his stillness.

'In the morning,' he whispered.

As he related all to me next morning, I thought about how far this was from the life we'd been accustomed to. The experience was already beginning to shape us.

Linc and Marlo had blended seamlessly into their new environment. Playing tirelessly with Juan and Christopher in their yard or house or our caravan, they were happy, as long as I was near to look after their needs. Early one morning however, they both woke way under par. Whether it was from drinking bore water or that they'd caught something from one of the other kids in the community, I couldn't be sure, but they were violently ill. I rushed them over to the nurses who lived nearby. Blood tests were done and a particularly severe strain of gastroenteritis diagnosed. It was unnerving to see my little ones so inflamed with fever. I stayed up with them for twenty-four hours – keeping them cool, cleaning up their exudations and helping them drink. We were acutely aware of the tyranny of distance from a proper hospital, and I prayed that they'd be restored to health quickly. It was five or six days before the terrible thing passed. They were pale and weak, and lay about for several more days after that, before regaining their full health and vigour.

After an overnight rain – an uncommon occurrence up here – the children were playing in a large puddle just outside Tony and Helen's enclave. By now all their clothes were rose-tinted

– stained from the red of the inland. Like dye, it was impossible to get rid of. I could only imagine what their clothes would look like at the end of this play session, but the sounds of delight kept me from calling them in. I looked out from time to time to make sure all was well. Then a silence alerted me. The puddle had been vacated. I went in to Helen to see if the children were with her. Juan and Christopher were, but not my two. With dread I remembered a nearby dam and sprinted towards it. On reaching the large expanse of water I stopped. With hands on my knees and gasping for breath, I scrutinised the mass of small footprints around the edge. There was no way I could tell if any of them belonged to my children. Fear had robbed my legs of strength so I careened towards Warren's workplace – a kilometre away.

I spotted him and yelled before reaching him. 'I can't find the children!'

He put his tools down and looked at me, trying to read the seriousness in my body language. I was at a loss, incapable of thinking.

'We'll go around the perimeter,' he said. 'They can't have gone far. You go that way and I'll head out this way.'

With heart thumping and my mouth dry with panic, I ran off, looking first out into the desert then back into home yards and along dirt "streets". As I passed the nurses' flat, one of the girls came out and said, 'Are you looking for Lincoln and Marlo?'

'Yes,' I said, with hope. Then sudden fury.

'They're in here having morning tea with us,' she said cheerfully. Then with timid realisation, 'Oh. Sorry.'

I saw Warren coming towards me from the other direction. The nurse went in to get the children who were oblivious, of course, to what we'd been through. We picked them up and loved them, like lost children found.

Prior to our leaving home, we'd bought a small tape recorder – a new concept in music listening. All we'd had previously were vinyl records. My brother, Dale, had lovingly and painstakingly made a tape of all our favourite music – Dylan, Hendrix, James Taylor, Joni Mitchell and more. Yuendumu had no radio or television reception, so music was king – from our cassette tapes or records. Most of the thirty-five Europeans running the settlement were under forty and so there was a party at someone's house nearly every Saturday night. We didn't go to many because of the children, but to hear Creedence Clearwater Revival, The Rolling Stones, Led Zeppelin et al blaring into the cosmos till the wee hours, was as comforting to me as a mother's lullaby.

Mount Allan Station was about eighty kilometres north-east of Yuendumu and Tony had made plans to pick up a side of beef from Did Smith, the station owner. He invited us to come with him. Helen offered to look after Linc and Marlo while we were away. It was late in the afternoon by the time we got there. When Tony introduced Warren as a farmer and grazier from down south, Did invited us to see some of his country and cattle. We got into his ute. The desert still frightened me. You could see so far. There were no comforting boundaries, and my children were more than an hour away. I knew they were under the best of care with Helen, but part of me was back there with them. After the drive around, we returned to the homestead for a beer and some history on the place, in response to our questions. Until recently, an Aboriginal mob had been living and working on the property, until a bill was passed in parliament to the effect that station owners had to pay for this labour. There was no way he could afford to pay them all, he told us, and consequently they had to leave their ancestral country, go into town and live on welfare.

Life out here was harsh but there was a rugged romance about it and for a few hours we were totally immersed. Did invited us to stay for tea. Tony and Warren accepted. My thoughts were with my children but I knew Helen would feed them. Did disappeared into the large coolroom adjacent his kitchen and emerged with four enormous T-bones. He cooked them to perfection – seared, succulent and sizzling, served with bread and butter only, on dinner plates obliterated by the meat.

We arrived home at eleven that night, still wide awake with our homeward chatter about the day, and the life and traditions of the Outback. We were about to go into the house to check on Linc and Marlo when Tony burst out laughing.

'Oh no.'

'What?' I asked, smiling at his handsome, happy face.

'We forgot what we went for. The beef.'

# TWELVE

After three months, it was time to leave the settlement. In preparation for the next leg of our journey, I cleaned the caravan thoroughly, washing everything, even curtains and blankets. With love and gratitude, we said goodbye to Tony and Helen, and many of the others we'd befriended in this amazing place. I knew the memories would be with us forever.

The road out was again horrendously corrugated and so, armed now with the knowledge of how far we could expect to travel in a day, we planned to spend the first night on the side of the road. We pulled up at five o'clock at a dry creek crossing, looking forward to the meal I'd prepared ahead and a good night's rest. I opened the caravan door. The sight before me made me groan. And swear. The back window had been smashed, probably by a rock picked up off the road. Slivers of glass covered the children's beds, and for incalculable kilometres, red bull dust had been sucked into every nook and cranny of the van.

I set the children up with toys and games just outside the van and told them not to leave that spot. It took us an hour to remove the glass we could see, and then we shook the blankets dismally. We were hungry, but before we could eat, all of our crockery and cutlery, now covered in bull dust, had to be washed. After tea we sponge-bathed the children and ourselves and went to bed finding it hard to breathe for the suffocating dust that remained.

About ten pm something woke me. The crunching sound of small river pebbles trodden. The moon was up. I sat up in bed and pushed the curtain aside. A dingo was circling our van. Even though this was before baby Azaria Chamberlain's theorised dingo abduction, I found this animal's interest in us chilling.

We wanted to see more of the Alice and the region surrounding her – Uluru (Ayer's Rock), The Olgas, Standley Chasm, Ross River homestead – so we booked into the caravan park from where we planned to do these day trips.

The first was out to The Rock – an almost eight hour drive. Even at first and distant sight, the monolith was stunning, and grew more so as we came nearer. Finally, we arrived at the best viewing site where I was shocked out of my reverie to see other people. We had not seen another soul on the road and somehow I expected the reward for daring to go to a place so remote would be solitude.

We got out of the car and sat on the ground. No-one was speaking – all of us in awe as we waited to see the mighty rock going to sleep. Then from the normal red of Australia's centre, its colour became even bolder with the setting sun – redder, blazing orange, the colour of fire. People gasped. Then it began to subside – to deep red, purple, indigo. Then in the end black, featureless silhouette.

It was immensely spiritual. We all sat there past her final bow.

We drove over to the camp grounds then, not far from the base of the rock and pitched our tent. With only a small community of fellow Argonauts there with us that night, we went to sleep with the comforting sound of human voices nearby and the flickering of lamps and campfires round about.

In the morning, as we sat on logs eating our homemade muesli, The Rock greeted us with her morning colours – waking from black to dark grey, lighter, to brown, then the red of her days. Again the show held me spellbound. The apprehensions I'd left home with had all gone. An impossible trip? Not at all.

The Olgas were next – just thirty kilometres west. We headed out early. These were such a strange and haunting sight – towering rounded rocks more than fifty metres high, rising from the desert floor. There were tracks within them and with almost breathless anticipation, we crept into this pristine pantheon of nature.

Inside we met another young couple – adventurers like ourselves – Anne and Ray. They were about to head out west along the Gunbarrel Highway into the Gibson Desert. We talked for half an hour, sharing stories of our trips so far, then wished each other good luck as we parted.

That afternoon, back at the campground, we were enjoying a beer when we saw a figure approaching from the west. It was Ray. Some distance out they'd broken an axle. Ray had left Anne – a porcelain-pale flower of a girl – out there with his rifle, and walked the forty kilometres back to camp. Although young and fit, he was dangerously languid from heat and thirst when we greeted him. Using the ranger's radio, he sourced a new axle to be flown in from Alice. Amazingly it arrived that same afternoon as the job had been given emergency status. There was no doubt Anne was in danger out there alone. Warren fired up his motorbike and took Ray and the axle back out to his car. I sat in the shade of ours watching Lincoln and Marlo at play with their toys – horse and pusher. I hoped to get my husband back by nightfall. He was gone again, out into the woop woop. I tried to be peaceful. I should have had no concerns. He got the job done and returned safely. We kept in touch with Anne and Ray by letter for the rest of our trip.

Next morning Warren climbed The Rock. Long before safety chains, it was a dangerous exercise, but on his return a few hours later, he was high with a sense of achievement and ready to move on. We returned to Alice that day.

Our next trip was out to Simpson's Gap and Standley Chasm. Driving through Namatjira's colours took my breath away. Red earth. Purpling distant hills. Noble, lustrous ghost gums. Green, red, green, red twisting shimmering leaves. An albino dingo, white as the gums, darted furtively out of the undergrowth into a clearing for a few seconds, then disappeared like a plastic bag in the wind. In a moment of nearness, my husband and I looked at each other in wonder.

Ross River homestead was next. We would take a circuitous route that day. With a little fresh fruit, some nuts packed for snacks and four litres of water, we set out from the caravan park. We'd planned a special treat – lunch at the homestead. However, when we arrived I discovered I'd left my purse and money in the van. So we sat under a tree and had our small snack and a drink of water for lunch. The homestead and surrounds were full of history – intriguing stories of pioneering and survival. Linc and Marlo were happy as always. It didn't matter to them where we were or what we were doing. Their world was us, and their immediate environment.

Around four o'clock we set out for home. Halfway back, the road began to deteriorate as we found ourselves navigating the dry Todd River bed. Driving over large boulders and through deep river sand, our pace slowed to a crawl. Night set in. We were hungry. Our water was gone and a full moon rose ominously through the scrawny scrub. I was tense with apprehension at the thought of getting stuck out here but did my best to hide it from the children. We sang and played games, and they were oblivious as usual to any sense of impending danger. Slowly and carefully we made tracks along the river bed until we arrived "home" safely at about nine o'clock. Linc and Marlo were fast asleep so we laid them gently in their beds. Next morning, they woke with raging appetites and ravenously consumed the hearty breakfast I had ready for them.

My brother Dale had written to ask if he and Heather could join us on our next leg, to Darwin. I was excited at the thought of seeing family again but as it would be two weeks before they'd be ready to come up, Warren would have to seek interim employment here in the Alice.

After speaking to a local in one of the pubs, he went to the yard of a trucking company – Blue Metal Industries. As he neared the office, he heard shouting. A driver was being sacked. The employee was leaving as Warren approached, and in passing shot him a sympathetic glance. Warren entered the office apprehensively. Red faced and fuming, the boss snapped, 'And what do you want?'

'I'm looking for a job,' said Warren, with little hope.

'Well, you'd have to be better than that bloody no-hoper,' he blared. 'Can ya drive a truck?'

'Yes,' replied Warren shortly.

'Got a licence?'

'Yep.'

'Well there's your truck,' pointing to a large vehicle in the yard. 'Foreman'll tell you what to do.'

Warren's trucking experience had peaked at driving the five ton Bedford full of grapes to the winery. This was a fifteen ton Diamond T.

Some of the workers were having lunch in the shade of their lorries. Warren walked over to them and could see amusement written all over their faces. There was one other Diamond T in the yard and Warren enquired as to its driver. A wiry bloke answered, 'That'd be me.'

'Would you show me how to drive the thing?' asked Warren.

Congenially he eased himself up off the ground and the two of them climbed into the cab together. Warren was unnerved at the thought of having to negotiate sixteen gears. The driver drew a diagram on the floor in the dust, taught him how to use the Joey box and double de-clutch. He told Warren never to come into the yard too fast or be heard grating the gears by the boss, Smithy.

'Or you'll suffer the same curtain fall as the bloke you just passed on his way out,' he offered with a sideways toss of his head towards the gate.

The job gave us the money we needed for the next three weeks.

We collected Dale and Heather from the airport. They were champing at the bit for adventure. We were now a family of six – ready for a two day trip in a Toyota tray-top with canopy. The back was full of our chattels – tools, jerry cans, water, spare tyres.

With three adults and two children squeezed into the cab's one bench seat, there would always have to be one adult in the back and so we took turns. We set a limit of eighty kilometres each. Within the stuffy, airless canopy, the heat, dust and petrol fumes were almost unbearable.

At one point we were relieved of some of our load. A long way from the nearest town, we came across a vehicle parked on the side of the road. We stopped. Warren asked the young couple if they needed help and they told him they'd run out of fuel. There weren't many petrol stations between Alice and Darwin, and Warren had calculated that we'd need at least one jerry can of fuel, if not two for this leg. We had two, and so Warren offered them some of ours. They filled their tank and placed the empty can on the back of their ute. We were at the top of a small hill and the lad said, 'I'll just run it downhill a bit to see if it starts.'

It did, and as he drove off at high speed, having gained a free jerry can and its contents, he waved and shouted, 'Thanks, mate.'

We were speechless, having learned another of those life lessons that never seem to stop coming by. I reckon we would have had little more than a cupful of fuel left in the tank before we reached the next roadhouse.

It was early August when we arrived in the cosmopolitan city of Darwin. Hippies from far and wide had gathered to live here, giving the city its unique vibe and colour. With the weather already hot and humid, the only site available for us in the caravan park was shadeless and within two days I was finding the heat almost unbearable. The six of us celebrated Marlo's second birthday with a party and a cake whose decorations melted in minutes.

Dale and Heather spent a week with us here and together we gave in to the temptations of Darwin's annual art festival, ingesting the city's visual and musical treats. Then it was time for them to go. I'd been expecting a painful draw towards home when they left, but surprisingly there was none. Although I missed my family, I'd become, I realised, the inveterate and spirited traveller.

Mum had waited for her three kids to become independent before moving out of the family home. She'd secured a teaching position in Adelaide and rented a small granny flat owned by friends. She and Dad had been miserable together for a long time, but life apart now was equally difficult for them. We urged them to seek professional help. We'd all enjoyed such a happy childhood. It was heartbreaking to see the marriage in its death throes. They agreed to give it one last shot and wrote asking if we could come and spend some time with them while they holidayed in Victoria's high country. They were missing us, especially with each wondrous stage of the children's development so fleeting.

Although it would be a huge trip for us – from Darwin to Myrtleford in Victoria through inland Queensland and New South Wales – we had no qualms about the value of making the journey.

Warren estimated he would need six weeks' work in Darwin to earn enough for the trek down and a week's holiday once we got there. The day Dale and Heather left and before Warren got his next job, however, we were down to ten cents in the kitty. It would buy us a litre of milk. We had enough food in the fridge for a few days but without Warren finding work that day, we would be in trouble. Throughout our trip, as we arrived at each new destination, we'd rush to the post office – hungry for news from home. On this day of the last ten cents, we received a letter from Mum. In it was ten dollars – the wonderful gift of a few more days' security. Mum has always been like this. She would give away her last cent if someone needed it, and simply trust there would soon be more.

Warren did find a job that day – welding. His employer was an Italian bloke of some impropriety – notably for having insufficient cash in his employees' pay packets each week. It was so tedious trying to get him to pay the shortfall that many gave up, which was probably the outcome he was hoping for. His company was building external steel staircases for houses in a big new housing estate. It would be only another sixteen months before all these houses, all these staircases and most of Darwin would be destroyed in Cyclone Tracy.

I was unwell in Darwin. I picked up a virus that lasted three weeks. Struggling through my days with near zero energy, I'd take the children to Mindil Beach – a hundred metres from our van – for a few hours each day. Even the walk there and back nearly did me in. When Warren came home from work, I'd collapse onto the bed and take the rest my body was screaming for. He'd take care of the kids then – play with them, feed them, bathe them. I lost half a stone.

Although it was still only August, an early wet season was in the air. Even the nights were so hot and humid that it was nearly impossible to sleep. We had no air-conditioning, not even a fan. Saturated with perspiration, we'd get up through the night to cool off with a cold shower.

The garbos would collect the rubbish at night. About two o'clock one morning when we'd finally dropped off to blissful sleep, there was a clatter and crashing to wake the dead. They were throwing the empty tin bins from the top of their truck onto the pavement. Warren stood in the doorway of our van and, drowning out their deafening din, described to them what he thought of their job skills.

On the day before we were to leave Darwin, I drove in to the post office to see if we had mail. It was difficult at the best of times to see what was directly behind me in this vehicle because of the windowless canopy over the tray. Inadvertently I turned into a tight dead-end street. There was nothing for me to do but reverse back out into the main thoroughfare – blindly. Even though I was driving slowly, there was a sickening crash as I reversed into an oncoming car. I climbed down out of the vehicle and was confronted with a ranting female driver who looked like Mrs Doubtfire with a voice like Johnny Cash. She demanded my details. I gave her my name and told her to come to the caravan park at seven-thirty that evening to work out compensation with my husband. Warren got home from work at five with his usual deficient pay packet. We had third party insurance but could afford no excess, or time waiting for insurance companies' red tape. We had a rendezvous with my parents in Victoria in ten days and it would take more than a week to get there. By six-thirty we were on the road to Katherine. I am really not proud of that, but at the time we considered it a matter of survival.

Karma came quickly. On our third day out, the Toyota developed valve trouble. We limped towards Mount Isa. Fifty-five kilometres an hour was the most we could get out of the old girl. It was six o'clock on the Friday night before we reached the Mount. All garages were closed for the weekend. We booked into the caravan park and prayed that we'd find a mechanic sympathetic enough to let Warren use his workshop next morning. Our prayers were answered, but together, Warren and the mechanic discovered two burnt out valves and there were no new ones closer than four days away.

Warren had spotted another Toyota – same model as ours – in the park, and went to have a chat with the bloke who owned it, with nothing more than faint hope he might have some spare valves. Amazingly, the guy said he thought he did have some somewhere, and after a short search, remembered he was using them as tent pegs for his annexe. He was happy to swap these for real pegs. Warren and the mechanic did a valve grind and within a couple of days we were on the road again.

Mount Isa's burnished beauty worked its way into my soul, and I ached at not being able to dawdle through this place of breathtaking geological contrasts. Boulders of rich brown, red and yellow lay about in heaps, caressed by native grasses varying from rich green to straw-coloured. Small mulga trees like giant parasols with their sculptural trunks and dense canopy of leaves cast pools of shade and dispersed across the landscape with bushes and grasses of such diverse textures and greenness that my artist's soul was singing. I hadn't written any poetry since leaving home, but the magnificence of this landscape stirred me once again. That night we camped at Boulia.

> Boulia Wind
> Your voice has the wisdom of time
> discloses doggedness
> unceasing wanderings
>
> You swoop between boundaries
> of bleak burdened skies
> and warm compact earth
> and brutally tear at my new peace of mind
>
> You seethe and you wail
> like a ghoul telling tales
> then whisper of all you have seen
>
> You are mocking
> and tell me my quest hasn't started
> I know
> that though you have your boundaries
> mine are more confining
> I cannot see it all
> I am not God
> or your peer
> Boulia Wind.

It was dusk before we arrived in this town whose main street was reminiscent of a Jeffrey Smart painting. Desolate. Population nowhere to be seen. The only pub had lost its vital signs. Brown with dust and age, its dim light glowed from three or four small windows. No cars. I thought I heard a horse and cart but it was only my mind in surrender. Three to four hundred kilometres in any direction from the nearest town – Mount Isa, Winton, or Birdsville – we were in Channel country, between the Diamantina and Simpson Desert, our small family like a speck of dust in a wasteland.

We pulled into a vacant paddock across from the pub and Warren walked the fifty metres across the unmade street to ask the publican if it was okay for us to camp there for the night. He and his one patron regarded Warren suspiciously and together gave their laconic permission.

Whilst in Mount Isa we'd been indulgent and bought two fillet steaks – a rare treat. We'd been looking forward to the eating and some quiet time together this night. After giving the children their tea and putting them to bed, we set up our small barbecue under the waking stars and sat in silence as the steaks seared. With little to look at other than the vast quietude of the town and the huge night blue sky, our eyes met. Our small smiles and slightly raised eyebrows suggested inconceivability. Had we expected this?

The barbecue plate had become too quiet. Before the steaks were ready to turn we were out of gas. Another excursion to the pub netted a good result. Warren exchanged our empty gas bottle for a full one and the two at the bar were happy we'd spent some money in their town. Needless to say, with the heat stoppage our steaks were pretty ordinary.

Next morning we set off for Winton. We'd heard about a supernatural phenomenon that sometimes occurs on this track. Over decades the "Min Min" lights have appeared to station owners and night travellers, dancing tauntingly just above the ground and out of reach, like playful ghosts.

As we drove through this spooky stretch, a monstrous, ink black cloud rose ominously from the vast horizon behind us. The flat, treeless landscape was alight with the might of the sun engaged in an arm wrestle with the cloud. The country was soft with grasses as we drove along the hard track, the great rolling mass of thunder snapping at our heels. Like running from a tornado, we kept just ahead of the rain.

As we pulled into Winton, a passer-by pointed to our outfit. We stopped. Warren walked around the van, kneeled down to look underneath it and discovered five broken leaf springs. Like a faithful kelpie, our van had gone till it dropped. We had taken her through hundreds of kilometres of punishing country and were lucky to have broken only springs. Warren managed to hire a welder and set to work on repairs.

'How long do you think it will be now before we reach Myrtleford?' I asked as he worked.

'Months!' he snapped.

Parked in the main street beside the memorial to Banjo Patterson, I planned an extended stay. Linc and Marlo were happy with the break. Horse and Pusher were unpacked and patient little legs put into action. Luckily the town toilets were nearby, with water – a chance to deal with dirty clothes. No laundry. Everything had to be washed by hand.

Again we were regarded with curiosity. As we went to sleep that night I knew the eyes of the town were upon us. I felt exposed and vulnerable as our outfit sat disabled in their street. It took Warren most of next day to complete the job and so we stayed another night, knowing there would be a full day's drive ahead before we'd reach the next town – Longreach.

The state of the roads was still horrendous. Averaging thirty kilometres an hour, we negotiated our way around enormous rocks, potholes, washouts the width of the track – some deep enough to bury a trailer. At one stage we passed a group of road workers who gestured in what was now a familiar manner – pointing. We pulled up. Our caravan door was swinging open – television set teetering on the step. All the cupboards were open and contents strewn across the floor. A heavy box of books had turned over. A tin of molasses had worked its way out of a cupboard, lost its lid and embellished the books beyond recovery. Only one did I rescue – my favourite recipe book, *Cook Right, Live Longer*. I had seriously doubted our chances of longevity as we'd set out five months earlier, but my fear of perishing in the Outback had diminished another notch when Warren completed the job on the springs. I'd developed a complete trust in him – in the way he regarded his responsibility as expedition leader, in his mechanical skills, and most of all, his life-saving resourcefulness.

From Darwin to Myrtleford we travelled inland – Blackall, Charleville, Cunnamulla, Bourke. It was September and the land under sentence of drought. Hollow, bony sheep nuzzled the bare earth without reward. I wondered how people could live out here in their huge silent spaces, with only the sound of the wind hooting through the Tagasaste trees. Equally though, I think the inlanders were puzzled by our presence here. Warren's hair was shoulder length. He had a full beard. My hair was long and we both wore flared jeans and body hugging tops. Onto my jeans I'd stitched leather stars and moons. We wore handmade sandals and beads. Our hair was bleached from the sun and we were brown as berries. A canoe was tied to the roof of our vehicle and a motorbike sat in a rack at the back. A picturesque sight I think.

One night we pulled into a little place called Frewena – pub, general store and fuel depot all in one. The owner was having a drink with a couple of station hands. Warren asked if he'd mind if we camped nearby for the night.

'As long as you're out of shotgun range!' he mocked with unnerving chill.

Warren took a bucket to a tap near the pub. The water was from a bore. We were going to use this one bucketful to bath the kids. The publican, too long in the bush, roared from the doorway, 'Turn that bloody tap off. Don't you know we're in drought out here!'

His attitude was brutal but he'd probably seen no-one like us before and could not have known we were actually farmers with an equal respect for water.

Since leaving Darwin we'd been on the road ten days. Having estimated, before our unscheduled stops, that we'd have two or three days in Myrtleford before Mum and Dad arrived, amazingly we all got there at exactly the same time. The children hadn't been told of the rendezvous as they'd have worn themselves out with excitement. Lincoln was now almost four and Marlo two. We passed my parents driving down the main street from the opposite direction. Looking out the window, Lincoln spotted my mum.

'Grandma!' he cried, as his big blue eyes filled with tears.

I hadn't ever considered the toll the separation from grandparents may have taken on the children, but the tears from this sensitive little guy told the story.

My parents' faces were aglow with love for us all but the two of them seemed strained with each other. How could this be, after twenty-seven years of marriage and having so lovingly brought up three children? It was a surreal time – for them as they struggled to present an illusion of normality, and for Warren and me to see their heartbreaking demise. We booked into the caravan park at Porepunkah, and Mum and Dad into a motel at Bright.

There'd been good snowfalls, and there was heavy fog as we drove up to Mount Buffalo – all of us somehow squeezed into our Toyota tray-top. I was nervous. There were no guardrails, only large red signs every fifty metres that read, "*Keep to Left of Poles*". I'd caught glimpses through the fog of the drop-offs over the edge into oblivion and could only think that if we didn't obey these signs we'd be in free-fall for hours.

The weather was perfect though, once we climbed out of the clouds. Warren, who'd never skied before, took to it like a duck to water. The kids and I did some tobogganing, and Mum and Dad tried skiing like two people who didn't know each other.

After four or five days, it was time for Mum and Dad to return to the Barossa. I knew the marriage was over. Even though I was an adult and had left home long ago, I had a deep sadness about the empty feeling my childhood home would now have without my mum there. I was often asked when we returned how I felt about my parents' parting. My answer was always the same.

'My dad was a lovely father, but not the best of husbands.'

Dad was affable with most people but with Mum was often cold, petulant and moody. He'd been deprived of love at an early age with the loss of his mother, and after her death his father had, to some extent, been unaffectionate and stern. With one World War past and another one brewing, my father's childhood had been in a time of men as soldiers. It was not masculine to show emotion. And I suspect my grandfather would not have known what to do with the grief of his six children. That my father knew how to love us was remarkable, I suppose.

He would be alone now. He would have to face the scrutiny of his community and would not cope well. Mum was devastated too but she would survive. I knew my brother and sister would be there for them, in my absence. The plan was for us to be away at least another year.

# THIRTEEN

Porepunkah was a picturesque town, but through the caravan park flowed a raging river – much too dangerous for our children – so we pulled up stakes and moved to the Myrtleford park. Here we planned an extended stay as again we were nearly out of money. Warren quickly picked up some work – shearing on a grazing property thirty kilometres out of town.

I discovered this park was full of young travellers like ourselves – friends to be made.

Lincoln, a reserved little boy, was slightly overwhelmed by the bold gang of pre-schoolers in the park. Even at this age there were initiation rites. On the first morning, after Warren had gone to work and the kids and I were dressed ready for the day, my little ones opened the door of the caravan to survey their new environment. Waiting outside was a group of six or seven seasoned park kids. My two quickly shut the door and proceeded to peek at them through the window. Marlo, being the gregarious girl she was (and still is), needed to be out there. Tiny of stature and a tad over two, she flung the door open and with real or feigned confidence strode towards them. She was in.

Linc took a little longer and there were a few dust-ups – seemingly necessary amongst boys – but within a couple of days he too had been accepted into the group. Marlo bonded with Kylie, daughter of Tony and Anne who lived in the caravan next door. Linc chummed up with Chris and Arnie whose parents, Rose and Leigh, lived in the van on the other side. And we were all welcomed into the larger fold. On weekends we'd get together for barbecues where invariably the conversation would settle on past adventures, and the contemplation of those still to come.

One morning on his way to shearing, Warren burnt out the motor of the Toyota. He'd been doing some engine maintenance the day before and failed to properly seat the distributor stem, the purpose of which is to activate the oil pump. An engine doesn't run well without oil! Next day we were amazed to have a dealer offer us what we'd paid for the car, despite the damage. As we weren't planning any bush bashing for a while, we drove away in a Ford Falcon panel van – a much more comfortable vehicle for us all. The children could now sit in the back instead of on my lap, for sometimes hundreds of kilometres at a time.

One morning while the children and I were having breakfast, I heard a ruckus outside. Shouting. I looked out to see smoke pouring from Tony and Anne's caravan. I dashed out to see Rose yanking at the caravan door which had jammed shut.

'The van's on fire,' she yelled. 'Kylie's inside. We've got to get her out.'

Rose ripped the flywire screen from one of the windows, and as I saw her heave herself up and through the window into the burning van, I raced to the office to phone for a fire brigade and ambulance. When I got back, out of breath and fearful for the safety of my own children, Rose was outside gasping for air – overcome by smoke. She'd managed to kick the door open to get out, but with zero visibility inside had been unable to find Kylie. A man we didn't know appeared and heroically entered the burning van. Within seconds he burst out through the door with

Kylie in his arms, just as Anne, who had been having a shower and been alerted by the commotion, arrived on the scene. She wrest her baby girl from the stranger and dropped to her knees. Her long, wet hair straggled over the smoke-blackened, tiny, lifeless figure. She screamed. And screamed.

'No... No... No...'

Rocking back and forth, she tried to love her only child back to life.

The ambulance took them both away – one dead, the other overwrought with grief.

Tony came in that evening. Still in his work overalls, he stood at a distance from what had been their home – his body convulsing in anguish. He stepped into the horrid, acrid van and stood motionless in the doorway. Rose and I were together. As Tony began to walk away, we approached him and in a circle of three we hugged each other and wept.

The fire had been caused by a faulty power point that had ignited the curtains hanging over it.

Rose and I tried to salvage some of the family's possessions. We washed bed linen and towels that hadn't been burned, but they fell to pieces with smoke damage.

My sadness and compassion for the parents of this precious little girl were overwhelming in the days to come. A black, gutted box sat beside our clean, shiny home – safe with children, love, and promise. Marlo, at the age of two, had lost a friend, and although she and Linc had witnessed the tragedy, they were bewildered by the concept of death. Where had the sweet little girl gone? I held them close, cherished them deeply, and did my best to explain it in their terms.

We saw neither Anne nor Tony again. The foul-smelling shell of a home sat beside ours for another two weeks until we could no longer bear the trauma of being near it. We had to move on.

Michael Fromm, Barossa born and bred, was managing a cotton and beef enterprise in New South Wales. He'd heard that we were travelling and offered Warren a job at this farm – about twenty-five kilometres out of the town of Wee Waa. Warren appreciated the offer and accepted.

The owner of the huge property, Harold Freer, had built an amenities block for some of his workers – a sheltered double caravan pad, with bathroom, toilet and laundry. One young family was already living there and there would be room for us as well.

John and Jan and their little girl, Tracy, who was Marlo's age, welcomed us warmly when we arrived.

Next day, Warren started work with John, and Jan and I, who would be living in each other's pockets, became acquainted over a coffee. Jan was petite, blonde, had a heart of gold, and swore like a trooper. A large, inflatable swimming pool was the centre of play for the three kids each day. It was November and the days relentlessly hot.

The landscape here was featureless. Cotton fields – tabletop flat as far as the eye could see. The only interruption to the plainness of the horizon was the small bump of the Nandewar Ranges in the far distance. The wind howled around our camp daily, playing eerie tunes in the slightly open windows of the van. Dust. We ate it, slept in it, wiped it from our eyes. And grasshoppers – huge missiles that they were– bombarded our vans in kamikaze fashion until we could barely see out of the windows. I wondered if I'd ever get rid of the glue-like substance of them.

Linc turned four here. He'd been talking incessantly about a bike so we bought him a brand new two-wheeler with jockey wheels. The joy on his face when he saw it on the morning of his birthday is something I'll remember forever – the start of his "love affair" with two-wheeled vehicles.

Warren and John were asked to do some night work. The crop-dusting pilots preferred to fly at night when the wind had subsided, and men were needed on the ground with flags and torches to indicate field boundaries. Warren had always found agricultural chemicals abhorrent, especially insecticides, and was very concerned about the safety of this job. It was hair-raising too, he said, having these aircraft flying straight at them only metres off the ground.

Early one morning John came in from work seriously ill. Jan rushed him to the hospital where he was diagnosed with pesticide poisoning. Suffering severe damage to his nervous system, he fell into a coma. It was three weeks before he regained consciousness. He was lucky to have survived, and we were acutely aware of how easily it could have been Warren working downwind of the spray that night.

An intense low had brought rain and thunderstorms to the area. I'd planned to go into town to buy food as we were getting low, but the Biscay soil here was renowned for getting horribly sticky and dangerous to drive on when wet. For two days it drizzled. I waited, hoping for it to stop and the roads to dry. Finally, with no sign of the rain letting up, and the pantry empty, I had to make the trip.

This farm was divided into large expanses of cotton crops – each field watered by canals running either side of a network of tracks. Before leaving for work that morning, Warren warned me, 'The tracks'll be treacherous. Be careful.'

When it was time to go I put Linc and Marlo in the back of the panel van. No seatbelts.

'Now I want you to hold on tight,' I said to them, 'and don't talk to me until we stop. Okay?'

They nodded. As we set out the car began to slide. It was vital not to get stuck. There was no help out here. So I kept up the revs, fighting the steering wheel from lock to lock, wheels spinning constantly. The car snaked and slid along the greasy tracks, precariously close to the full channels on either side, for several kilometres. When we finally reached the farm gate and hit the gravel road to town, I stopped. Still trembling, I turned to see if the kids were okay. Their little knuckles were white with obedience. After shopping, I had to do it all again to get back to camp.

'How'd you go?' asked Warren when he got home that night.

I knew he cared, but at the same time expected me, as always, to do what it took. I still often wonder if he knows how scared I've been – doing what it takes.

For the first time since leaving home, Warren was dissatisfied with his pay. He wasn't making enough for us to eat, travel and make our mortgage payments. We'd received a letter from our new friends Rose and Leigh. Leigh had gained employment as a boilermaker at North West Vegetable Oils in Narrabri. The company was looking for more tradesmen, and knowing Warren could weld, Leigh suggested he apply. He did and was given a job. The money was good. He gave notice at the cotton farm and within a week we were on our way to Narrabri. We booked into the caravan park where Rose and Leigh had set camp before us.

Warren's first job on a big industrial site, it was an eye-opener for him. Huge capacitors had to be kept going twenty-four-seven. If the machinery stopped, the oil would coagulate and have to be physically scraped from inside the works before it could be started up again. It was as a result of this job that we stopped eating margarine. The quantity and nature of substances added in order to make it look appetising was beyond belief.

One of Warren's workmates considered himself God's gift to women. Swinger had been living with a girl who'd had enough of his philandering. On the day she left, he was filled with remorse.

He elected Warren his confidante and talked incessantly about how much his partner had meant to him and how determined he was to get her back. She'd left the district but he would go and find her. He devised a plan. He was contracted to work here for six months and without seeing out the term, would relinquish substantial financial benefits, unless he was injured. So, he asked Warren to cut off one of his fingers.

'Sure!' said Warren, facetiously.

They were working on a knife-sharp auger at the time. Swinger went to his toolbox and came back with a heavy hammer which he handed to Warren. Placing his little finger on the auger edge, he looked away and said, 'Now go on, belt it hard and don't miss!'

'You're mad, mate,' said Warren.

And with no-one prepared to inflict the injury upon him, he stayed. Within days, he'd fallen in love with another girl.

It would soon be Christmas – our first ever without extended family. A melancholy had settled on me about this, but a couple of weeks into December we received a letter from Warren's mum, asking if she and Otto could come to spend a week with us. We were all elated at the prospect. Warren and his dad hadn't spoken to each other since the day of their row.

A day or two later we received a letter from my dad asking if he too could join us for Christmas. My spirits soared.

On the night Dad was to arrive, the kids went to bed before he got there. I'd made up one of the three bunks for him. Marlo had been promoted to top bunk. Next morning she woke early, peered down to the bed below, and with the cutest hope-filled voice said, 'You're Grandad, aren't you?'

He lifted her down. Lincoln woke too and the love between the three of them warmed the cockles of my heart. For as long as we were away, Dad wrote weekly and would always send a special note and cartoon drawing for the children. My mum and Lin wrote regularly too. We looked forward so much to this news from home whenever we reached civilisation.

Otto and Lin had booked a cabin in the park. On their first day with us, Lin came to our van to be with the children and left Warren and his dad to talk. Otto told his son he'd been offered a good price for the farm at Copeville and if Warren agreed, he would sell it. Warren hadn't seen the property as part of his future and told his father he was happy for him to sell it. Otto wanted to know if we intended coming home. Of course, said Warren. The positive reply must have relieved Otto immensely. He relaxed and seemed happy. I imagine he would have suffered deep remorse over the argument that drove his son away and must have wondered if he would ever return.

'But there'll need to be changes,' said Warren.

He explained how he had dreams and plans for his life. The two of them would have to run separate businesses. He didn't want to be "the boy" forever. And he was a grazier, not a vigneron. They'd had this talk before. Although he was nodding, his dad said he didn't know how we could survive on sheep alone. But it was their moment of reconciliation, and Otto's acceptance of his son's desired direction – or so it seemed.

The children were showered with love and had lots to give in return. We had a joyful Christmas, and as our three parents left, there was hope for us all.

About nine o'clock one morning, Warren and Leigh came driving into the park in a state of high anxiety. Once they'd left for work in the morning they usually only returned at the end of the day. Something was wrong.

'Start packing,' Warren shouted as he pulled up on his motorbike.

'What's going on?' I shouted back over the noise of the bike.

'The river's rising. We've got an hour to get out.'

It normally took us two to three hours to pack up ready for a shift, but right then we just began hauling our stuff out from under the van and throwing everything inside – tools, jerry cans, shovels, hoses, spare tyres. Then toys, outdoor furniture, motorbike on the back. When all was done we hooked our van up to the car. Rose and Leigh had more stuff to pack so we helped them. In an hour we had finished and as we drove out of the park, we saw the Namoi River just across the road, breaking its banks. The speed with which this had happened was frightening.

We drove to the North West Vegetable Oils factory on high ground, unhooked our vans, then Rose and I drove into town to buy supplies for what we'd been told could be a week's isolation – or more. The town was in chaos. Supermarket aisles were full of people preparing for a disaster. By that afternoon, the caravan park we'd left was six feet under water.

We were isolated alright at our factory on the hill, with flood waters as far as the eye could see. Five families in caravans had made it here. We were fortunate to have electricity and the use of the workmen's wash room – one toilet, a basin and shower. Within two days this room was thick with crickets. Before we showered, we had to kick clear an area to stand in – clear of the black shiny things, some dead, some still alive. Rose and I still had the plastic baby baths we'd bathed our kids in when water had been scarce in the Outback. Now we used them for doing our laundry. We'd carry water in buckets from the bathroom and stand side by side outside our vans, chatting and laughing as we tried to get our husbands' overalls clean in these tiny tubs. We'd look out over the vast flood waters below, wondering how long we'd have to live like this. The kids were oblivious to the disaster and accepted the change without question or complaint. They played happily all day with new playmates, few toys and lots of imagination. In the evenings, our small cloistered community would cook on barbecues and eat, drink and be merry together. We were aware though of how many devastated families there must have been below.

It was ten days before the flood waters receded. So much had simply been washed away – roads, cars, homes, livestock. Some of the people in our camp had run out of food in a week and a helicopter had brought in basics for them – tinned meat, bread, potatoes, milk, dried vegies. I'd bought enough to last us the ten days.

The stench of the aftermath was sickening – rotting food and vegetation, animal carcasses, and sewage. All of this combined with the smell of warm vegetable oil being processed at the factory was enough to cause me horrible nausea. I was so relieved to finally be able to leave this place. The caravan park we'd escaped before the flood was destroyed, uninhabitable, so we booked into the shire park – conveniently right next to the town's swimming pool.

On this trip, our environment and the landscape were forever changing. I'd take the children for walks and talk about everything we saw along the way. There was much to learn from Nature. I read them stories, sang with them, always had materials ready for their creativity – Textas, paper, paint, homemade play dough. I taught them how to swim. We cooked together. Like clay, my children were being shaped.

We needed to spend a little longer here while Warren worked to earn enough money for the next leg of our journey. Most

Saturday nights we'd enjoy a barbecue with Rose and Leigh and several other families like ourselves. We'd put the kids to bed after tea and check on them periodically. There were no concerns for their safety.

Warren and Leigh's work at the factory was nearing an end but they'd heard of prospects with a mining company in Townsville. They applied for jobs there and with their skills in high demand were employed immediately. Rose and Leigh planned to go directly there but we wanted to take our time and see a little more of Australia along the way.

My father's sister and her husband lived in Grafton. We planned to visit them. Dad had always been close to his sister Joan, but since he and his siblings had left the family farm as kids, they hadn't seen much of each other. Aunty Joan had met her husband during the war and they'd settled in his home town, Grafton, New South Wales. They'd been back to visit their South Australian family maybe twice in twenty years. Uncle Ted was an ambitious person who'd built an engineering business so successful that he could never get away. Our family had made the huge journey to see them when I was about fourteen – the five of us bundled into our FJ Holden. I remember it as a magnificent three week adventure – one of my happiest childhood memories. I didn't need car games. Just looking out of the window at the passing scenery was enough to keep me well entertained. I loved the quaint towns, each one different from the next, paddocks of sheep, forests of towering trees and ferns, country kids at play on bikes, in creeks. Townsfolk gathered. Roaming dogs.

I had always felt a particular fondness for this aunt and uncle. Aunty Joan had missed her southern family terribly and there'd been emotional goodbyes at each of those few visits. I was looking forward to seeing them again and introducing them to my little family. On the banks of the Clarence River, their home was a modern two-storey "Queenslander" on a few acres where, as a sideline, they grew vegetables and ran cattle. Warren and Uncle Ted hit it off immediately with a common interest in farming and European cars. Uncle Ted owned a Porsche and Rolls Royce. For three days he and my aunt took us out sightseeing in their everyday car – a Mercedes Benz! They showered us with love and the best of country hospitality.

Our visit was short as Warren needed to get to his next job. Knowing it would probably be years before we'd see each other again, there were tears as Aunty Joan and I hugged each other goodbye.

Our next stop was Proserpine. We pulled into the caravan park at dark. After we'd eaten, I bathed the kids in the baby bath, put them to bed and then went to have a shower myself. The night was balmy, the air heavy with the perfume of frangipanis and hibiscus as I strolled across the palm tree strewn lawns, swinging my toiletry bag and smiling while the beautiful tropical environment worked its magic on me.

The shower was good and hot. I shampooed my hair, rinsed off the suds, opened my eyes and there on the floor, between me and the door, was the most enormous toad I have ever seen. I'd never seen a cane toad. A scream lurched in my chest but I clapped a hand over my mouth before it escaped. We looked at each other – the toad and I. Had it not been at my exit, I would have run out of the building naked.

'Shoo,' I gurgled.

I flicked water at it. It loved that.

'Shoo,' I stamped.

It gave me a disdainful scowl and hopped heavily out, under the door. Warren laughed from his belly when I told him. As it turned out, we'd have to live with these creatures for the next five months.

We reached Townsville in early March, had a brief look around the city then drove up to Yabulu – twenty kilometres north-west. Warren was to work here on the construction of a huge nickel refinery, for a company called Greenvale Nickel.

There was a caravan "city" for the families. It comprised four blocks, each with its own amenities, and separate dongas for the single men, while many of the workers rented homes in Townsville. Rose and Leigh had been here two weeks when we arrived. Their sons, Chris and Arnie, had already chummed up with a few of the park kids and they welcomed Linc and Marlo into the new group.

This workplace had Warren in awe of its size. There were hundreds of tradesmen – boilermakers, riggers, fitters and turners, engineers, and technical assistants for them all. From sitting alone on a tractor all day or working in a shearing shed, this was a far cry, and Warren must have been way out of his comfort zone.

He began by welding checker plate flooring for the two seven-storey buildings that were to house the machinery. After a couple of days of having his skills scrutinised by a foreman, he was promoted to welding pipes together and assigned an assistant. These were ten metres long and two metres in diameter. Nothing was small on this job. At this stage the pipes were still on the ground. Another boilermaker was working from the other end, several pipe lengths away, and after a couple of days he walked through the pipes to where Warren was welding.

'Hey mate,' he said as Warren flipped his welder's mask up. 'Slow down. What're ya tryin' to do – show me up? You've done more in a day than I've done all week.'

The energy of the union was in the air. Warren had always been used to doing an honest day's work, but here the premise seemed to be – "let's see how little work we can do for this really good money". Warren hated this "go slow" principle. Working fast made the day go quicker and he propounded his view on it whenever he had a chance.

New friends were made through the children. Linc and Marlo had befriended Mark and Ruth who were similar ages and we soon got to know their parents, Jenn and Terry, whose caravan was quite near ours. They too were travellers and before long we felt we'd known each other all our lives. Having come to Australia in the late sixties as Ten Pound Poms, Jenn and Terry were rich with life experiences. Terry and Warren had a love of motorbikes in common and often took the children out for rides on their bikes after work.

The men were paid weekly – cash in an envelope. The pay office was a tin shed with four windows. There were hundreds of workers. On Warren's first Thursday there, the knock-off siren went at four. Men downed tools and ran for their pay. It became a stampede and the momentum of the mob took out the shed. Warren could only look on in disbelief.

One Thursday afternoon I was on my way back to camp after shopping in Townsville. Driving along the dirt road, children in the back, I could see a cloud of dust ahead. As I came up over a hill, I saw a monstrous mass of utes and four-wheel drives coming towards me, two abreast across the whole road. I yanked the wheel and pulled up onto a three foot embankment to avoid a head-on collision. As the first driver passed – window down, elbow out, he yelled, 'Ya tryin' to commit suicide, lady?'

The workers were on their way home.

Cane toads lived here by the thousands. They inhabited the amenities block – under the building, in the showers, toilets and on the lawns. I thought I would never get used to the constant grumbling chorus but eventually the noise became just another part of the environment.

We loved Townsville and its climate – twenty-six degrees most days. On weekends we'd often go exploring, and early one Saturday, packed up with our small tent and all we needed for two days' camping, we set out for the Burdekin River. By now we had a short wheelbase Nissan Patrol after trading in the panel van at Narrabri.

Before the era of mobile phones, many people were loath to go into these remote places and hence we often found ourselves utterly and delightfully alone on these excursions.

On this particular weekend we pulled up at a glorious spot on the grassy banks of the Burdekin – just a trickle in the dry northern winter. The thin stream shone like a giant serpent sunning itself on a pristine bed of sand. Again, we had the feeling of being just a dot on the landscape.

The children played with found objects, slid down sand hills and swam in the clear, shallow water. A confection of lilting bird song came out of the bush. Nearly camouflaged kangaroos stood still with ears twitching. We called out our names to hear them come back to us from across the river. Warren had envisaged times like these, he told me, in his dreams, before he'd taken us away from home.

# FOURTEEN

Dale and Heather were to be married in June, and Warren was to be best man. I think our families were hoping our adventure would end then and we'd resume life as it had been before. But there was still half of Australia to see, and if Warren was to receive his full financial entitlements from Greenvale Nickel, we'd have to put in at least another two months in Townsville. He arranged to take two weeks' leave without pay.

We set out on a Friday afternoon, having planned to drive non-stop and as the crow flies so we'd have as much family time at home as possible.

Warren drove the first eight hundred kilometres, then in the wee hours stopped for fuel at Aramac – a tiny, lonely speck on the map. We'd seen the dim light of its one bowser fuel station from some distance and as we pulled up we could hear the knock of a diesel generator – their only source of power. The fuel gravitated silently from a tank at the back of the hut.

Our vehicle had only a canvas top and the chill of the inland night had caught us by surprise. The car had no heating. As Warren refuelled, I lay over the bonnet, hungering after the warmth of the engine. Linc and Marlo began to stir with the cold. I hadn't brought enough warm clothes. I opened our two suitcases and retrieved towels, light jackets and the nappies I was bringing home to store. All this I lay over the children in their beds – all but one nappy which I tied scarf-like round my head.

Now it was my turn to drive while Warren slept. Lonely in the silence of the car, I drove with one hand whilst sitting on the other to keep it warm. When my driving hand had lost all feeling I'd use the other. Warren slept fitfully.

'Pull over,' he grouched, shattering the icy atmosphere.

I obeyed. He grabbed our only map and took it to the front of the vehicle where he tied it to the radiator to stop it from cooling.

'The engine might give us some warmth now,' he muttered.

It didn't. The children slept comfortably, aided by the contents of the cases and each other's body heat. I drove for the next six or seven hours – rigid and shivering with the cold. Warren was never quite asleep. We agreed in the warmth of the next day that we had never been so cold for so long.

I slept restlessly through the next morning until we stopped for more fuel, something to eat, and a break for the kids. I'd packed enough food for the journey. Although tired from lack of sleep, Warren drove the next leg – about five hours – until it was time again for exercise and to have our evening meal. Longreach, Charleville, Cunnamulla were all behind us. I was to drive through that night but after four hours I couldn't stay awake. Warren had slept reasonably well so we swapped. He drove until two am by which time the temperature was again plummeting. I drove for the next three hours until dog-tired and in pain with the cold. Warren took the wheel once more. As dawn broke we saw Broken Hill in the distance and ice on the landscape.

We'd come through Bourke, Cobar, Wilcannia in the night. We pulled up for breakfast – homemade muesli with powdered milk and cold water. Sitting on jerry cans and the step of the vehicle, we tried to get our frozen fingers to hold our plates and spoons. The sun was still no match for the ice but promised us relief as it began to light the flatland.

The cold had deprived us of so much sleep that from Broken Hill to home, neither of us could stay awake at the wheel for more than an hour. After forty-five hours on the road, we arrived at Dad's house at two pm. Everyone was there, except Mum. The tragedy and emptiness of divorce was now in the place. We would see Mum next day after a *long, warm, comfortable sleep*.

It was wonderful to be back. Little by little we caught up with all our family and friends. On our second day home, Lincoln fell into a torpor. As he lay on the couch at Dad's house, his temperature suddenly went through the roof and he became delirious. I rushed him to the doctors' clinic. Our lovely family doctor of old asked me about my son's legs. He'd scratched them whilst playing in the bush at Townsville, I told him. The scratches hadn't healed. Doc felt his glands, took his temperature, and said to himself, 'Hmmm,' and then to me, 'It's a good thing you brought him in today. He has blood poisoning.'

'*What?*' I said as I looked at my son's glazed eyes.

I held him close, kissed him and stroked his head as the doctor prepared a syringe of penicillin. As he administered it, Lincoln barely flinched. He was so ill. What a blessing we were home and near our wonderfully caring family GP. For another two days our precious son slept, and then on the third, began to stir towards recovery. I still shudder to think of what might have happened had we arrived home a day or two later.

We had a week to help Dale get ready for his wedding. I was happy to see my brother preparing to spend his life with Heather – an intelligent, adventurous and ambitious girl. The wedding was a happy occasion, but my parents were in a bad state emotionally. It was difficult for me to leave them at the end of our time home, but I believed they would survive and grow through this time of hardship.

We drove back to Townsville more sensibly – via a different route and stopping at caravan parks for two nights.

On Warren's first day back at work, a union meeting was called. The single men were unhappy with the size of oranges in their lunch packs, and as the meeting gathered momentum, they found more and more to gripe about. They voted to go out the gate – for better conditions and more money. Warren was earning more than four times the basic wage. It was amazing money and had helped us enormously in reducing our mortgages.

Ultimately there was a two week strike. Wrenching to think we could have stayed home that much longer. Remarkably though, after the dust had settled and the wheels were back in motion, Warren discovered that he'd been paid for the two weeks he'd been away. He told his boss.

'As far as I'm concerned,' said the foreman, 'you never left the place. In the two weeks you were gone, the rest of the crew didn't even catch up to where you were before you left.'

Warren had heard about an upcoming motorbike scramble to be held in Cairns. He succumbed to the enticement of competing in it and began to prepare his TM Suzuki 125.

It was a three hour drive to get to the event so we left on the Friday after work. Jenn and Terry, keen as always for another new experience, came with us. We set camp in the bush near the track – our four kids like pups amongst the melee of motorbikes, riders and their families.

Early next morning Warren wheeled his bike to the starting line with a hundred or more others. On the starter's instructions, the mass of machines were kicked into life. The noise was deafening. A huge cloud of dust began to rise as the bikes took off. As they crackled and zigzagged across the face of a large hill, I tried in vain to keep my husband in sight. I couldn't wait for it to be over, but for Warren the adrenalin had taken effect and although he finished in the middle of the field, a fifteen year passion was launched.

A couple of young musicians lived on our block in the caravan park. Larry was tall and thin with long hair, beard, sandals, cheese-cloth tops and brightly-coloured, baggy cotton pants – the whole hippy package. A guitarist and singer, he'd been a member of a well-known blues band in Canada. Jude, his "Kiwi" partner, had met Larry in Canada whilst hitchhiking around the world. She too was a gifted guitarist/singer/songwriter. We became friends and I fell under the spell of their enchanting music. One Saturday they invited us to the folk club in Townsville where they were to sing that night. Jenn and Terry offered to look after Linc and Marlo. The wonderful nights of live folk music we'd enjoyed at The Catacombs in Adelaide seemed a lifetime ago.

The ambience of the Townsville club did its work on me – candlelight, sandalwood, newly written songs. Art. Our friends' singing drew enthusiastic applause.

The following Saturday night I found myself on this stage. Larry and Jude had invited me to read some of my poetry. One of their friends accompanied me on acoustic guitar – his hauntingly beautiful ad lib strains embellishing my words in the dim, hushed room full of alternative people. Oddly I wasn't nervous. This was my genre. These were my observations, my truths, from my marrow. The audience was hungry for art. This was the seventies. Poetry was revered. It felt wonderful to have my work heard.

After five months at Yabulu it was time to move on and say goodbye once more to friends. Warren received all his severance pay which, together with what we'd saved, was enough to give us three weeks' travelling before the next job.

Fearing we may not get to some of these North Queensland places again, we planned to forge even further north. Although we would travel these parts again in later years, they would be vastly different from the unspoiled wildernesses of the seventies.

The Atherton Tablelands were picture-book glorious – rolling green hills dotted with dairy cows and quirky weatherboard houses. Towns more like villages. Narrow streets undulating. Slightly slumped wooden shops showing their age, while locals gathered in twos and threes to look after their parochial solidarity.

Kuranda was hippy heaven – a haven for anti-war, peace-loving people of all ages. They'd bought land in the rainforest – five to ten acre lots – and settled in communities. Along forest edged roads they walked – barefooted, dreadlocked, bedecked with beads and tinkling shoulder bags, smelling of garlic and sandalwood. At street markets in town their produce was bought and sold – fresh vegetables, tropical fruits and berries, eggs, honey, jams and bread. Idyllic.

The day we arrived in Port Douglas we were soon in awe of the small, sleepy town whose people had been there for generations and seemed almost unaware that they were living in one of the most beautiful places on earth. The place was appealingly unkempt – its main street shady on the beach side with enormous mango trees. Free of edges, the road and footpath melded as leaf litter and old fruit softened the earth that led to the sea.

The sign "Fresh Fish Daily" encouraged us into the local fish and chip shop. Out the front an ice cream placard stood askew. Our feet were noisy on the floorboards and we heard the sea. Not much else. I'm glad we saw it then, before it was "discovered".

After our brief pause in paradise we headed south west. Then from Ravenshoe into deep inland North Queensland – harsh, lonely terrain.

First night out we found an exquisite camping spot – Millstream Falls. We'd seen an old handpainted sign for it, half hidden in the bush and leaning with indifference. On sudden impulse, Warren turned into the even rougher track with twenty foot caravan in tow. Again we were rewarded for his sense of adventure. The falls were some fifteen feet high and sixty wide. Later that night as I lay in our comfy caravan bed, their music lulled me to sleep and coloured my dreams.

Next morning we set out for Normanton on the Gulf of Carpentaria – a nine hour drive. Here we found hot springs – a swimming hole whose surrounds had been beautified and cared for by the town. We were so very far from any other form of civilisation, yet again we felt watched.

After our long, hot drive we were thankful for the luxury of a swim after tea. In the thick damp air under a caramel gold sky, we were acutely aware of the insular locals whispering and wondering what on earth had brought us here.

Karumba was an hour's drive to the coast, which we did next morning. A cyclone had hit the town a week earlier and the sea had claimed the esplanade and some fishermen's sheds. It was from here that people were granted the only access to Weipa, the next town north – about eight hundred kilometres, but by ferry only. The wharf would have to be repaired before there was any more sea traffic, and that could be weeks they said. We returned to Normanton from where we headed for Cloncurry along the Bourke Developmental Road. Camooweal was our next day's destination and the day after that Three Ways, where we expected to find amenities. We were champing at the bit for our first shower in days. Water had been, as always, scarce, and we'd had to make do with sponge baths the previous nights. At Three Ways we set camp near a *Besser* brick ablutions block – part of the pub – and hurried for the clean hot water we'd been longing for. It became quickly obvious there'd been plumbing problems for a while. Water from other people's showers lay as sewage, four inches deep, in the only cubicle. Swimming in it were several pale, soap-affected frogs. I stood on the raised edge, straining towards a dribble of hot water while the comforts of home seemed a million miles away.

Our goal for the next night was Daly Waters. These were long, scorching days of travel and as usual our little ones were champions. Air-conditioning was "windows down". We'd stop for an hour at lunchtime, run and play to burn up their burgeoning energy and then return to the road where they'd play car games and then sleep. They accepted each day as normal, no matter what.

Darkness fell before we reached our destination. Driving speed always depended on the conditions of the road so it was almost impossible to estimate a time of arrival. While still a hundred kilometres out of Daly Waters and driving along a newly made section of gravel road built up three or four feet above the plains, our headlights failed. In the ink black night, Warren hit the brakes for fear of going over the edge. He stopped on the road. By torchlight he searched under the bonnet, discovered a blown fuse and replaced it. Barrelling along at ninety kilometres an hour, it happened again. It was a helpless feeling to be suddenly driving blind without room for error. Obviously, the problem was more than a blown fuse and so we limped into Daly, nerves on edge, as periodically we'd find ourselves, in an instant, in total blackness on this high and narrow, unfinished road.

That night in Daly Waters, after Warren had fixed the headlight problem, we tried to estimate how long it would take to get to Port Hedland where Warren had a job lined up. We were beginning to contemplate end days. After Port Hedland we would make our way down the west coast, trusting there'd be enough work along the way to get us home by Christmas. Linc was to start school in the new year.

There was no track through the Tanami and Central Desert Aboriginal Land, so we would have to drive a long way north before turning west to Port Hedland.

We wanted to see Kununurra and Broome, but it looked like we'd be cutting it fine money-wise before getting there. So we'd need to stop in Katherine where we hoped Warren could find a week's work.

By the time we reached Katherine we were exhausted. We'd been on the road in excruciating heat for more than a week. Warren pulled up at the pub and went in for a quick beer and chat, hoping to find out about job prospects. Ten minutes later he returned to the car, shaking his head.

'What's up?' I said.

'The publican told me I was in the wrong pub.'

'What do you mean?'

'Black fellas only.'

When he'd walked through the door Warren had seen that, apart from the barman, he was the only white fella in there, but of course it had been no issue for him. He hoped it hadn't been for the patrons either. He had a beer and a yarn anyway.

We set up in the caravan park and Warren headed back into town, about five kilometres away, to the "right" pub to find out about work. We were out of food so I asked him to bring back something for tea. We would do a big replenishing food shop next day.

The days of travel in above forty degree heat with no cooling had been taxing. I wondered how we'd cope with this heat for the next week or so. Our caravan was in the blazing sun as there was little shade in the park. The kids and I went for a walk and spent some time at the two swings where there was a little shade.

By six o'clock Warren still wasn't back. He'd left at three. This was unusual. The kids were hungry so I gave them the last of our food – dry biscuits with Vegemite. By seven I was concerned. If something had happened to him, no-one would know who he was or that he had a family waiting for him. How would I look for him without a vehicle?

The kids were spent so I put them to bed. I would now have to ask the park manager for help. Just as I was leaving the van for the office my husband pulled up – his face beaming. He saw my face – not beaming – and with sudden realisation said, 'Oh. Sorry. I met the most amazing blokes. Buffalo hunters. You wouldn't believe their stories.'

He'd found the yarns about their lifestyle so riveting that he'd not wanted to leave until the telling was done. This was part of what he'd expected to find on this trip, he told me. He'd brought no food. I was furious, but more than that, relieved.

In the "right" pub, Warren had learned that the manager of the town's power station was looking for someone to undertake machinery maintenance there, so he went to see him next day. He was given the job.

We bought a fan – the first we'd ever owned. It felt like an incredible luxury. While it was comforting to know it was there if we needed it, someone in the park had told me about a swimming hole not far away, in the Katherine River. The Aboriginal children swam there and didn't seem to mind sharing it with us.

Crystal clear water about two feet deep flowed over a sandy bed. Shady trees leaned protectively towards the carefree children. I took Linc and Marlo there most days. Playmates were found, logs climbed, bark boats sailed.

We got to know another young couple of travellers in the park – Dennis and Karen – and enjoyed a beer and a yarn with them most evenings.

After three weeks in Katherine, Warren felt financially secure enough to set out for Port Hedland. Time again to move on.

# FIFTEEN

Our destination first day out was Kununurra – a full day's drive. By mid-afternoon we'd reached the turn-off to the mighty Lake Argyle – a modern and amazing feat of engineering, built to conserve the massive amount of rain that fell each wet season. We drove the twenty-five kilometres in to see it. Warren and I stood in wonder as we looked out over the immense expanse of sparkling water. Linc and Marlo, always ecstatic to be out of the car, danced and sang.

On our way back out to the main road we crossed Overflow Creek. It looked so inviting that, despite the "No Swimming" signs, we stripped bare and lay on the pebbly bed with the cold clear water rushing and pummelling over us.

The next leg would be hot, long and arduous as we headed for Broome across the top end. With Halls Creek in our sights that day, we left Kununurra early. On our left was a vast and desolate plain, on our right the harsh and rocky Durack Range. In a long-distance film shot, our outfit would have appeared as a speck, flat-lining silently across the foot of the range – a titanic tick of dust leaving the road behind us. The landscape made us silent. There was *no-one* else out here. But then, way off in the distance we saw an indistinguishable object in the shimmer of the road. As we got closer we could see it was a vehicle. A woman stepped out from the front of her Land Rover. She and an Aboriginal female companion had the bonnet up. We stopped. They'd hit a 'roo and put a hole in their radiator, and were loath to put in the water they may have needed for drinking. We'd filled our caravan's water tank before leaving Kununurra and so Warren had no qualms about filling their radiator for them. The white woman told us they lived on Mabel Downs – a cattle station sixty-five kilometres further on and then another few off the highway. She asked us where we were headed and when we told her Hall's Creek she said, 'It'll be late before you get there. I wouldn't recommend being out here after dark. You're welcome to follow me in and spend the night with us.'

Warren was nodding.

'Let me cook you a meal.'

The offer sounded wonderful.

The woman had come from Sydney to work as governess to the widowed station owner's two kids. She'd fallen in love with the place and the man, and they had married.

The homestead was large and comfortable with wide verandahs, closed in on all sides with flywire. A few small trees softened the harsh and rocky landscape. Linc and Marlo quickly spotted a corrugated iron swimming pool – a tank in its previous life – and then caught sight of the two station kids who'd emerged shyly from the house. Our two, always delighted with playmates and water, seized the last of the day and before long the four of them were like pups in a litter.

After a generous barbecue, we tucked the kids into their beds and sat outside with our hosts. For a moment I had to sit back and take in my surroundings – sprawling corrugated iron homestead nestled in a hollow of rocks, a riot of sunset colours creeping across a nearby jagged hillside, the exotic scent of desert flora and the chaotic going down of birds. All manna for my senses.

For a moment I thought, as I often did these days, "what if we had never done this." The four of us chatted comfortably. There was much to learn about life out here.

A small Aboriginal community lived in camp a hundred metres or so from the house. The men helped with the stock work and the women with the home and garden. We were told a story about our hosts' "dogger" – Old Jack, not Aboriginal. He'd spent most of his life here on Mabel Downs, travelling long distances as he checked and repaired the dog fences. His staple diet was tinned food warmed over his camp fires each night. Once a week however, he would return to the homestead to report on the fences, have a tub, enjoy a hearty meal cooked by the "missus" and sleep in a comfortable bed. This had been his routine for years. One Sunday he failed to return. A search party went out. Old Jack had broken an axle on his ute the second day out and set out on foot in the direction of home. The days were searing and he'd soon run out of water. They found his body not far from the highway. He'd written on Bex powder papers that he knew the road was nearby but didn't have the strength to crawl to it. Those who found him, disconnected the tail shaft of his vehicle and drove it home. His lack of mechanical knowledge had cost him his life.

Like a child who's heard a scary fairytale, I was on tenterhooks about water as we left next morning.

We drove until lunch time and pulled up beneath the shade of a solitary tree, rare as they were out here. We hadn't seen another soul on the road. While I was unpacking the food I'd prepared that morning, Warren lay down on the dirt and dragged himself under the caravan.

'What's up?' I asked.

'There's a wet patch. I think there's a hole in the water tank.'

'What?'

'Yep. Here it is.'

I gasped. 'How much water's left?'

'About half I reckon.'

He dragged himself back out and stood up. We were silent as he mentally assessed the situation. Even the children sensed it was dire. He walked to a nearby tuft of spinifex, pulled off a handful of its straw, folded it into a wad, crawled back under the van and plugged the hole with it.

'I think we'll have enough water,' he said, 'to get us to Fitzroy Crossing tonight.'

Every kilometre closer to that town was a relief and finally, we arrived on schedule.

The Crossing was sparsely populated – a store-owner/publican and another small community of black folk. We hadn't showered since Kununurra, two nights earlier, and so once again anticipated the luxury of hot running water in the camp area. After showering and putting on clean clothes, we walked back to our van through six inch deep bulldust that, with each step, rose in small puffs like talcum powder. We lived in sandals and so before bed, in a basin of warm water, four pairs of very dirty feet were re-washed. Thankfully we were granted access to a rainwater tank here and in the morning filled our depleted one.

Next day we reached Broome. Like something from an old western movie, the main street was wide and unsealed, the buildings weatherboard or corrugated iron. It was dead quiet. A dog or two lay about in the shade of shop verandahs. We asked a local if there was somewhere we could camp for the night. He directed us to a small caravan park near the beach. With the boom of big surf in our ears we quickly set up for a short stay and then hurried towards the enticing sound. Looking down from the top of a cliff we were in awe of the magnificent beach before us. Thousands of tons of snow white sand, recently washed up by a cyclone, had been spread as far as the eye could see. Pristine, wild, deserted, this was Cable Beach. What a privilege to have seen it before it became the bustling, thriving tourist mecca it is today. I was so intrigued with the unique architecture of this town that next day, while Warren took the children to the beach, I sat on a stool in the street and did some sketching.

With our travelling funds almost depleted, we had to get to Port Hedland soon. An old associate, David Simpson, was living and working here and had assured Warren of good job prospects. On the map it looked like a day's drive, but within an hour of leaving Broome we could not hazard a guess at how long it would take. The road was the worst we'd travelled – enormous potholes, corrugations, wash-outs. By five pm we were exhausted and not yet halfway there. We spent the night at Sandfire – a fitting name. A graveyard for wrecked and abandoned vehicles, it was hot, dirty, and remote.

The next day's travelling was a replica, but the reward at the end was Port Hedland. We stopped at the entrance to the caravan park. Another van pulled up right next to us. Warren looked out of the window and said, 'Look, there's a caravan exactly the same as ours.'

It *was* ours. The towbar had broken and the van had come to rest right beside us. Lucky it happened here and not out in the God-forsaken country we'd just come from.

David Simpson was working in this town as a heavy diesel mechanic for Brambles Transport. Warren looked him up next day and with his help secured a job – welding for an engineering company. We had enough money to pay a week's rent in advance at the caravan park, and to frugally replenish our food supply. On leaving the grocery store, I had ten cents left in my purse. Our children who'd been so patient and well-behaved, asked me for an iceblock when they saw other kids in the park eating them. I explained that we'd have to wait until their daddy's next pay day. Later that afternoon Warren came back with mail from home. I opened the letter from Mum and out fell another of her life-saving ten dollar notes. It would feed us for another week. The first thing I did was to buy Linc and Marlo their iceblocks.

Linc was the only child in the park with a two-wheeled bike which put him high on the popularity ladder. All the kids wanted to ride it. Our son's inherent business bent must have begun there. With absolutely no coaxing from us, he began to sell rides – two laps around the park for twenty cents. Kids scurried off to their mothers for the money. After each ride, Linc took his "customer" to the kiosk to buy him or her a fifteen cent iceblock. After he'd been paid for three rides, he could buy an iceblock for himself. After the next three he bought one for Marlo.

We'd been there three weeks with almost enough money saved to get to Perth. After work one day, Warren called in to the post office to see if we had mail. He was handed a telegram. It read, 'Warren. Please ring. Urgent. Dad had accident. Mum.'

I knew something was wrong as soon as I saw his face.

'I need to call Mum. Dad has had an accident.'

'What's happened? Is he ok?'

'I don't know. I have to ring.'

He headed for the public phone in the park. I followed. His mother answered the phone and, in tears, told him what had happened.

Otto had been spraying the vineyard. He'd pulled up outside their house to make some machinery adjustments and had leaned across the slowly turning power take-off shaft between the tractor and the spray plant. A protruding grease nipple on the rotating shaft had become hooked in the leg of his new overalls. Because the fabric was so tough, he'd been unable to rip it to get free. The engaged shaft just kept turning while twisting the overalls tighter and tighter until they tore, but not before rolling off Otto's flesh from knee to ankle, to the bone. It's hard to imagine the trauma or how he finally got free. Lin, who was inside the house, thought she heard a cry. She went to the back door and saw her husband dragging himself across the lawn – a shocking trail of blood behind him. As she ran to him, she saw the mutilated leg. She rushed back inside to phone for an ambulance, then back to Otto with towels to try to stop the bleeding. He was rushed to Adelaide and given transfusions along the way. The blood loss was enormous. That night amazing micro-surgery was performed by highly skilled surgeons to try to save his leg. We were told later that had it happened a few months earlier, no-one in Adelaide would have had the skills to perform this operation and he would have become an amputee. Lin begged Warren to come home as soon as possible.

It took two days for us to reach Carnarvon, with the roads no better than the previous. From here we phoned Lin again. She told us Otto was in the best of care but would be in hospital for weeks.

Prior to this accident we'd planned to visit my aunt and uncle on their sheep station – a hundred kilometres inland from Carnarvon. We hadn't seen them since they'd left their property at Corny Point where I'd holidayed as a girl.

Every second Friday they'd come into town to do their shopping. Coincidentally it was on this very day that we were in town and bumped into them. We'd planned to call them via pedal radio to let them know we wouldn't be coming in to see them. Although they understood our need to get home, they were bitterly disappointed. Like her sister whom we'd caught up with some months earlier in Grafton, my aunt missed her South Australian family. So, knowing it was unlikely we'd ever get back to this place, and having been reassured by Lin that Otto was in good hands, we considered a couple of days with my aunt and uncle a possibility. After her initial trauma, Lin had taken stock and told us she'd be okay until we got home.

Aunty Roma had a doctor's appointment at four but had no idea how long it would take, so Uncle Vern suggested we head out before them. They were totally familiar with the track and would do it much quicker than we would. For us it would be a two hour drive, as long as we got there before dark. Rough road. Nothing new.

'You can't go wrong,' said Uncle Vern. 'Just keep to the main track. There's a few gates. Leave 'em as you find 'em. We should be back by seven.'

We headed due east into dense, low scrubland. The track was narrow, winding, sandy, and by five pm, with no sign of the sun in an overcast sky, we'd lost our sense of direction. We came to a fork in the road and couldn't determine which was the main track. The fear of getting lost caused us to be terse with each other. Warren sensed my anxiety and said, 'I'm going to follow my instincts. We'll have to trust that.'

Kangaroos came out and softened the landscape in the fading light – cheeky with their bush sense. Tense with the knowledge we were in danger, we drove in silence, opening and shutting gates every so often until we rounded a bend and saw a small but proud-hearted homestead – welcoming in the twilight. Three sheep dogs greeted us ecstatically. As seemed to be Aunty Roma's lot, she again had only one shady tree in the yard. We parked our caravan beneath it. Crossing the lawn she'd created from one square foot of turf, we went into the house. My aunt and uncle had cleared the scrub here and built themselves a home. Aunty Roma had given it her touch – cosy and gracious with her good furniture and chattels brought with them from South Australia.

After tea in the caravan and putting the kids to bed, we sat outside to watch the huge sky darken and come alive with stars. We were happy to be there. The enjoyment of our whole trip had been sharpened by these constant, periodic states of release after tension.

'What's the time?' I asked.

Warren looked at his watch.

'Eight o'clock.'

'That's strange. They said they'd be back by seven.'

We had a beer and listened to the distant bleat of sheep, a late bird looking for its mate, the creaking of the van still coming to rest.

By nine the tension was back. Perhaps Aunty Roma had been admitted to hospital, or maybe they'd broken down out there.

We went back into the house, and in the dim battery light stood looking at the pedal radio. Warren switched it on. It hummed into life and we raised our eyebrows at each other. Then after a while, 'Hello, Jean. Jean are you there?'

We studied the device.

'Yes. Hello, Nance,' – one of those crackling voices from old Australian movies.

'How'd Jack get on with that busted mill today?' Crackle and static.

'All fixed there, Nance. They replaced the buckets. Lucky he checked it Tuesday.'

Warren leant in, fingering the knobs and switches, hoping to be able to ask these doyens of station life for some clue on what may have happened to Roma and Vern.

There was an eruption of barking outside as the dogs heard their master's vehicle approaching. We left the radio to greet them.

About to leave Carnarvon, Vern had noticed a pool of water under the car.

'Water pump,' he told us.

Luckily the garage had one in stock and the mechanic had been able to replace it in time for their trip home that night.

Next morning, we enjoyed a full station breakfast together, sitting at the same table my aunt and I had sat at fifteen years earlier as we waited past nightfall for Vern to come in from reaping, to start the generator so we would have light. There was so much to tell. They wanted to hear all about our travels and we were absolutely taken with their stories of pioneering out here.

My aunt had bravely followed the ambitions of her husband, to this place that must have seemed like the end of the earth to her. Here she kept house and garden, cooked, sewed, read. When asked to, she'd drive to the nearer bores to check the water. In defiance of her environment, she wore frocks and varnished her nails.

One day she'd been out watering her tiny plot of lawn when she'd had a feeling of being watched. She looked up to see a small group of naked Aborigines standing in the bush no more than thirty metres away. On eye contact with her they quickly disappeared. There was no known community anywhere near here. My aunt believed she might have been the first white person they had ever seen.

Vern wanted to show us some of his country. The station covered seven hundred and fifty thousand acres. There was a beautiful lake out a bit, he told us, so we packed some lunch and set out. My uncle drove at speed, with confidence to spare, giving the wheel its way in the soft deep sand. Tea trees brushed and scratched the bush-beaten four-wheel drive as the track narrowed. Wrenches and spades clattered in the back. We drove for two hours until finally coming to a clearing where, sparkling in the midday sun, lay a small shallow lake – an utter oasis in this bony country.

It was spring and there were wildflowers, and in the huge Outback silence, a festival of birdsong. A generous mulga shaded us as we ate our lunch – six people on a tartan rug on three quarters of a million acres. So small us. So big the land.

My aunt and uncle were softened by this temporary extension of family, I could tell. They took the children paddling in the lake.

The homeward run was by a different route. The maze of tracks, deviations, forks and crossroads was negotiated by my uncle with great bushmanship. It wouldn't take much to get lost out here. Driving beside a new fence we spotted a feathered head bobbing above the tea trees. We rounded the next bend and saw a baby emu pounding along the track – its mother on the other side of the fence. The chick was terrified, its mother panicking. I wished Vern would stop to let them have their way. He was not a man you could say that to. He just kept driving as a matter of course as they fled ahead, then powered past them once they were exhausted.

Aunty Roma cooked a lamb roast for tea and we talked into the night. It had been a long time since we'd seen them – back on their farm near the sea, at Corny Point in South Australia.

After a sound sleep we got up early, prepared our van for the trip out and sat down to another superb breakfast in the homestead. A workman who lived here on the station came in as we were having coffee.

'I want you to go out and check number three bore, Neil,' my uncle said to him.

Our little ones had latched onto the young bushman who seemed to have a flare with kids.

'Can we go too?' they asked.

'No,' I said, 'We'll be leaving soon.'

'Neil won't be long,' said my uncle. 'They'll be fine with him.'

They skipped out to the open Jeep with him and off they went. I felt uneasy.

'Are you sure they'll be okay?' I asked.

'He's very responsible,' my uncle assured me. We had another cup of coffee and resumed our chatter.

An hour later we heard the vehicle return. I was relieved. Neil and Lincoln walked into the kitchen.

'Where's Marlo?' I asked.

'She didn't come with us,' said Neil.

'*What?*'

I stood up as terror pounded through me. She was three years old. There were no fences around the homestead, only hundreds of thousands of acres of dense bush.

She's wearing blue, I thought. We won't even be able to see her from the air. My uncle rose from the head of the table.

'We'll find her. Neil, take the ute and head out east. Warren, come with me. We'll head west.'

Warren's face was pale as he shot through the door with the man I'd always seen as larger than life – tall, strong, and above all supremely bush-wise. But in that moment I could not imagine how even he could find our little girl out there.

In panic I ran around the yard shouting for her. My aunt did the same. To see this normally calm and placid woman in such a state, filled me with even more dread. Our baby girl had disappeared.

Something made me go back inside the house. I dashed through, looking in every room. Finally, the bathroom. I opened the door and standing on a stool at the basin washing her doll was our baby. I grabbed her into my arms and hugged and kissed her – my tears of relief wetting our faces. She was startled by the fuss.

I rushed with her out into the yard and caught the men just as they were leaving. The looks on their faces spoke a thousand words. Warren took her from me and hugged her with closed eyes.

It was time for us to go and there were tears as we said goodbye to our station folk. I couldn't imagine us ever returning to this remote place.

Two days later we reached Perth but Warren had become ill. Whether it was a virus or a reaction to his nearing the end of our magnificent odyssey, I couldn't be sure, but he was incapable of driving. At my suggestion of seeing a doctor, he said, 'No. We have to get home now, but you'll have to drive.'

The thought of towing our twenty foot caravan out of the city through the winding, hilly roads of the national parks, was daunting, but I took on the task bravely. I was returning home a lion, albeit a cub, compared with the lamb that had left home nearly two years earlier.

Linc and Marlo sat in the front with me and Warren slept in the back. I asked the children not to speak to me until I spoke to them. I didn't want to make any wrong turns and have to turn our large outfit around in a street. I drove for two hours until we were finally out on the highway and heading for Kalgoorlie. I stopped to see how Warren was. He'd been sleeping like a baby but was still very ill. He asked if I'd be okay to keep driving. I was nervous at the thought of heading into the Nullarbor where I knew medical help would be non-existent. Again I asked if he'd like to see a doctor but he was adamant. Home was his goal.

Now that we were out of the city, I was more relaxed behind the wheel. I pulled into Coolgardie late in the afternoon. Warren was feeling a little better, he said, although weak, and I hoped that with a good night's sleep he'd be back to normal in the morning. He was.

From here we planned to head down to Norseman and the Eyre Highway, but not before driving forty kilometres north to see Kalgoorlie.

Kalgoorlie was a mining town to the core. Having thrived in boom times, its former grandeur was now just a memory. Old buildings – town halls, police stations, boarding houses and pubs – were languid and eerie. Peeling paint. Rusty iron. Tattered curtains at the windows. Dead bushes against the walls.

We took some photos, did a U-turn and drove out. The Nullarbor was ahead, the road unsealed and rough. The monotonous, treeless landscape gave us nothing to do but contemplate the life that lay ahead.

> I've known winds in Outback places
> scorching sun that breaks the ground
> tears of parting
> new horizons
> railroad yards and five man towns
>
> I've known thirst and many hungers
> followed signs that have long blown down
> worn a thousand miles of road dust
> stolen jewels from the desert's crown

I've known rain on lonely mornings
cotton fields and lack of trees
I've known fear and isolation
I've known wealth and poverty

I've known campsites filled with workers
bellyaching
acid rain
searched dense bush for missing children
sat with blacks on their own terrain

I've known mornings ripe with hunting
waiting coals on icy grass
gorging fish with thawing fingers
makings ends of rations last

I've known bruised canoes in rapids
whirlpools of the mind and day
trekking home through summer forests
wordless plans a breath away

I've known flood slush in my cornflakes
in my books and in my boots
shower alcoves black with crickets
pub fights
wenches' wrath let loose

I've known hippies on the north shore
kids now buried in the east
pioneers in Outback west land
a southern farmer's restless feet

I've known waste of a poet's thinking
I've known times when the machine has slowed
to little more than a dying idle
before the fuel of the open road.

# SIXTEEN

In late October, nineteen seventy-four, we arrived home – travel weary and hungering for the warmth of extended family and community. As we pulled into the farm driveway, tears welled in me just as they had when we'd left. With seventy thousand kilometres of road behind us, we had grown beyond belief.

An hour from home we had phoned my dad, and as we approached the house, I saw him waiting with Warren's Mum on the hill. There were hugs, tears and an instant pampering of children.

Our house in the gully had been vacated a week earlier and Lin had given it a welcoming spruce up. The energy of the tenants however was still about the place and I couldn't wait to get our things back in, to get us back into the fabric of our wonderful old home. The first night back we slept in the van. For the children's sake we would have to extricate ourselves from it gradually.

Early next morning we drove to Adelaide to see Warren's dad in hospital. If you looked carefully you could see it was a happy reunion, but there was no visible emotion – just the necessary talk of what needed to be done in the vineyard. We were horrified by the extent of Otto's leg injury. We could see it would be weeks before he'd be ready to come home.

The very next day Warren changed hats and went back to work. The vineyard had to be sprayed for mildew. I dropped Linc and Marlo off to spend some time with their adoring nanna while I went up the street to buy food. How comforting it was to be back in my beloved Barossa Valley. Townsfolk greeted me like the lost lamb found and I knew without doubt that this was my home. Today we are called Barossans – those whose ancestors settled here. There is something intangible that unites us.

> Show me a valley where history lies
> slumbering passively amid sagacious old vines
> where it creeps amongst casks and ages the wine
> a valley that filters tradition through streets
> steeped in old secrets – a valley of peace.

It was time to re-establish our business. Warren heard of some land for lease in the Barossa Ranges – an opportunity he quickly acted upon. The Grocke family had dealt with Elder Smith pastoral company for decades, and so Warren approached them with the proposition of borrowing enough money to buy several hundred sheep and to make necessary land lease payments until shearing, when we'd sell the wool through them and pay back the loan. They agreed to the proposal. We purchased seven hundred wethers over which Elders held security. This would provide a solid restart for us and we were grateful for the support of this old and proven rural company.

Warren renewed his old share-farming arrangements with neighbours. It wasn't a slow start. In Warren's way, it was pedal to the metal. The three thousand acre dream farm was back in his sights.

The children were bewildered by this extreme change of lifestyle and quite overwhelmed by the size of our house. They could, by now, only relate to the dimensions of a caravan, and having their mother that near at any time. One day I was rushing about – washing, unpacking boxes, re-installing furniture. Marlo had been following me around like a shadow – insecure and a little afraid, I sensed. At one stage she lost track of me, and on finding me again, stood in the doorway with her hands on her hips.

'Will you stop sneaking around?' she chastised.

We gradually caught up with family and friends. Warren returned to Apex and we went back to church where, without delay, Warren was asked to be secretary. He rejoined the Country Fire Service, the Show Society and the Archery Club. On Saturday afternoons Warren looked after the children while I went back to playing tennis for our town team.

Like displaced pieces of a jigsaw puzzle, we were joggling our way back into the community. But never again would we fit the shapes we had come from.

Correspondence began with close friends we'd made on our trip, including Jenn and Terry whom we'd met in Townsville.

One day Warren was walking up our driveway for lunch. I could see he'd called for mail as he had a bunch of letters under his arm. He was reading one. He stopped walking. Something was wrong. He looked up at me as I watched him through the kitchen window. There was something in his eyes I couldn't read. I went out to him.

'What's happened?'

'Little Ruth has died,' he murmured in disbelief.

I took the short letter and read it aloud to hear my voice saying the words I couldn't believe.

Jenn and Terry had gone to a new construction site in Sale, Victoria. They'd arrived at the caravan park two days before Terry was due to begin work there. On his first day, Terry had got up early. Ruth had been coughing through the night with a cold, and Jenn and Terry had brought her into bed with them.

Terry had left for work in the dark. Jenn got up a little later and made herself a cup of coffee. She was pleased that Ruth was sleeping at last. She peeped in at her. The small shape in their bed was still. Too still. Jenn tried to wake her, but her adored little girl was without life.

There were no mobile phones. Jenn tried to locate Terry on this huge work site where he was unknown. It was a nightmare.

An autopsy revealed that Ruth had died from a lump of phlegm lodged in her windpipe.

We asked our parents if they'd look after Linc and Marlo for a few days while we went to Sale to be with our friends. Their grief was gut-wrenching. They took us to a beautiful spot beside a lake where we sat in the shade of a big tree. Clouds scudded across a strange sky, continually changing the mood of the lake, as Jenn and Terry's emotions ran the gamut of light and darkness. In waves they wept, and sometimes smiled past their broken hearts as they remembered Ruth's angelic ways. At times we were simply silent. My heart ached as I watched Mark, a shy little boy, without his playmate now. A tragedy beyond comprehension, and indescribably painful for them to have to bury their daughter in a place that was never going to be their home.

We still spend time with Jenn and Terry, and although decades have passed, the pain of this terrible loss is still in their eyes.

Linc started school and Marlo went to kindergarten. I was in that zone of broken days – running children in and picking them up at different times.

Warren's dad returned home. It was almost Christmas. He'd spent nine weeks in hospital. Apricots had to be picked, barley harvested and vintage prepared for. Otto was frustrated at not being able to help, and so there were more criticisms, words in anger. Warren was stretched to his limit. The old tensions were back.

I took on the responsibility of the bookwork. I knew Warren appreciated it. He was working long hours and often went out to meetings in the evenings.

I developed a love for gardening and would spend two or three hours a morning at it before doing anything inside. I planted trees, shrubs, cottage gardens and gradually created the park-like environment I'd envisioned for our place. I mowed the lawns with a push mower and cared for my roses. Now and then I'd need Warren's help – in lifting heavy rocks, chainsawing or pruning trees, but he hated gardening.

'If you can't complete the job yourself, don't start it,' he'd berate.

Compared with the simple life we'd enjoyed whilst travelling, our days were now hectic, intense, full of small and large irritations. Otto was back at work. Warren was shearing again in some local sheds, growing and irrigating lucerne, tending our sheep and share-farming. He was happy with all of that, but despite the talks he'd had with his father, he could still not escape a feeling of obligation to help in the vineyard. The innuendo was *still* that our business was secondary.

Often, by seven at night, Warren would not be home from the hills and I'd be frantic with worry that he'd fallen off the edge of a cliff on his motorbike. The track into our range country was treacherous. Barely one vehicle's width, it had been excavated by timber cutters of old. At one point it hair-pinned off-camber around a huge red gum tree and the wheels of our ute would be so close to the soft edge of a thirty metre drop-off that I feared we'd go over each time we went up there. One day I had to do it alone. We were to spend the day cutting firewood and Warren needed me to bring up a second vehicle – a ute that I was unaccustomed to driving.

'But it's so dangerous,' I said. 'I'm scared I'll go over the edge.'

'It's all in your mind,' said he who had done it a hundred times. 'Just don't think about it.'

I remembered that in the life I had chosen with this man, some things were not negotiable. I followed him up the hill, around the gum tree – slowly, carefully – and down into a deep gully where we worked for most of the day. Later, with my manual-geared ute full of wood, I had to renegotiate this long steep hill and this horrible bend at the top. I knew I could miss no gear or I would meet my Maker. The fear was enormous, but I completed the trial. On top of the ridge I stopped to bask in the triumph. I was still learning courage.

Warren often asked me to help him – tailing lambs, fencing, driving the tractor or truck, running all sorts of errands. He needed to be able to call on me at any time. I understood we were a team.

It was time for old friendships to be renewed. We'd kept in touch with Sue and David as we travelled – a letter between us once in a while. They'd had a baby boy while we'd been away. Now Sue and I caught up with each other once a week – usually before school pick up. Our friendship had been built on a foundation of humour. I'd be smiling with anticipation as I knocked on her door, or as she pulled into my driveway. Over a glass of wine, we'd share the happenings of our lives that week. No matter how onerous the trials of motherhood and marriage, it all ended up as comedy with Sue.

The two of them were still having their loud, lively parties and on summer weekends we'd play tennis on the court that David kept in superb condition. Their home was grand with a large formal garden which David tended each day after work.

Mum had made new friends through her work at the kindergarten. One of them was Rita who, somewhere between Mum's age and mine, became my friend too. Rita loved the arts, wrote poetry and read incessantly. She and her husband had built themselves a magnificent stone home. Set into a hillside, it was on two levels – living area on the upper, and a garage and well-stocked cellar of character below. Each time I pulled up in their driveway, I'd close my eyes and draw in deep draughts of heady perfume, not only of the countless varieties of flowers, shrubs and trees but of rich, composted earth.

Rita had books on every subject, scattered tokens of European folklore in the form of sculpture and pottery, and her garden was filled with the unusual and exotic plants she'd read about. Her house was always filled with fresh flowers, brought in by the arm-full and placed lovingly in vases of stamp. There were floor lamps, wall lamps, reading lamps. Every wall was lined with books, paintings or fabrics. Their furniture was made by hand and upholstered in aged leather. Glorious rugs covered the recycled wooden floors. Coffee brewed and fresh cakes rose in a warm wood oven. A generous fire burned in the stone fireplace on any cold day.

As Rita and I shared our poetry and garnished our thoughts on music, literature and art, great musicians played on her turntable – from Brahms to Baez, Dvorak to Dylan.

I was always taken on a tour of the garden before I left and would come home with at least a bucketful of flowers.

Rita had spent her childhood in war-torn Germany. Through the terrible hardships of war, she had sought and found beauty in her surroundings, in books, in music and a handful of people of her stripe. This quality was still in her. She was a woman of substance and a wonderful friend.

# SEVENTEEN

Warren and I had little time together now. To fill my lonely evenings while my husband was at meetings, I would read, write or listen to the radio, or my records. I cherished my children and gave them all the time they needed. One of my strongest tenets has always been that children need time with their parents to thrive and feel loved.

Marlo had developed an uncommon interest in performance – from the day she'd starred as Mary in the nativity play at kindergarten – and Lincoln, for anything with two wheels. We bought him a motorbike for his seventh birthday. I felt it was one of my life purposes now to nurture and encourage their inclinations and gifts.

Returning to the Tanunda Public School precinct as a parent was remarkable. How different life would be here for Linc and Marlo, from my school days. Even in the span of just one generation, children had become more cosseted. I drove my kids to school each day. I'd had to walk. There was talk of corporal punishment being abolished. We'd been smacked if we misbehaved – or even if we hadn't.

~

My very first teacher, Mrs Rodin, had nurtured and loved her brood through grades one and two, but for every saint there is a villain. Grade Three brought Mrs Custance – robust as a wrestler, hair in a plait, wrapped scarf-like round her head. We, her pupils, lived in fear of her incessant wrath. In later years, from the safety of other distant classrooms, there'd be times lessons had to be stopped while we waited for her raucous fury to subside. In the two years she was my teacher, I found every minute in the same room with her terrifying. In her class the good children sat at the back and the "naughty" ones, mostly boys, at the front. I was having trouble seeing what was written on the blackboard so she shifted me forward. After several shifts, I ended up in the front row. One day we were having a test. There were sums written on the board that we had to copy into our books and solve. I couldn't see them and was too terrified to tell her that even the front row wasn't close enough, so I looked at the page of the boy sitting next to me. The murderous woman's scream was ear-splitting.

*'Susan Hancock. You were cheating. Go to the back of the room with your face to the wall.'*

When the bell went, I turned to see if I was to go out for recess with the rest of the kids.

*'Stay there,'* she shrieked.

For most of recess I stood with my face to the wall, trembling with fear in the empty room. Just before the bell, she came back in. I saw her pick up a ruler from a nearby desk. She began hitting me with it. My bare legs burned with the pain and with each blow she screamed at me about the evils of "cheating". I was eight years old. For years afterwards I would be traumatised by any personal injustice.

It was my Grade Five teacher, Mr Hoffman, who recognised my short-sightedness. Mum took me to have my eyes tested and within a short time I was wearing glasses. This was no small event. There weren't many myopic children at school and I felt quite self-conscious in my new spectacles. But despite my now being different in this way, I was ecstatic at seeing, for the first time, the full and exquisite beauty of my environment.

We walked to and from school most days. Extreme weather never bothered me. I was too preoccupied with what was going on around me – the industry of the town and vineyards, Mother Nature at work. We wore hooded plastic raincoats if it was raining. Plastic was new then. Getting my feet wet in unavoidable puddles or rushing water was the worst (and best) as my feet stayed wet then for most of the day. Chilblains.

The morning walk was always brisk but the homeward trek delightfully unhurried. There was the creek to explore and wild fare to be had along its course – loquats, pomegranates, quinces. In winter the waterway became a deep, dark, hurrying thing, frothing tawny white at its red gum-lined edges. One day Roger Lange, in an unprovoked moment of mischief, snatched my school case from me and hurled it into the raging water from the bridge. It bobbed out of sight in seconds and I ran home to tell my mother. I knew it was an important item not easily or cheaply replaced. When Dad came home from work that night he went to look for it, and much to our surprise (although we shouldn't have been), he returned with the soaked, bedraggled thing, telling us how he'd found it wedged in a tree root, a hundred metres or so downstream. There was no confrontation with the perpetrator. It was part of childhood.

Once every two years the school maypole would be brought out as our biennial money raising Continental approached.

We'd spend weeks practising the Polka to a scratchy seventy-eight rpm record. The teacher would carefully lower the arm of the gramophone until the worn needle touched the revolving Bakelite disc. The static would explode into the yard through large speakers before a crackly British voice announced, "See me dance the Polka."

It thrilled me as we danced, to see the wide muslin sashes weaving together to form a brightly coloured umbrella of fabric.

There was a girl at school who suffered from epilepsy and one day had a seizure whilst we were dancing. Our teacher must have ducked inside for a minute as he wasn't there, but knowing how important it was to get the pattern right, the boy who was partnering her, just held her hand tighter and kept dancing, wide-eyed, using all his strength to drag her along until the thing was finished.

An atmosphere of industry whipped up as The Continental approached. Most of the school "family" contributed in some way. Girls made sweets. Mothers made cakes. Boys organised the Cheap Jack stall and on the night, teachers hurried about officiously and fathers gathered in small groups – smoking and shifting uncomfortably like builders at a flower show.

The November evening was usually balmy and there'd be an exciting atmosphere of carnival – music, bright lights and the camaraderie of people who knew each other and had gathered for a common cause. For me the highlight was the picture show. In preparation for this, large carpet squares were laid on the asphalt and a screen hung on the blank southern wall of the old stone building. With eyes wide with delight, we'd watch Laurel and Hardy, Pete Smith and the *Movietone News*.

Until the late fifties, pictures were shown every Saturday night in our town hall. We children would have been too young for many of the films, so we didn't go often, but when we did, it was an experience like no other. *War and Peace* and the romantic musicals *Rose Marie*, *Oklahoma* and *The Student Prince* are engraved in my memory.

On arriving at the hall, we'd join a queue that threaded its way to the ticket office while Mum and Dad chatted to whoever was in front of and behind us. On reaching the theatre door, we'd wait for one of the usherettes – dressed in long gown and bolero top – to show us to our seats. On cold winter nights the Art Deco heaters high up on the walls would be visually comforting though virtually ineffective, and so Mum usually brought a travelling rug for our laps. I loved the ambience of the theatre. At interval, the canteen boy walked up and down the aisles carrying his large, heavy tray of ice creams, soft drinks, peanuts and cigarettes. Most of the men smoked through the show, including my dad who usually bought us a packet of peanuts – something we could share.

The children's film extravaganza was at the Tanunda (working man's) Club annual Christmas party, traditionally held on a Saturday afternoon in the hall. We'd be given a bag of lollies on arrival – a rare treat – and after a tumultuous time of excited greetings, changing of seating positions, and banging of hinged wooden seats, the lights would dim, noise subside, and the show begin. Again, we watched Laurel and Hardy, Pete Smith, and sometimes Ma and Pa Kettle. At interval we'd be given a soda drink and ice-cream, and at the end of the show, an envelope of money – the amount of which depended on the club's profits for the year. It could be anything from five to ten shillings – something substantial to go straight into our piggy banks. With a happy feeling of excess, Erica and I would walk the two kilometres home in the late afternoon shadows, crunching through the fallen carob beans that littered the unpaved footpath, and running our hands along the lavender and rosemary hedges.

Life changed the Christmas I received my bright blue Malvern Star bicycle. I was seven. After breakfast on Christmas day, Dad took me out into the street to teach me how to ride it. Being the kind of father he was, he talked to me about the principles of momentum, balance and stopping. I was rearing to go. I sat on the seat as Dad held me upright and began to push the bike forward.

'Now pedal,' he said.

I did, looking down at my feet. I felt secure with my dad running alongside of me, but at an unannounced moment he let go and I was riding unaided. It was truly exhilarating. A bike. A country town. A yearning for discovery. Two days later I pedalled the two kilometres into town to pick up *The Sunday Mail* for Dad.

Erica inherited my bike when she was old enough, and I was given the privilege of riding Dad's racer. One cold, blustery morning I was riding it to school, pushing hard against the wind. My right foot slipped off the serrated metal pedal. Attached to a fixed-wheel mechanism, the pedal came around with such force that it hacked into the back of my leg. I stopped to inspect the damage – a terrible gash. Hopping on one leg to the nearby solicitor's office for help, I felt faint at the sight of the blood trail I was leaving. The receptionist there rushed me to hospital in her car. Our family doctor saw me immediately. He told me my hamstring was holding by a thread. Over the next hour and with great skill he performed remarkable surgery to secure it. Had it been completely severed, I would have lost the use of my leg, permanently. For me, who loved to run, this would have been a catastrophic disaster.

It was crucial for me not to use the leg for at least three weeks, the doctor had instructed, so I was confined to home for that period.

Although there was still school work for me to complete each day, I'd get that done quickly and spend the rest of the day in a euphoria of freedom. I'd taken to reading *The Advertiser* newspaper. Strange for an eleven year old perhaps, but the inherent writer in me was already hungry for knowledge and stories of all kinds. Anzac Day fell during my time of recuperation and on this particular day I came across several pages of memorials to fallen soldiers. These outpourings of grief and remembrance were so poignant that I was burdened with melancholy for the rest of the day.

~

From an early age I'd been endowed with a strange mix of my father's pensiveness and my mother's joie de vivre. Even before I'd started school, with the tailings of war still in the air, my father had shown me books of photographs – ships in battle, lifeboats full of striped sailors with grief-stricken faces, fighter planes going down in trails of smoke and fire. He'd told me of rations, curfews, blackouts, families who'd lost sons, husbands, fathers. Riveting.

Brenton Meyer and his toy soldiers had lived a few doors away from me. A little older than me and not really a playmate, the boy seemed happy, nevertheless, to let me line up his wee men in their lounge room and murmur to myself about death and bravery. The stories of war had aroused a deep pathos in me.

Dad had not gone to war. He'd enlisted to join the Air Force with his brother and best mate. The three had been at the railway station ready to leave for training when Dad was withdrawn from the group and told that his welding skills were needed in the munitions factory at Islington in Adelaide. He'd been devastated to see his brother and mate go off without him.

~

During the days of recovery from my leg injury, I'd sit in the sun on our back verandah and lose myself in the fantastic adventures of Enid Blyton's *Famous Five* or *Secret Seven*, Hans Christian Andersen's fairytales, the *Little Women* stories and Lewis Carroll's *Alice in Wonderland*. *Princess Magazine*, read till ragged, was a publication I'd subscribed to with money earned from cutting apricots for drying during the holidays.

To nurture my interest in designing clothes and motifs for fabric, Mum had bought me a tin of Staedtler coloured pencils, and in a state of bliss, I'd sit at my small table in the sun, creating countless exotic designs.

When finally allowed to put some pressure on my foot, I was sent back to school, albeit still on crutches. For two or three weeks I had the privilege of being driven there and home again by Mr Hoffman, a teacher who lived in our street. A small, eccentric man, he drove a self-important green and orange Austin Seven that he parked ostentatiously in the school yard rather than in the street.

My return to school did not go under the radar. A throng gathered to inspect my injury. Everything seemed surreal to me for a while. Routines and friendships had to be re-established.

Soon a walking stick replaced my crutches and after a few more weeks my leg had healed completely. I'd been manacled for so long that on the day I got back on my bike and went back to play, I felt I'd grown wings.

Year's end, biennially, was time for the school concert. A day or two before the big night, we'd skip down the road to the town hall for full dress rehearsal. Once through the doors of that imposing old brick and stone building, I'd draw in deep breaths of the sweet smell of aged timber – floors, seats, dressing room walls. The huge black backdrop curtain had a presence, always moving with a breeze or the passing of a wayward child running their hands along it. The dressing room walls were painted dragon green and lined with the customary lights and mirrors. I'd be in a state of near ecstasy as my make-up was applied and costume donned. Why is it so much fun as a child to be a nurse, a crinoline lady, a fairy with cellophane wings?

While I was in Grade Seven, our class put on the operetta *Snow White*. In the beginning, each of us was given a copy of the libretto and asked to learn one particular song from it. I loved singing so much that I dreamed of being given the lead role. After a few days of rehearsals it was time for Mr Colebatch, our headmaster, to choose his principals. He asked us to sing the song we'd learned and as we sang it over and over, he walked amongst us, listening carefully and writing notes in a small book. Finally, he stopped us and told us he'd made his choices. He announced the supporting characters first. Then the prince. My heart walloped my rib cage as I waited to hear who would be Snow White. The sound of my name in the room brought my hands to my mouth as I tried to hide the smile that was threatening to overthrow my face.

My feet hardly touched the ground as I walked home from school that day, and that night I dreamed of being on a magnificent stage, singing like a film star.

At school next day it was time for me to sing alone, but a feeling of unspeakable terror came over me – the fear of being the centre of attention. I couldn't utter a sound. Mr Colebatch told me to relax. He gave me a little time and I tried again. The result was the same.

I was devastated. Next day he announced that Suzanne Rogasch would be Snow White and I would be her understudy. Although I was bitterly disappointed with myself, the weeks of rehearsals and voice training that Suzanne and I were given by one of the Barossa's most accomplished sopranos, were a joy for me. I'm not sure though what would have happened if I'd been called on to sing on the night of the production.

A little later, I entered a South Australian Schools' writing competition and submitted an essay titled "The Barossa Valley". The winning entry was to be read out over ABC radio. My essay won and I was duly recorded, reading confidently to a microphone – an invisible audience.

Three years earlier, one performance had made a deep impression on me – the Grade Seven production of *Hiawatha*. A beautiful Indian brave had held me spellbound, and the memory of him been indelibly etched.

~

# EIGHTEEN

Marlo was the actress extraordinaire – in school, at play, on her front verandah stage at home. For and with friends, cousins, pets, she was writer, director, lead actor.

While there was a parochialism about Linc and Marlo going to the same school Warren and I had, and even Otto had, our big trip had unfolded us, given us a bigger surface on which to write the story of our lives. As I helped with various school activities, I knew I was a different parent from the one I would have been without the journey. Linc and Marlo too had been marked by it and I loved watching their unique individuality stand out. Linc was gaining amazing skills on bikes. He'd joined a BMX club and we often took him to the track to compete. One day he entered a slow race, to demonstrate adeptness at staying upright on a bike whilst travelling extremely slowly without putting a foot down. Ten or more competitors left the starting line and with a slight sense of disappointment and surprise, I thought Linc was going to come in at last place by being first over the line. However, at about a metre from the finish, he turned his front wheel at an angle against a tiny ridge he'd spotted on the track, and balanced there until every other rider passed him. To loud applause, he crossed the line last.

Warren had joined a motorcycle club in the Barossa and helped organise a family event one weekend. Lincoln entered and was to ride his small motorbike in a three hour Enduro. It was high winter and conditions were harsh – muddy, slippery and soon boggy. A large log, slimy with moss, was to be negotiated each lap. Most riders jumped it, but Linc and his bike were too small for that, so each time he came to it, he'd have to lift his motorcycle over. He was nine years old and slightly built. It was such a demanding event that only a few riders finished the course and most of the competitors were adults. Our son won a trophy for coming third outright and being the youngest to finish. The hand-carved wooden trophy is the only one of his I couldn't part with. He has the rest. To me it speaks of so many of his qualities – particularly his determination to give each of his undertakings his absolute best.

Our carefree years of early marriage had gone – the magic of new love worn to a sliver. Financially we were still committed to our mortgages, but in contrast to having a good and regular wage as we'd had on the road, we now had to work with the seasonal payments that are a farmer's lot.

Warren was putting long hours into the vineyard and having to find time outside of that for our business. He was strong and fit enough for the work but being unable to pursue his dreams freely was causing him frustration that, ultimately, I had to wear. I felt I had lost my mate, and we lacked the time and skills to communicate it. I longed to be able to talk to my husband about my concerns for our marriage, but I'd learned that any attempt usually ended in a flare up and then days of not talking to each other at all.

We'd bought a few head of cattle and had been supplement feeding them on our shearing shed block. They were prime now and it was time to get them yarded for sale. But they were flighty – spooked by the dogs and Warren on his motorbike. I was in our four-wheel drive. Each time we got the steers to the yard gate, they'd break away and flee to the freedom of the open paddock. When they broke back from the gate for the third time I reversed in an effort to cut them off. By now Warren was busting his boiler – yelling at me for driving in reverse too far and too fast. I did a U-turn and drove home. Our work together often ended this way – especially sheep work.

It was a nightmare too bringing a mob of sheep down from the hills to the shearing shed, past properties with ancient fences easily stepped over by the animals. If that happened, our two wonderful dogs, Ernie and Willie, would get through the fence and run full tilt to head off any escapees before they reached the neighbour's flock in that paddock. Had our sheep mixed in with them, it would have taken half a day to bring them all in, separate them and put them all back where they belonged.

Ernie was a border collie kelpie cross. The kids could do anything with him. His bed was on the verandah next to the winter warm chimney wall. An old chook, Geri, who followed me around the garden whenever I was out there, slept beside this wall too, in winter. She'd taken a fancy to Ernie and if he was there, she'd nestle in beside him. Apart from a little embarrassment if spotted, he'd take it on the chin.

Willie was a highly intelligent kelpie coolie cross. Fragile when he'd first come to live with us as a one year old, he'd been nervous and unsure of his new environment. We'd given him the tender loving care he needed and he'd soon become a faithful and hardworking team member.

One day Warren was mustering in the forest – a tricky task with no open country to see where the sheep were. Eventually he found them and was bringing them out with the help of the dogs. Without instruction, Willie headed back into the trees. Warren called him back. With unusual disregard and a backwards glance at his master, Willie disappeared. With whistling and calling ineffectual, Warren continued driving the sheep without him. About three hundred metres further on, Willie emerged with three sheep that had been missed. With head held slightly aloft, and a "just trust me" look, he brought them quietly in to join the mob.

'Okay, sorry mate,' said Warren. 'Good boy.'

His assertiveness wasn't always appreciated, however. Warren had asked me to bring a mob of sheep down from the hills. 'Willie'll do most of the work,' he said. 'I want them on Nitschke's.'

Warren brought them out of the paddock and onto the road for me, then headed off to the shearing shed – five kilometres away, where he was getting ready for shearing. There wasn't enough room in the yards or shed for this mob, but Warren wanted them close at hand, on Nitschke's, so he could quickly bring them in when they were needed.

Willie and I and the sheep had been heading down Rifle Range Road for an hour or more when we reached the turn off to the shearing shed. Nitschke's block was further down Rifle Range Road, and so I gave the required instruction to Willie for him to keep going – i.e. no left turn. He gave me a disdainful look.

'Don't you know we're shearing?' said the look. 'These sheep need to go to the shearing shed.' And he started to turn them left.

'No. Fetch 'em back, Willie!' I yelled. '*Fetch 'em back.*'

But he was adamant.

When Willie and I and the sheep arrived at the shearing shed half an hour later, Warren said, 'I told you to take them to Nitschke's.'

'Don't tell me,' I said. 'Tell your dog.'

Willie and I often sat together on the front step of our house – me sipping coffee, he leaning slightly against me, looking off into the distance with ears twitching at sounds that only dogs can hear. We were close. Willie did not live to be an old dog. At the age of eight he contracted encephalitis, and with broken hearts we had to say thank you and goodbye.

Mum and Dad had divorced. Mum had returned to the Barossa and was living in a barn on a friend's property. It was little more than camping. Whilst in Adelaide she'd met Sandy. On weekends he'd ride his BMW motorbike to the Barossa, and together he and Mum restored the barn and made it weatherproof and cosy.

Dad was fending for himself, still in our childhood home and now working for a large winery as engineering draughtsman. Every week or two we'd invite him to join us for a meal. It must have distressed me to see him living alone as I often dreamt of having deserted and neglected him.

I was miserable. It seemed so much of what was precious to me had been lost. The unique love that Warren and I once shared was almost too small to be seen – imploded like a black hole. What had happened to us was as mysterious and unfathomable. The inherent love of life that had always made me want to sing, lay buried.

Disappointed and disillusioned with my lifelong safe haven, the Church, I abandoned it. I simply began seeking my own answers. Listening unquestioningly to a judgemental pastor each Sunday seemed unintelligent. I wanted to study Christianity for myself, but not only that, other religions too – Buddhism, Hinduism, Spiritualism.

In dim, unruly book shops I found the tomes I needed. I discovered the beat poets – Ginsberg, Ferlinghetti, Burroughs. I was inflamed with inspiration, and floodgates opened as I rediscovered the joy of creating word pictures, and the absoluteness of doing what I needed to do. I loved the sight of my finished poems on the page, the way they sounded when read aloud. And I was grateful for my God-given gift of observing and interpreting my environment – how I could see that a fox and her cub moving across a hillside through long grass looked like "the toys that boys pull home on coloured strings".

I discovered the writing of Henry Miller. Hungrily I devoured his philosophical ravings. Furiously I scribbled comments in the margins, underlined his thoughts on education, religion, work, play, money, friendship, love – all those that struck a chord. I sucked the blood of the works of D.H. Lawrence, Hermann Hesse, Anais Nin, Carl Jung. And oh the delight of Dylan Thomas's prose – each page a feast for me. I rediscovered classical music. Dvorak's stirring passionate expressions were like an emery at my emotions. Although seeking therapy this way for my consuming sadness and emptiness, I was only fanning the flames by listening to Janis Ian, Leonard Cohen, reading the melancholy poetry of Sylvia Plath, Jack Kerouac. But writing became my strongest medicine.

One night a poem woke me from deep sleep. I stumbled out of bed half awake, fumbled for a pen and paper and spilled a torrent of strange words onto the page. Next morning, I picked up the work and read the prose that had come from somewhere deep within – or maybe without.

Something has been lost
irretrievably
Lost as yesterday's loose covers
It could have been a lullaby
or a sleepy river ride
but the water salves my gaping wounds
and slows a nation's bleeding

The concertina blow and suck
just takes
and gives
and takes away
From cosy groups their solidarity
To Dadaists their daily bread
From the duty bound their grappling irons

My lantern swings awaiting dawn
while the jungle tangles round me
Catching
Tearing
cloths of blood red weave

I pillage skies
and time spans' layers
with hoping hands
plunged deep
in sorrow brewed with tea leaves
telling
time has come for mime
and social lies

Root out the superficial garble
as metal jaws devouring earth
Dump the refuse largely
into mounds of madness
crawling

Exonerate and hail as gods
these murky mounds
but plunge the ore back deep
Enigmatic
Black and glowing
Buried deep
Then in its own time oozing
urging second comings.

Over the years I often received beginnings or ends of poems this way but never again an entire one like this. It was a bleak piece, but times were so. My Indian brave and I were worlds apart. The pain was drowning me. Who was this man I woke up to each morning? And what had become of the alive-with-music, happy country girl he'd married.

While reading our local newspaper one day, I spotted a small ad. The person who'd placed it was looking to bring together a few people who had a love of folk music, and a guitar. His idea was to meet one evening a week, play some music, sing some songs and help each other along. Something leapt in me. Warren had an old guitar that had been languishing in a corner of our house for years. Perhaps I could bring it back to life. I went to the first gathering. After ten years of giving myself entirely as a wife and mother, I was intoxicated by the thought of now taking something this good for myself. Through The Apex Club I'd met

Carol. She and her husband, John, had recently settled in the Barossa, having lived in Sydney till then. John was the manager of a large winery, and he and Warren became mates. It hadn't taken long for Carol and me to realise we had a love of music in common. As the mother of four young children, Carol too was aching for some time away from the humdrum of domesticity. She joined the group.

The handful of us who'd responded to the ad, began to play some chords and pick some melodies. We sourced our own music to songs we loved and shared in an achingly raw way, our beginnings in musicianship. Once in a while we'd gather at each other's homes, and sometimes others who were a little further along would join us.

From early childhood, hearing even just one note from a musical instrument had sent a wave of joy through me. Each day now I cradled this guitar, with its woody smell and beautiful tone, in my arms and with it, my voice issued songs that I loved. It was more than enough to begin to restore me. Carol would call in a couple of mornings a week or I'd visit her, and we'd play and sing together.

Trevor, the person who'd put the ad in the paper, had become our group leader. Skilfully, he'd encouraged us not to be nervous about performing for each other, reassuring us that we'd all come from the same starting place.

I began writing songs. Trevor was writing too – not only songs, but poetry. Although I thought I'd done so before, I now reached into even deeper places and wrote anew as we shared our work.

I discovered Joan Baez, bought her records, learned her songs. Bob Dylan was never far away as an influence. I'd found myself a hallowed niche – a small quiet space where I could indulge in the bounty awaiting release from my creative depths.

# NINETEEN

Once in a while an opportunity would present itself and instinctively Warren would know that it fitted into his life plan. A large tract of land had come up for sale. Over a thousand acres in the hills was to be sold in several lots. Buying the whole parcel was out of our league, but perhaps we could afford one of the titles. Warren spoke to our bank manager about another loan. Within two weeks it had been approved.

My father had always taught me never to buy anything unless I could pay cash for it – remnant philosophy from the Depression years, I suppose, so I'd been edgy about this new proposition. I tried to hold Warren back. There was no stopping him of course. He was encouraged by the fact that we were making good money from lambs and wool, and banks were lending freely.

'It won't be long and we'll have the house paid off,' he said. 'Trust me, it's a good thing.'

Auction day came, and I was twitchy. Warren seemed relaxed and confident. As the auctioneer's voice ricocheted around the hall, it felt like a game – big money, big stakes. Out of the corner of my eye I could see Warren nodding. For a minute or two, there was shouting like rapid gunfire. I was forgetting to breathe. The auctioneer banged his gavel on the lectern and I nearly jumped out of my skin.

'Lot One goes to you, Sir.'

I looked at my husband questioningly. He nodded and smiled – not too much emotion in a room full of farmers. We'd purchased another hundred and fifty acres.

This block too was a picture – heavily wooded and in need of some clearing if we were to use it for grazing, which was Warren's plan. When we got home that afternoon, Otto asked how much we'd paid for it.

'A hundred and seventy-five dollars an acre,' said Warren, brimming with enthusiasm over his purchase.

'You've paid too much,' said Otto.

We'll see, thought Warren.

A couple of days later he met with the young fellow who'd bought the title next to ours. He too was a grazier. They discussed their plans. They would hire machinery to clear the prolific wattle, fallen branches and woody weeds, and leave the stately gum trees and creek verge flora for shade and shelter. They worked together for a week until the block was a picture with pasture, trees and indigenous flora.

We bought a few more sheep. Our flock now totalled around thirteen hundred. It was time for them to be divested of their wool. As our shearing shed was a five kilometre drive from home, I'd get up early to make morning smoko and send it off with Warren first up. I'd rush the children off to school and return to begin preparing a two course midday meal for the team in the shed. While all was simmering, I'd prepare afternoon smoko – same as for the morning. I'd then drive to the shed and arrive at five to twelve. This would give me time to unpack everything from the car, wend my way through a couple of yards full of sheep whilst struggling to unlatch and re-latch gates with arms full of food, then lay the table, ready for "tools down".

The shearers would consume their main course, dessert, coffee, and a long neck bottle of beer in fifteen minutes. I'd sit with them as they ate and, as always, the chatter would be about people of the district – who had died, who'd had a baby, who'd bought more land, who had sold some, who had married and who had parted. This caring need to know is one of the things that binds a rural community together.

We met a couple who had bought a property in the foothills. Peter and Warren had become acquainted on Rifle Range Road during a sheep shifting exercise. Peter was a cabinet-maker and Margo a hairstylist who'd set up a chic salon in the main street of our town. On their hundred acres they'd built a beautiful new home and two bed and breakfast cottages. The four of us hit it off. Peter, like Warren, loved animals and the land. Margo and I talked about the arts, books, metaphysics. Peter and Margo, like our friends John and Carol, had acquired that rare skill of knowing how to integrate quickly and successfully into a community. Some struggle with this for years.

Peter was a horseman, and happy to help Warren with our cattle when it came to a muster. It saved Warren and me getting cranky with each other. And because of his carpentry and building skills, we employed him to renovate our bathroom. Out went the flamingo pink wall tiles with black trim, so too the lily-pad green bath, basin and built-in linen press. These were replaced with all white bath, basin and wall tiles, and a western red cedar full length vanity cupboard. A cedar ceiling replaced the saggy plaster one. Bronze taps were installed. A bevel-edged mirror in an old picture frame hung over the basin. Room number two had been renovated and I was delighted.

Motorcycle racing was still high on Warren's agenda and during the cold winter months of each year he would compete in the South Australian Motorcycle Enduro (dirt bike) series, some interstate events, and *The News* Twenty-four Hour Reliability Trial. There was usually an event a month and in preparation he'd work on his bike till all hours for several nights – the number of which depended on the degree of damage from the previous race. He kitted out a camping trailer for our accommodation. Linc and Marlo had a wonderful time on these excursions – quite at home in the bush and playing with other kids. I was Warren's crew and drove my own Enduro at each event. Following mud maps, and with my driving skills tested to the limits, I'd navigate my way along rough, boggy bush tracks to checkpoints where Warren would need fuel, tools, a drink, and encouragement. I knew he appreciated my support. At night, we'd sit around campfires as riders related their own personal highlights and horrors of the event.

During the Enduro series of 'seventy-seven, we went to an event in the ACT. Andy Sherwood, a young rider from Warren's club, came with us. We'd become friends with Andy and his fiancée, Heather. Tragically Heather had been killed in a freak accident. A truck going around a bend had lost an unsecured grape bin that landed on top of her small car as she drove past. Andy was in deep grief and had thrown himself into riding.

In Canberra we hired a small caravan to take up to Brindabella Station where the event was to be held. Andy had a tent.

This two day event was an Enduro in every sense of the word. Under an ominous black sky, we suffered rain and snow all weekend. The organisers had miscalculated the distance between two of the fuel stops, and on day one, eighty percent of riders ran out of fuel and had to push their bikes through mountainous terrain to the next pit stop. That evening many were coming in late. By six pm all were accounted for, except Andy. It was dark before two sweep riders from the host club went out to look for him. Warren had wanted to search earlier but for safety reasons had not been permitted to ride against incoming riders. We waited anxiously, fearing for Andy's safety. At about eight o'clock he walked into our van – soaking wet, shivering and exhausted. He'd thrown a chain, miles from any control, and had been sitting in the mountains for hours, waiting for help. He told us later how desperately he'd wished for a box of matches so he could light a fire, and how frighteningly the bush had come alive with the sounds of animals as darkness blindfolded him. He could only hope he'd be rescued that night.

We were so relieved to see him. After he'd shed his wet leathers and warmed up in the shower, he was finally restored by the hot meal I'd saved for him. In our cosy van we talked of the ride, as riders do.

Andy died a year or two ago – of a brain tumour. We hadn't known he was ill and felt so sad at the news. We wished, and still wish, we could have said goodbye.

Dad had met Kath – a work associate and single mother of two boys. I could see they enjoyed each other's company. Dad had been in the doldrums for so long, it was wonderful to see him picking up. After a courtship of a year or so, they decided to sell their homes and buy a farm together. Strangely, I don't remember our house being sold, or the shift. I guess we weren't invited to take part, or perhaps we should have offered. Today I wonder what happened to my Grandma's porcelain doll, my first plein air painting done at Corny Point, and the small iron chairs that Dad made for Erica and me when we were children – springy chairs that we bounced around on, trying to topple each other, and laughing till we wet our pants.

The farm was a dream come true for Dad. He'd wanted one since leaving his "Woodlands" as a teenager while still in deep grief over the loss of his mother.

This one in the Barossa was only a hundred acres or so but on it was a lovely old stone home with sheds, water and enough pasture for a few sheep. Dad bought a ute and a motorbike and began a new life with Kath and her boys.

Mum was now renting a lovely old cottage in the Barossa. Owned by close friends, it was in need of some loving care when she first moved in. Mum of course was delighted to give it her touch. With her passion for gardening, she planted native trees, flowers and shrubs. The interior was made cosy with her few pieces of restored furniture and treasured artwork and bric-a-brac. Here she entertained friends and family with her special brand of love and welcoming. Her years of teaching kindergarten had provided her with a wealth of songs, stories and games that she spent on her adoring grandchildren. She was still seeing Sandy who rode his motorbike from the city to be with her one night during the week, and then on the weekends.

It was obvious how badly the divorce had affected Dad, but Mum, with her "always look on the bright side" attitude had seemed to handle it okay. She only shared with me years later that she too had been devastated. She had loved Dad for so long but their life together had become intolerable. She told me how she had wept with grief for months after the separation. And life as a single woman of that generation was punishing. But she had met Sandy, a lovely man who cherished her, and as the relationship deepened, I could sense a deep peace and happiness in her.

# TWENTY

By nineteen seventy-eight, my own marriage had deteriorated to its lowest ebb. It was time for the two of us to make a commitment to do the work to repair it, or to part. There was so much pain, but we began to remember how much we'd once loved each other. We knew we had to find those two people again. It was time to talk. Time to listen. We had two beautiful children, and with our love for them foremost, we decided to start again – with a belief that we could become a devoted family, second to none.

What changed? We spent more time together. Warren gave up a couple of his committees. I gave up my guitar group. For a long time my days were grey, surreal. So much pain. So many tears. So much sad music. To cope, I kept busy. I kept Linc and Marlo close to me and whenever I could, I took them out. I wanted to help them really see their marvellous world, to teach them things they would never learn at school.

We went to the city by train. As a child I had travelled on trains with my mother, to buy hats and coats. My children and I explored the Adelaide railway station from top to bottom while I shared my love of its architecture. In the dark, reverberating terminal, the muck from the nostrils of old engines had been thumbed into everything.

We went to lunch at Cranks, the best health food restaurant in town, and to Grumpy's who made the best hamburgers – Linc's favourite. We explored the streets of Kapunda – an old mining town on the edge of the Barossa – peeped through the grimy windows of the town's deserted convent, reputed to be haunted. We went to concerts and films, into the hills for picnics and nature walks. I played my guitar and we sang.

Warren and I talked for a year. Marlo said to us years later that she wondered what we were talking about in bed on all those Sunday mornings. We were getting to truly know each other. We were so at odds in character and spirit. I was introspective, contemplative, artistic. Warren was practical, outgoing, his world and dreams limitless. We had to accept that we were different but had to find some common ground which, we agreed, was our love of rural life and travel.

This crisis had sharpened my senses and I began to look further out. Part of my healing was to experience something new each day.

One day I visited our local historical museum. Stepping into the building, I closed my eyes with pleasure as I breathed in the smell of old timber and leather, fragile pages, fireplaces, the blood, sweat and tears of our ancestors. The smell of history. I imagined the pride of craftsmanship in the collected artefacts worn smooth with use. I looked long at the photographs of the town as I remembered it twenty-five years earlier, squeezed images from deep within my memory.

Something palpably spiritual emanated from the marble altar, pews and heavily engraved wooden pulpit in the small room set up as a chapel. Religion wrapped itself around me – my ancestors' religion, their blind faith, and the fear and uncertainty that must have come with them from their homes across the sea.

The history of our community was still young. I knew people who were only second and third generation since white settlement here. I became lost in thought as I returned to my childhood.

~

Living in our street had been more recent immigrants. Mr and Mrs Weiss and their quiet, studious daughter, Gretel, lived in a modest bungalow across the road from us. A German family, they'd been deported from Palestine by the British just after the Second World War. They spoke little English.

With the uncanny way kids have of knowing what's going on in their street, we discovered one summer day that they'd bought an electric refrigerator – the first in the neighbourhood. Next day, Erica and I summoned up the courage to knock on their door and ask if we could see this amazing new appliance. Mrs Weiss invited us in. She opened the freezer compartment, took out a plastic tray of water iceblocks and gave us each one. It was a special treat and from then on, on particularly hot days, we'd tiptoe down their driveway, knock on their door and ask if we could have a water iceblock – please.

They were elderly people and Mum had told us not to disturb them, especially if their blinds were pulled down in the afternoons as they rested. Mr Weiss, a white-haired old man, was my Geppetto from the Pinocchio story. He was a shoemaker and it was to him that all neighbourhood shoes were taken to be mended. Attached to the back of his house was a small lean-to room where he worked. A rich smell of tannin and boot polish filled the place. Piles of shoes and remnants languished on small homebuilt tables.

The shoemaker wore a leather apron as he worked. Sitting on a stool and looking over the top of his little gold-rimmed glasses, he'd fish tacks out of his mouth, one at a time. With a small hammer, he'd tap these into the sole of the shoe he was working on. It always concerned me he might swallow one if he should cough or sneeze. It was his way to work silently except for a barely audible grunt every now and then – the sound of an old man at labour. When he'd finished, he'd scrutinise his work, remove the tacks from his mouth, reach for a tin of leather dressing and polish the shoes slowly. He'd hand them over then, with a twinkle of satisfaction in his eye.

'How much, Mr Weiss?' I'd ask.

His answer was always the same. 'Mmm, two shillings,' which was always the coin I had clasped in my hand.

We were a little different from the seven other families in our street. Mum was of Polish/Danish descent – fourth generation in Australia – and we had Dad's English surname. All other names in the street were German. We went to the Methodist church. Our neighbours were all Lutheran. Mum was so outgoing however, that despite these differences we felt completely integrated.

The Pursche's lived at the end of our street, and Karin and Christine were our friends. There were days of snail races in their enchanted garden. A chook shed in their backyard – a dry, crusty place that smelled of feathers and ammonia – was like the house that Jack built, extended often and full of tantalising nooks and crannies. Roosters, hens and chicks creaked and fossicked in their runs, and it was only ever a privilege to be asked to help collect the eggs.

Mr Pursche grew lucerne for his poultry and in one end of the shed was a green-feed cutter (a machine to produce green-feed not a green machine!). We'd feed the scythed herbage into the hopper whilst turning the handle, and watch the fine cut stuff spill out. Plunging our hands into the fluffy, moist green feed, we'd spread it evenly along troughs as the warm hustling hens brushed boisterously past our legs.

We spent a lot of time with Christine and Karin. Their father had built them a playhouse that seemed large when we were little – a great place for playing doctors and nurses.

Our next door neighbours were the Kloses. They owned an old pump organ that sat groaning with family photographs in a corner of their lounge room. Mrs Klose played the organ at church and practised her hymns every Saturday. Often, on weekends or during school holidays, I would ask if I could play it, and graciously she would invite me in. I taught myself to play many tunes on that organ. I wonder what the good Christian woman thought when she heard me pedalling away on the small intense instrument singing...

> 'Why are the stars always winkin' and blinkin' above
> What makes a fella start thinkin' of fallin' in love
> It's not the season the reason's as plain as the moon
> It's just Elmer's tune.'

Knowing Mrs Klose, she would have been smiling.

One of her two sons, Brendon, was a reserved boy, except when it came to street warfare. The Lange boys had somehow ostracised themselves from the rest of us and there were frequent rock throwing episodes on the unsealed street that was full of good ammunition. Often, on their way home from school, Brendon Klose and Roger Lange (the boy who'd thrown my school case in the river) would have a dust-up in Roenfeldt's vineyard behind the houses.

It was during one summer holidays that there was an altercation in full swing – Lange Boys v Rest of Street. We were all out on the street. Lucky for us we had reinforcements from town. Robert McCorry threw a large rock at Roger who by now had retreated to his front yard. The missile missed him but hit the magnificent cut glass window of their lounge room. The sound of broken glass tinkling onto the concrete path caused an immediate evacuation of all kids from the area. This was a huge expense for Robert who took weeks to pay for the damage out of his pocket money.

~

Museums intend to do this to us – to take us back in time. I walked to a small window and looked out to the street below. What a bursting of the bubble of daydreams to see sleek cars, cream brick buildings and brightly painted modern signs. Trying to reclaim my former mood, I descended the stairs thoughtfully, caressing the bannister rail worn smooth by the hands of those whose olden privacy I had slightly glimpsed, and with affection and a kind of possessiveness, I slowly turned the big brass door knob and stepped out, into nineteen seventy-nine.

*Me with Lincoln*

*My parents 1945*

*Leon and me*

*Me at 18*

*Warren and me - early courting*

*Our bridal party - L-R Cousins John, Jack and Rob, us two, Erica, Rose and Jill*

*Our wedding day*

*Warren, Rose and Jack (left), & other friends behind*

*Me with Erica and Dale*

*Grocke Homestead 1915*

Grocke Homestead 2010

Linc with friends at Yuendumu

Marlo in bush bath

Otto and Lin

Linc competing at age 9

Long drop at Kiah. Ready to go

One mob in for crutching Kiah

Carol and me at Kiah - a little bit tiddly

Warren with Ernie and Willie

Boys' Camp Kiah

Marlo - An early performance

Linc at 15

Dad 1986

Mum 1996

Me looking over Birribi

Feeding cattle at Birribi

Our Wenlock crossing

*Marlo at sixteen*

*Marlo (right) in Medea*

*Warren and me 1990*

*Warren competing*

*Linc competing*

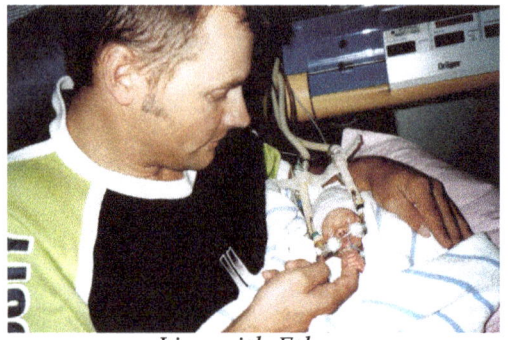
*Linc with Ethan*

*Linc and Nic with Ethan*

*Marlo, Mark and Otto*

*Warren and me 2018*

*Eversden*

Some of our flock - with Glen

Jeppi at the work she loved

Me - just finished harrowing

Shearing at Eversden

Foreseeing coming weather

Crops failing

*Ethan*

*Jacinte*

*Otto*

*Claudia*

*Sylvie*

## TWENTY-ONE

Our sheep were providing us with a good income. Our house was almost paid for, and so was the hills block we'd purchased before our big trip.

Close friend, Malcolm Semmler, called in to see us one day. He had a business proposition. He and a mate wanted to buy a section of the hundred and fifty acres we'd recently purchased. Ideal for growing Riesling, he propounded. They needed forty acres and would give us a thousand dollars an acre. On top of the hundred and seventy-five dollars an acre we'd paid for it, we'd put in another hundred per acre to improve it. This would be an amazing capital gain.

We were really just flying by the seat of our pants, business wise, but Warren's passionate dream was still to own three thousand acres on which to run prime sheep and do a little cropping. It didn't take him long to figure this would get him closer to that goal. He gave the nod to Malcolm.

With the proceeds of this sale, we paid off what we owed on the rest of that parcel, and also on "Lance's" – the hills block. And with the change, Warren bought his dream car – a white nineteen sixty-eight Porsche 911.

Peter and Margo were looking to expand. Their life path was similar to ours. They'd bought, renovated and sold properties, and Peter too wanted a large grazing farm. He called in to see us one day.

'I'm going down south to look at some properties,' he told Warren. 'Do you want to come?'

'Sure,' said Warren, 'when are you going?'

'Tomorrow. Pick you up at seven?'

Warren shot me a glance and nodded at Peter.

As they left next morning I said to my husband, 'Just remember who's buying the property!' The two of them grinned like school boys.

When Warren walked in later that night, he was charged with excitement.

'How'd it go?' I asked.

'We looked at this block near Frances – seventeen hundred acres of good country. It needs developing but there's four hundred acres ready to go. It doesn't suit Peter. He wants something bigger.'

I'd enjoyed the feeling of being debt free. I now sensed it was to be short-lived.

'I wonder if John and Carol would like to go in with us.'

I shook my head. 'I don't think it's a good idea to go into business with friends.'

'Well, why don't we just go and talk to them, and see what they say?'

Warren went to see them next day. They were both keen, so John and Warren drove down that day for a closer look. In the four hours it took to drive there, they talked about their dreams and goals and the prospect of owning a farm together. Before they left the property to come home they'd signed a contract – settlement in seven days, subject to nothing.

Next day, a Friday, Warren went to the bank. He told our manager how much money he needed to purchase our half share of this property and said he'd signed a contract.

'It's subject to finance, of course?' said George.

'Well, no,' said Warren.

George became wide-eyed. 'When's settlement?'

'Seven days,' said Warren, by now starting to get an idea of the gravity of the situation.

George folded his hands on his chest and became silent. 'Leave it with me,' he sighed.

The following Thursday he called us into his office.

'Your loan has been approved,' said George, 'but don't ever do that to me again. In future, if you're going to sign a contract, make sure it's subject to finance and settlement in no less than twenty-one days.'

That weekend our two families went to explore the new asset – the first of countless trips to this farm throughout our partnership.

We named the property Kiah and planned to crop some of it that first year. Sheep were bought. Apart from the four hundred arable acres, about nine hundred acres of virgin country had been pushed down prior to our purchase. Of this, we would prepare and pasture a hundred acres a year.

There were no dwellings on the place so we considered buying a caravan for shelter. A chain-wide stretch of bushland which we named The Nature Strip, ran the three kilometre length of the property, and within this we began to establish a camp. After looking at dozens of vans, Warren and I finally walked into the one that would be our home away from home at Kiah. We towed it to the property and parked it twenty metres from where John and Carol had set theirs up earlier. There was no electricity so we bought a small generator to run lights. We had gas to the caravans but most of our cooking was done over the campfire around which life revolved. The fire was lit upon each arrival and doused when it was time to leave. We erected benches made of railway sleepers for the kids. Deck chairs for the adults. Dinner was eaten from our laps each night whilst the kids straddled the sleepers. It had taken only a couple of upturned meals for us to realise that the plate-on-lap deal was too difficult for most of the kids. Geoff was the eldest at about twelve. Linc was next at eleven, Marlo and Ian were nine, Jenny, seven, and Trevor, three.

John's managerial job was demanding, as was Warren's work in the Barossa, so the time they had to invest in this farm was limited. However, we went there most weekends and school holidays.

A contractor was employed to put in first year's crops. Had we thought about the immensity of the task of equipping a bush property from scratch to run efficiently, we may never have set out. But John and Warren, with similar natures and spirits of adventure, took the necessary steps, a day at a time, and were rarely daunted.

On our way to Kiah one weekend, we stopped at the Keith general store as we often did, to purchase last minute groceries. John and Warren crossed the road for these items while Carol and I stayed with the kids, chatting to each other as we waited. After about twenty minutes we presumed our husbands had gone into the motorcycle shop next to the store. Fifteen minutes later they emerged from that premises wheeling a motorbike each. The Yamaha AG175 bikes were cheaper by the pair and were needed on the farm for mustering and general getting about. Carol and I went across to buy our bread and milk while the boys loaded the bikes.

John bought his first tractor, we took one of ours down, and over the ensuing months an assortment of machinery and plant were purchased by the partnership. The men worked and planned as if their lives depended on it. Carol and I, loving the environment and freedom from normal housework, took care of the children's needs, ran countless errands for the men and generally kept the home fires burning.

Our family hadn't been on holiday since returning from our big Outback adventure six years earlier, so when Warren's cousin Rob invited us on a houseboat trip, we didn't need to be asked twice. However, underlying my enthusiasm was an inexplicable mistrust of the River Murray. To me this big river seemed to have no interest in accommodating people. Its sparkling surface appeared enticing, but its murky alter ego seemed ready to suck down victims at a whim. This impression of the river so many people love had been with me for as long as I could remember.

Rob and Wendy and their two little girls, Bindi and Santha, called for us one hot morning in January. Our cars were packed with the prerequisites of an indulgent holiday and, buoyed at the prospect of a week of recreation, we set off.

It was midday by the time we arrived in Waikerie and boarded the big comfortable houseboat. Soon after pushing off, Wendy and I began to unpack food, bedding, clothes, books, games. Warren had brought our canoe which he tied to the side of the houseboat at water level. After an hour or so, Rob, who'd been at the helm, said to Warren, 'Your turn, mate. I'm gonna get in that canoe for a bit.'

Warren took the wheel and Rob climbed down into the little vessel. Within five minutes he was back up again. 'It's too rough,' he said, 'I'll tie it to the back. Linc, do you want to hop in?'

Linc asked me if he could. I didn't like the idea of him being out on the brown river without me or Warren, so I said, 'It seems a little dangerous to me. I'd rather you stayed on board.' So Rob got in alone.

'Now let the rope out, mate,' he called to Linc.

I went to join Warren at the helm. After a couple of minutes Wendy came in and said, 'Come and have a look at this, Sue.'

I followed her out to the rear deck. Rob was in the canoe about thirty metres out, his face beaming. 'I haven't seen him this happy for so long,' said Wendy. 'He's been working like a slave. He really needs this break.'

A little later he pulled himself in and asked Wendy to hand Santha, their five year old, down to him. Again he said to Linc, 'Let the rope out mate.'

This time he set out with the canoe and the two of them facing away from the mother vessel. When the rope ran out of slack and became suddenly taut, the canoe whipped around violently. Rob and Santha – neither wearing life jackets – were thrown into the water. Wendy came running through the houseboat.

'Stop,' she yelled. 'Stop. Rob and Santha are in the water.'

Warren began a U-turn. I ran to the stern and grabbed the lifebuoy, but we were too far away for it to reach them if I threw it. I had to wait until we got closer. Rob was a strong swimmer. Why was I filled with this terrible dread? Then I heard Rob cry out. His head and Santha's were just out of the water.

'*Help!*' he called.

The sound of his cry walloped me. Everything changed, became instantly surreal. I ran through to Warren.

'They're drowning,' I yelled.

Warren threw the gears into neutral, ripped off his shoes and jeans and dived in. As he swam towards them, I saw Rob push Santha up out of the water to her waist. Then he disappeared.

Warren reached Santha just as her head was almost out of sight. He side-stroked with her towards the bank. I rushed to the helm, found the boat's forward gear and steered it towards the shore, my heart thumping wildly as I tried to keep the huge vessel away from the two of them in the water. Rob was still nowhere to be seen. Warren reached the shallows and struggled with Santha through reeds to safety. As the boat bumped into the bank, Wendy jumped off and ran to take her daughter in her arms.

'Where's Rob?' asked Warren, gasping for breath.

The silent river feigned innocence.

I jumped down onto the shore. Wendy thrust Santha into my arms.

'Rob, *Rob!*' she shouted as she bolted up and down the bank, stumbling over logs, looking in the reeds. '*Rob, Rob!*'

'Where's Rob?' Warren asked again.

'He's gone,' I said.

'What do you mean?'

'He's drowned,' I whimpered.

'*No*,' yelled Warren, looking at me wildly. His frantic eyes searched the river.

'*He can't have. Look, bubbles.*'

He waded furiously through the reeds, swam to the disturbance and dived. He came up for air and dived again. And again. And again.

'*It's too deep,*' he shouted. '*I can't see a thing.*'

I looked back to the boat to see the children's grave little faces watching the tragedy unfold. Warren stumbled out of the water and stood beside me, shivering uncontrollably. Wendy was still reeling up and down the river, searching, wailing for her mate. Then, '*I've found him. He's here.*'

Warren ran to where she was standing, frozen with fear. Again he waded into the reeds, and stopped.

'It's a log,' he uttered, as the last remnant of hope flowed out of him.

Rob was gone.

We all went back on board and stood in a huddle against the trauma of grief and unspeakable pain.

'Where's Daddy?' asked Bindi in a small, small voice.

Wendy had no words. Warren was silent. From somewhere I had to find an answer for the little girl who had just lost her Daddy. I picked her up and said, 'He's gone to Heaven, darling.' But I could see in her beautiful, innocent face that in this moment, these words to her were meaningless.

It was getting dark. Using the two-way radio we called the houseboat owner. He told us he'd send the police immediately. They were there in twenty minutes. Huddled, shivering and immobilised, we waited – for someone to drag us out of this nightmare.

In filling out their initial report, the police were as sensitive and compassionate as we could have wished for. With their questioning over, they asked if we were okay to go to Berri, forty kilometres upstream, in the houseboat. With the strength and leadership men must find when they least have it in them, Warren said yes. The officers tied a bucket to a log on the bank as a marker and told us they'd send out an aqualung squad next morning to search for Rob's body. As we pulled away from the terrible place, Wendy hurled a hideous scream at the river. With callousness, the river hurled it back.

Still we could find no words. Between us there were only primal sounds of grief. Some of Warren's happiest times as a child had been with Rob, whose parents were delivered the shocking news that night.

At Berri, we were met by a warm and empathetic doctor. He assessed Wendy who was by now barely able to stand. The sedative he administered took effect within minutes. Warren and I put the children to bed and collapsed onto our bare mattress. Through the long hours of night, we held each other close – not sleeping, but every now and then one of us breaking into uncontrollable trembling.

At the hint of the dawn of our first day without Rob, we left our beds. Wendy was the first to see the silhouette of Rob's father standing on the bank. Statuesque. She left the boat and ran into his arms. Their weeping was heart sickening.

The divers retrieved Rob's body later that morning. It was almost exactly where he had gone down – not where Warren had seen bubbles. We were all questioned extensively then, even Lincoln, as the police completed their report.

For weeks afterwards we found sleep elusive, and when it came, it was infected by nightmares. A few months later, Warren, who'd been almost undone by not being able to save his cousin, received a letter from the Royal Humane Society. He was to receive a commendation for bravery – for saving Santha.

# TWENTY-TWO

Having the farm and the company of our friends and business partners helped with our healing. Sitting in the campfire light each night, we talked well with our wise and caring friends. The kids were usually tucked into bed by seven-thirty – exhausted from play and without protest.

The three older boys rode motorbikes, built huts – one of these from tree branches and as big as a single car shed. All the kids helped their dads, learning job and life skills along the way. Marlo and Jenny explored the bush, picking up treasures from its floor – wild flowers, moss-covered twigs, insects – all to be studied and preserved in jars. They created hides in the thick native brush, the whereabouts of which were divulged to no-one. The boys spent a part of each day searching for them but were never successful. I don't know how the two little girls found their way back to them each day. They obviously had their own Hansel and Gretel trail.

Marlo's love for acting was blossoming. She and Jenny produced plays – usually performed for an audience of two mothers, the odd father and an assortment of kids who invariably disrupted the flow with coming and going and mucking around. School friends were often invited for a weekend, so it wasn't uncommon for there to be eight or more kids in camp.

A long drop toilet was dug. In hard clay soil the job took hours – each of us taking turns at digging. Finally, with great satisfaction, we placed the "little house" that Warren had built at home, over the pit and tried it out. A bush shower was slung over a sturdy tree branch behind John and Carol's caravan. The men used this at the end of each day. Water simmered constantly at the fire's edge – for washing dishes, clothes, kids, and for the showers. We'd bought a galvanised iron tub just big enough for one small person to sit in, and one by one in the evenings, the kids would be whisked through it – most of them deeply concerned about privacy and demanding it before disrobing. After Warren and John had gone to bed, Carol and I would take our turn at bathing. The generator would be switched off and by the light and warmth of the fire, one would ease into the small tub of hot clean water while the other sat with her back to the ablutions, playing guitar and singing – most often Joan Baez songs from me and Linda Ronstadt from Carol.

We met our neighbours, Fred and Winnie East, who welcomed us into the district. An older couple, they were genial and well-to-do. One evening they called in to our camp to say hello. Warren was showering when he heard their vehicle approaching. Covered in suds, he had only a minute or two of hot water left in the bag. The track in to camp was behind the caravan and as our new acquaintances drove past within four metres of Warren, he just turned his back and waved a backhander. Winnie was still blushing when she got out of the car. We invited them to sit at our fire and as they were teetotallers made them a tea. Winnie was wearing a floral nylon dress and as the red gum logs spat and crackled over the fire, sparks and small embers landed like missiles in her lap. By the time they left, her frock was peppered with holes and ready for the rag bag.

They invited us over to their place to see their slides.

'But there are so many kids,' we said.

'That's okay,' said Winnie. 'Bring them all.'

We arrived at seven-thirty next night, the kids dead tired from their day's play. All the chairs Fred and Winnie owned were lined up around the edge of their lounge room. When we were all seated, Fred brought in a huge bowl of sweets which, as we talked, was handed round and round the room until the entire contents had been consumed. By now all the kids were wide awake and convulsing with sugar-induced giggling.

We were shown slides of their property being developed. And then pictures of their son's wedding, his twenty-first birthday party, their twenty-fifth wedding anniversary, their parents' golden wedding anniversaries… Within an hour the kids were all asleep – some snoring. We four were in a soporific stupor by ten. Suddenly the lights came on and we snapped back into conversation, groping for our intelligence.

'Time for supper!' Fred announced cheerfully.

The kids straggled awake and followed us into the kitchen. Two throw-overs were whisked from the huge country table and before us lay an immense supper. Three or four large bottles of homemade flavoured soda stood along the centre of the table. There were fritz and pickle sandwiches, Jatz biscuits with cheese and tomato, hundreds and thousands on bread and butter triangles, home-baked lamingtons, cream puffs, and strawberry and cream sponge cakes. The kids thought they were dreaming.

'Come on everyone, tuck in,' said Fred as Winnie poured the tea.

It was a night to remember, and we never failed to appreciate the goodwill and generosity of these fine country people.

One day we were using their stock yards to treat our sheep for lice prevention. The sheep had to run through a race, slide down a chute into a long narrow trough full of sheep dip, swim the six or seven metre length of it and haul themselves out at the other end. It was my job to dunk them under with a forked tree branch to make sure each one was completely submerged, but every now and then two would jump in together and consequently one on top of the other. Seeing even animals disappear under water was still traumatic for me.

'They're drowning!' I shouted to Warren who was pushing them from the yards.

'They'll be right!' he yelled back.

Running up and down the sluice with my fork, it took all my strength to lift soaked sheep from on top of others. At the end of the day as we were packing up, apart from being exhausted, I was so thankful none had died.

Friends and family often came to spend time with us here at Kiah. It was such a beautiful place, dotted with hundreds of majestic blue gums. In spring, the pasture was thick with clover and small lakes appeared. The nature strip produced a masterwork of wildflowers. There were emus, echidnas and just a few kangaroos. One day I was walking through the bush alone. Moving slowly and delighting in the colours of the bush, the textures of bark, the architecture of banksias, I heard the snapping of a twig nearby. I stopped and looked to where the sound had come from. Camouflaged, and not three metres from me, was the most enormous kangaroo I had ever seen. I looked up at him. Our eyes met. I greeted him and told him I was leaving. He was calm and watched me as I backed away. A scintillating encounter.

The lifestyle here was something we all loved. The kids would disappear after breakfast and return when they were hungry, reliably about midday, then meld into the bush again after lunch. By around four, the smaller ones would be back in. Carol and I would wrap potatoes in foil and place them carefully in the coals near the fire's edge. Guitars would be tuned, a melody struck – our repertoire by now extensive.

There was never a shortage of fortified wine in the camp – Cream Sherry, Muscat or Port – from which we'd trickle our afternoon aperitifs. Our singing would be without inhibition then. I think the children returned for it as, weary from play, they'd come in close to their mothers' music and nurturing. We'd play and sing for an hour or more before dispersing to our caravans to prepare the evening meal. Kids' meat would be put in racks over the fire, and salad or steamed vegies put together. By the time all little ones had been fed and bathed and some put to bed, the men would be in. We'd have another aperitif with them and settle into our chairs around the fire. Then, after the men had showered, we'd sit down for our meal – also cooked over the coals – a good red wine and lots of laughter. I don't think I have ever laughed as much as I did with Carol in that camp, and whenever we went into the Frances store.

About twelve kilometres south, Frances was a sleepy town. There were silos, a railway station, garage, pub, general store and post office. The store had been there for a century or more – solid stone walls, small windows, low ceilings, old front door thick with paint, and creaking floor boards. Sagging wooden shelves were laden with all that we needed, and leftovers of generations past, including jars of ointment labelled "For Bad Breasts". From the cover of the stack of toiletries and laundry products, Carol and I would take these dusty jars and bottles from the shelves one at a time, and with tears streaming down our faces, legs crossed, convulsing in silent laughter, hand them to each other to read. This laughter was *our* medicine.

Carol had been very close to her father who had died too young – just before Carol and I had met. And her caring for four young children was a solid task. For me, laughter had always been a tonic, giving sad memories a nudge.

For our first twelve months here, Warren would drive our Bedford down most times – the truck laden with tools, machinery and equipment. I'd collect Linc and Marlo from school on a Friday afternoon and then drive the three of us down with a ute-load of extras – fertiliser, fuel, small machinery. And even four rams one day. We'd arrive typically after dark and be greeted happily by Warren who was always relieved we'd arrived safely.

For our first shearing here, we were grateful for the use of a neighbour's facilities. We'd bought an old army tent and erected it in our camp – shearers' quarters. Each evening all the men showered under the big tree. The campfire was stoked substantially enough to accommodate the fifteen or more of us who sat and ate around it each night until the job was done.

We needed a bathroom, and so after shearing, Warren built one of corrugated iron. He and John plumbed water to it from the nearby bore, installed a shower, chip heater and an old claw foot bath – all clearing sale purchases. It was a wonderful extravagance. At my shower time I'd stoke the chip heater till the water was almost boiling. I'd undress and lay my clothes over the small camp stool behind the door. Steaming heavy water, tempered with cold, sparkled out of the chrome shower head as I stood on the latticed rubber mat over dirt, to wash. I loved the sound of the water singing in the copper cylinder. The luxury of it. A small breeze, or sometimes icy wind, sliced in under the door. A window facing east framed the branches of a big old stringy bark. One morning, unaware of me, an Azure kingfisher sat in the tree – a vibrant splash of blue in the grey-green bush.

It doesn't get much better than this, I thought, as the ambrosial water ran over my sun-dappled body.

Warren had a cousin who owned a farm about fifty kilometres from Kiah. A dyed-in-the-wool bachelor, he'd sometimes drop in of an evening. He was a night owl and one could always count on a late night and some interesting stories when Glen was in camp. One night, after quite a few ports, he was in the middle of a story and trying to think of someone's name.

'McDonald,' he said. 'No, not McDonald. McGregor. McInnes. Nope. McBurnie. McDougall? (looking at the group questioningly – no reaction). McAllister. No, no, not McAllister. McFarlane. Nope. McGuire. McClure. *McClure.*'

His eyes lit up. '*McClure.* How does that sound?'

By the time he'd got it, the rest of us were in fits of laughter over the string of "Mc" names that had flowed periodically and seriously over half an hour.

One day Warren asked me to go over to Glen's to bring back a seed drill that he'd offered to lend us. Glen hooked it up to the tow bar for me and I headed off. The monstrous implement was the full width of the narrow road from his farm to the highway – several kilometres, with dense bush on either side. It was an infrequently used road but as luck would have it, on this afternoon I rounded a bend to see a ute coming towards me. We both stopped, and because it was impossible for us to pass there, I had to back up until I came to a slight clearing I'd noticed a little earlier, so that the other driver could go around me. It was a slow process as I manoeuvred the huge thing in reverse. When he finally drove by, I saw a look of amusement on the farmer's face, but also respect.

'Thanks love!' he shouted, and then another forty kilometres along the highway for me before I reached our farm.

On another occasion Warren asked me to go into Frances to pick up some buckets for the windmill. 'Hang on,' he said as I was about to drive off. 'I'll get one, so you can show Gibbsy what we want.'

I'd imagined large water-carrying containers, but these were small leather containers not much bigger than an egg cup – bucket *washers* in fact. Gibbsy was the local mechanic – his workshop a relic. Built of corrugated iron, it slumped in its weed-filled yard. Above the door, a tin sign, faded to near illegibility read "L. Gibbs – Motor Repairer". It was dark inside – the dirt floor soaked in engine oil. Rows of shelves sagged with spark-plugs, bearings, tyre tubes, belts, headlights, globes, filters – all covered in dust, some in oily cardboard boxes with ornate labels. A light bulb hung over it all and filled the space with moving shadows as Gibbsy yanked the switch cord next to it. His overalls were damp with the same dust and grease. The office was all paper – hardly a clear space to be seen. Somewhere under it all was a desk. Great wads of invoices bunched together with alligator clips hung from nails on the walls. Girlie calendars from the past several years added colour. The price book with dog-eared pages and grimy cover was usually as hard to find as the telephone. The docket book was more at hand, and as he handed me the invoice, I handed him a cheque. This was how business was done – psychologically more rewarding than the direct transfers of today.

With the property becoming more productive it was time to buy more sheep. Warren went to an off-shears sale with an Elders stock agent. Sheep auctions are a grazier's delight. Amid the loud and furious calling, Warren successfully bid for four hundred wethers and then hired one of the waiting truckies to deliver them. Because the new sheep would have to be branded next day and put in one of the back paddocks on good pasture, Warren went with him. After the five hundred kilometre journey, it was late by the time they got there, and the stock were unloaded in the dark.

I thought I'd have to make the four hour trip to bring Warren back next day but he decided to come home by train. The only problem was he didn't have any clean clothes. The ones he'd left home in, the morning before, were now dirty and smelled of sheep. The only clean clothing in camp was a pair of Carol's flares (three inches too short for Warren), and one of her striped tops. He donned these, climbed onto the tractor and drove into town. As he neared the railway station, he saw the train coming. He pulled up in front of the store, dashed in to ask Bob Beagley, the shop owner, if he'd mind parking the tractor out the back till we came down next, and ran for the train. Bob's mouth fell open at the sight of him in Carol's clothes and we could only imagine how this story was told about town.

After this we bought an old Nissan ute to use as a farm runabout. Most of the kids learned to drive in this vehicle but because it had no brakes, special skills had to be learned to avoid crashing into gates etc. Even so, there was a terrible arc in one of the newly made gates that smacked of too enthusiastic an approach.

Life was busy. We had our properties in the Barossa, this one in the South East and Warren was still working in the vineyard.

When we were at home in the Barossa, Warren's cousin Jack would often call in seeking a sympathetic ear. He had fallen into disrepair after his divorce from Rosemary, and more often than not, he'd be three sheets to the wind. There were times he'd let himself into our house in the middle of the night and scare us out of our wits as he crashed into furniture. It distressed Warren to see Jack destroying himself. They'd been like brothers as kids and had lived through enough adventures to fill a book.

We were at home watching television one night when Warren announced, out of the blue, 'I don't feel well.'

'What's up?' I asked.

'I don't know,' he said, 'I just feel really strange.'

This was unusual for Warren who was more inclined to suffer in silence if feeling under par.

At about eleven that night the phone rang. It was Warren's mum telling us that Jack had died. He'd passed away at the very time Warren had begun to feel unwell.

Jack was forty years old. Although we were shocked and saddened at the news, we weren't surprised. He'd been committing a slow suicide for years.

As we said our goodbyes at his graveside, no more than a dozen people stood with us.

Warren had three close boy cousins as a child. Now two were dead – Rob and Jack. John, the third, had been conscripted to the war in Vietnam. Because of his slight build he'd been a "tunnel rat" and had come back a changed man. But like most vets, he'd kept the horror of war largely to himself. His wife Jen is an angel who is still in love with him and has had the strength and wisdom to ease him carefully through life as they found it, once he returned.

## TWENTY-THREE

By the early eighties, our children were finding their niches – Linc in the world of bike racing, and Marlo in performing arts. Our daughter's gift had been recognised by the community when, at the age of ten, she'd played the lead in a short humorous play performed in our main street during a Vintage Festival. Standing back, I'd watched the gathering audience whom she had in the palm of her hand. Afterwards I heard comments from the crowd.

'Wasn't she wonderful,' said someone.

'So vibrant and confident,' effused someone else.

She had a charisma, an artisan-ship that would see her become single-minded about becoming an actress. And one of my roles, I still believed, was to help my two talented children pursue their dreams.

Our friends Peter and Margo had sold their property to an out-of-town couple. Fred was a retired newspaper editor. Peter must have told him to contact Warren if he needed help and/or advice with farming. Although Fred and Marjory were several years our senior, we struck up a warm association with them as Warren helped them with some of their sheep and farming work. One morning Fred called in to see us. Over a coffee he asked if we'd consider selling them some of our land.

As one who never fails to weigh up what could be an opportunity, Warren asked, 'Which block are you interested in?'

'The one you bought recently in the hills.'

'Could be a possibility, I suppose.'

'Can we go up and have a look?' asked Fred.

That night Warren and I talked about the prospect and agreed that if we got a good price for it, we would sell the remainder of this land. Considering we'd paid a hundred and seventy-five dollars an acre for it three or four years earlier, that Malcolm and Steve had paid us a thousand dollars an acre for their bit, and that this section had a few more moss rocks and was not as arable, we would let it go for five hundred an acre. We called for Fred and Marjory next morning, drove up and walked over the block. It was a glorious piece of country. When we got back to their place, they invited us in for a coffee. They'd realised by now that the property was on the market and asked the price.

'Well we really hadn't planned to sell it,' said Warren, 'but if you're happy with five hundred dollars an acre, we'd let it go.'

'Get the cheque book, Marjory,' said Fred, and wrote out a cheque for the deposit then and there.

Selling the property was, in one way, moving away from Warren's dream three thousand acres, but this wasn't the property of his dreams. The income from it hadn't been outstanding, so he began to think of doing something more productive with the proceeds. He would buy a new tractor, a mower and baler, and establish a hay contracting business, which he hoped would be lucrative enough for us to save for a larger parcel of land.

Farming at Kiah had had its challenges. The soil was different from the Barossa's and the rainfall higher. We had to be vigilant for foot rot and other unfamiliar ovine diseases. Early one morning Warren went out to check the flock as he often did. When he returned, he told us he'd found three or four dead sheep. He went out again next morning and found another two or three, stuck in the mud at the edge of the dam – too weak to get out.

'There's something wrong,' he said. 'These aren't natural deaths. We'll have to call the vet.'

It didn't take the vet long to diagnose Barber's Pole worm. It was imperative that we inject the entire flock immediately. By the time they started to recover, we'd lost fifty. It was heartbreaking to see them die. A pall settled over our psyches.

Each spring, gigantic heaps of pushed up virgin scrub would be lit – one or two at a time, generally towards evening. Carol and I would see the horizon aglow from the camp and hope the kids were safe – either with their fathers or well away from the fires, which were enormous.

One evening our neighbour Fred came over. There were none of his usual cheery overtures. This visit was of a serious nature.

'Have you heard the news?'

'What news?' asked Warren, alarmed by the gravity in his voice.

'The government has brought in a clearing act. There's to be no more scrub cleared in South Australia.' Warren and John were silent as they tried to process the announcement. 'And any bush that's been pushed down,' continued Fred, 'has to be cleaned up within twelve months or not at all.'

Our plan had been to develop a small portion of Kiah each year as we could afford it. Nine hundred acres of scrub had been chained before we bought it and we'd developed about two hundred acres of that. The property would never be viable if we could only ever use half of it. We agreed to approach a bank for a loan big enough to complete the job within the stipulated twelve months.

A bank manager from Naracoorte came to look at the property and discuss our plans. They lent us the money we needed at an interest rate of eleven percent. We purchased a wake rake, blade plough and Caterpillar D7 bulldozer – all second-hand.

Lawry Bensch had a small farm near our shearing shed block in Tanunda. He'd been an earth moving contractor most of his life and was now semi-retired. We asked him if he'd be interested in doing some dozer work for us there. He was a solitary man who loved the bush and his answer was a resounding yes.

He and dog Rover set up camp near our caravans, and Lawry spent eight hours a day over several weeks doing a sensitive job of tidying what had been a tangled, ravaged pile of chained scrub. With all significant trees and stands of native bush left, it was rewarding for us to see the fertile, productive farming land emerge.

I was by now firmly entrenched in a farming life, motorcycle crewing on winter weekends, and motherhood. A notice in our local rag caught my attention. Someone was offering watercolour painting lessons. The medium had always appealed to me. How wonderful it would be to add another string to my artistic bow and take some time for myself again. I enrolled in the course.

Florence Peitsch, our tutor, was vibrant, outgoing and warm. A truly gifted artist, her painting style matched her personality. Her pictures were full of life, colour and courage.

At our first session, seven or eight enthusiastic women from diverse walks of life gathered – all of us optimistic about what we might achieve. Florence asked us to introduce ourselves, give a little of our background and our reasons for being there.

This took me by surprise. I found myself confronted by that old fear of being focussed on by a group. I was the last to speak – my heart thumping, knees shaking. Where did this fear come from? I wanted so much to conquer it. Even my painting was controlled, restrained. I longed to be as courageous and free with my work as Florence was with hers.

One spring day she brought in a huge bunch of flowers picked in haste from her cottage garden. In their delightful disarray, she plunged them into a bucket of water, and said, 'This is what we're painting today.'

I gasped with the enormity of the task. She saw the look on my face and said, 'Sue, you don't have to paint them all! Just pick the ones that take your fancy, even if it's only three or four.'

I don't think my tutor had any idea of how powerful her words were, for me. In that instant I was freed – to see things in their simplicity, not necessarily their complexity.

I began to paint with glorious abandon. I bought tubes of amazing colours that thrilled me as I brushed them boldly onto sheets of damp watercolour paper, using plump brushes. The fact that I often started a stroke and the paints themselves finished it, held me in a state of constant surprise and wonder.

Florence told us that if we were to paint well, we'd need to develop our drawing skills. She suggested an hour's sketching a day. There was wonderful opportunity for this at the farm. Joyfully I sketched people, dogs, sheep, vehicles, sheds, the bush.

Because watercolours can be so quickly executed, it wasn't long before I'd completed quite a few, and I was pleased with many of them. An exhibition was to be held at a local contemporary gallery – part of a Barossa Arts Programme. I was invited to take part. I picked out twenty or more of my favourites. It was incredibly satisfying to see my framed works hanging in a gallery. At the exhibition opening I sold enough to pay for the framing.

Over the next seven or eight years, I painted and sketched in any spare time I could find. My paintings still hang in the homes of friends and family members, and in our own.

Warren had established a clientele for his hay contracting business which brought us a lifestyle hitherto unknown. For Warren it meant nights followed by days without sleep. For me, sleeping on the couch near the two-way radio so I could hear clients call in the middle of the night to inform us their hay was ready to bale. By radio then I'd relay the message to Warren who'd be working somewhere out in hay land where the only light would be from the stars, the moon and the odd burning car.

In the beginning, I'd pack enough food for him for twenty-four hours and take it out to wherever he was working. When the hay was too dry, he'd attend to repairs and maintenance and then perhaps roll out his swag and grab forty winks under his tractor. Sleeping fitfully, he'd reach out to feel the moisture content of the hay. When it was damp enough, he'd continue the job. The kids missed him. One day I heard Marlo crying in her room. I sat on her bed beside her.

'I miss Dad,' she sobbed.

'I know,' I said. 'Me too. But it won't be forever. Hay season will be finished soon.'

I wanted to comfort her, and the season did end soon after that, but the job spanned several months of each year, and Warren would continue with it for the next nine years.

Since returning from our big trip eight years earlier, we'd not had a holiday. The motorbike trips were never relaxing, and the houseboat holiday had been over before it started. Lincoln was thirteen and Marlo eleven.

'You know,' I said to Warren one day, 'it won't be long before the kids won't want to come on holidays with us. We need to take a break, with them.'

My husband would not have stopped work had I not organised it, but I could see he was tired. I planned a two week trip through Tasmania. Warren's sister and her husband were still living and working there. They were now principals at the Missionary Training College in St Leonard's – a beautiful hamlet on the outskirts of Launceston. We flew across, and after a few day trips with them and their two children, Jonathan and Andrea, and hours of catching up chatter, our family set out to see the big island. The college folk kindly lent us a car and as we toured, we fell in love with the island – its European-influenced architecture, its forests, beaches, mountains and wilderness. We wandered through art galleries and studios that were nestled in woodland nooks and crannies. Early one morning, a colourful sign on the roadside tempted us into an orchard. Dewy cherries as big as plums filled crates that were stacked to the ceiling in an enormous shed. We couldn't resist a purchase. Throughout the day we popped the fruit, bursting with sweetness, into our mouths. Food in season.

Making our way down to the Huon Valley a couple of days later and contemplating breakfast, we spotted a roadside stall advertising fresh crayfish. Selling them from the back of his van, a salt-haired fisherman served us just-cooked, succulent tails in that morning's bread rolls, with lashings of butter, a little salt and pepper and a squeeze of lemon. One of those looks that don't need words passed between my husband and me. We were in a moment of rare contentment and happiness.

Warren returned home from this holiday with his mind clear enough to reflect upon another move towards his dream. He talked to me about the prospect of buying some more of the range country, this time from his parents. Times were tough for the vignerons in the Barossa and the idea of a state-wide vine pull was being mooted. Supply was beginning to outstrip demand for red grapes and the Valley was in an uproar. There was dissent about the vine pull amongst those in the industry. Warren was still involved in Apex and many of his fellows were winemakers, but none more passionate about the situation than winemaker David Wardlaw who expounded that it would be a travesty to destroy the magnificent old Shiraz vines. He believed that a demand for reds, beyond comprehension, was just around the corner.

In desperation, many growers began to lay waste the gardens of their ancestors – making a place for the new whites. A mass pain hung in the air as the gnarly old vines, alive with the stories of a century of harvests, were wrenched from the earth, domineered into heaps, poisoned with petrol and lit.

None of our vines were pulled. Otto just couldn't bear to do it, and was probably with the David Wardlaw school of thought.

We bought the Kaiser Stuhl country from Otto and Lin. They offered us the opportunity to buy the vineyard they called Schlenks' as well. We did the sums, and even at mates' rates, considering the money we'd have to borrow, it would not be viable.

Warren loved to work. His disinterest in grapes was never about the work. He had grown up through hard times in the industry. But it was not even that he expected there not to be tough times in sheep farming by comparison. It was that he had a passion for it.

Schlenks' was put on the market, but the economic climate was not right for selling a vineyard. After a few weeks the agent said, 'Pull out the vines Otto, and I'll sell it for you.'

Still Otto resisted, even though he was over seventy and considering retirement.

Out of the blue, our friends and Kiah business partners, John and Carol, asked to have a look at the vineyard. They tramped along the rows through the Biscay soil after a rain. Their shoes became so huge and heavy with the sticky mud that they were never to be worn again. But they fell in love with the place, the space and the views, and bought it. No vines were pulled, and the red wines that John and Carol have made from that vineyard have won prizes and accolades to be proud of.

# TWENTY-FOUR

Change was in the wind. Otto could see we were doing well and seemed *at last* to accept that his son would never have the connection with grape growing that he did. Without prelude, he engaged a share-farmer.

Warren had begun work with his father at the age of fifteen. Now, twenty-seven years later, he was finally able to devote his time entirely to his own ventures, to drive through the vineyard on his way to *his* work without the pressure of wondering how he was going to get everything done. Some other competent person whose only job now was to toil among the rows of vines would wave to Warren as he passed, oblivious to the difference he had made to our lives.

Otto and Lin had invested their proceeds of the vineyard sale and should have been relieved of the worries associated with growing and selling grapes, but Otto could not extricate himself entirely. He had been a hardworking man all his life and could not give it up. They took the trips that Lin had dreamed of but still Otto was never happier than when in his overalls helping the share-farmer, driving his tractor up and down the rows, always in hope of a better harvest, better prices, a frost-free year.

Warren tendered for and won a contract to cut and bale four hundred acres of irrigated lucerne, four to five times a year. Lincoln was sixteen and champing at the bit to begin work. He was au fait with tractors and farming so the obvious starting point was as his father's off-sider. He left school to become a working man.

The lucerne property was an hour from our home so the owner offered Warren accommodation in the once grand but now almost derelict homestead. My husband was grateful. It would be better than sleeping under the tractor.

The house had some fifteen main rooms. Great empty rooms with lofty ceilings and board floors. Any conversation echoed along passageways that were long and wide enough to pitch a cricket ball. As the sun went down the place creaked with cabinetry.

Lincoln had a terrifying paranormal experience there alone one night. He'd just gone to bed on a mattress on the floor in one of the huge empty rooms. Something began to choke him. It felt like hands around his throat, he told me. He tried to sit up but something heavy was holding him down. Gasping for air and struggling to escape, he was just as abruptly released. Despite not having slept and being dog-tired, he was happy to go out to the safety of his tractor and keep working till dawn.

On another occasion he came into the house at about two am, exhausted after a whole day and half the night of raking hay. He switched on the kettle to make himself a coffee, then decided to have a shower first. He didn't realise the kettle was not automatic. Before he got back to the kitchen he could smell smoke. The kettle had boiled dry and was on fire. So too the cupboards above it. He raced down the passage to get a blanket and back to the kitchen where he beat frantically at the flames. It took him several minutes to put out the fire. His lungs were filled with smoke and he was spent – not only from lack of sleep but from the fear of the experience.

My maternal heart was often heavy with seeing him in a man's world so soon after being just a boy.

With his earnings, our son bought himself a second-hand tractor and, with one of our implements hooked up to it, raked the mown hay. Warren followed with the baler. With repairs, maintenance and customer liaison on top of baling, it wasn't unusual for Warren to work thirty or forty hours without a break. Linc's mate Ben had left school too and worked for Warren for a while. He drove one of our tractors and mowed the lucerne.

Every two or three days I'd drive down with food for them all – prepared meals that they only had to heat. I'd try to time it so that Warren and I could eat together and talk about upcoming jobs, invoices to go out, fuel deliveries, machinery parts to be ordered etc. Still no mobile phones. The pace was fast and furious. Everyone wanted their hay baled at once and there was nothing more frustrating than to have a machine break down and no replacement parts in South Australia. In that case I'd notify and try to pacify all clients. Warren and the boys would sleep like the dead – sometimes for twenty-four hours straight.

Marlo had gone to New Zealand on a Rotary Exchange, and while I missed her terribly, at least I didn't have the concern of leaving her home alone while I made these excursions into the night.

Between lucerne cuts, we'd drive down to Kiah to undertake the jobs that were imminent there.

Lincoln had been riding Enduros for a while but his first road event was *The News* Twenty-four Hour Reliability Trial.

On the first day of this trial, he left the starter's podium as the youngest in a field of hundreds. He was sixteen. Warren was riding the event too. The conditions were appalling. There'd been heavy rain and the track was treacherous. They started around midday on the Saturday and were to finish around the same time next day.

In the wee hours of Sunday morning I headed for a checkpoint way out in the back blocks. The roads were wet, boggy, slippery. In the pitch black night I had trouble finding the place. Eventually I saw lights in the distance and headed for them, following what appeared to be the most used track. I loosened my knuckle-whitening grip on the steering wheel and took a deep breath of relief when I came to a paddock of parked cars and scattered campfires.

> Rugged up against a blizzard's child
> I stood beside a roaring fire
> gloved hands covering my frozen face
> Slowly I turned in an effort to thaw
>
> Under coats, hats and scarves
> a rotisserie of figures
> unrecognisable as bank robbers
> circled with me
> in the fire's genial light.

At these checkpoints riders were required to hand in their time-cards to a steward who'd note their time of arrival. It was rare for anyone to reach a control ahead of time. Points were lost and tallied for degrees of lateness. Lincoln came roaring in – a few minutes overdue. Waiting to help him refuel his bike, give him a drink and clean his goggles, I was by now standing three metres past the official's desk. He spotted his mother, rode straight past the steward, pulled up in front of me and with fatigue-glazed eyes gave me a look that said, "Mum. Home."

'Go back,' I shouted as I helped him push his bike back to the clock where the steward stamped his card.

I ached at seeing him take off into the sleety black night. He'd been riding – but not only riding, *battling* the terrain for twelve hours, and despite the fatigue, was committed to his goal – another twelve hours of the same. Both he and Warren finished that event, and in fact Lincoln became the youngest rider ever to have finished a "Twenty-four Hour" – the beginning of a long and successful career in motorcycle racing, culminating in his being fully sponsored, riding the Australian Four Day (world class) event, and being South Australian Rider of the Year in nineteen ninety-five. He and Warren competed together for years and Warren too won many awards. I loved seeing them so bonded in the sport they loved.

Throughout the racing season each year, we still had to go to the farm regularly and I tried to fit in the odd Sunday lunch in the Barossa so that we could catch up with the rest of the family.

Dad had retired. Kaiser Stuhl Wines had been taken over by Penfolds and there'd been retrenchments. Dad had been safe after the first wave and still had his job as engineering draughtsman after the second, but he'd grown progressively uneasy, sensing it would only be a matter of time before the axe fell on him. He was sixty-one when it came, and although he received a good pay-out and had retirement projects lined up, it affected him badly. For forty-five years he'd been part of his country's workforce. I could see that being out of it was gut-wrenching for him.

He'd been wrest from the farm of his boyhood, had dreamed all his life of owning his own, and now, even though he had his farm and all the time he needed to run it, he was grieving the loss of his job. He bought some more grazing land and a few more sheep, and in his workshop began to bring an Austin Seven car and Royal Enfield motorcycle back to life. He'd restored an E-type Jaguar prior to this, and it was now winning concourses and being written about in motoring magazines. He had the patience of a saint when it came to restoration – a quality he often lacked, in his own quiet way, with people, although never his kids.

I was with him one day when he told me he'd been to see his doctor about a persistent cough. X-rays had picked up a shadow on one of his lungs. I had no idea what the implications were. I took Dad to the Royal Adelaide Hospital for tests. Through the course of that day, one doctor after another came into his room, each one a little more qualified than the last, all of them asking the same questions and all looking extremely grave. Suddenly something that felt like dread hit me. Adrenalin went to the tips of my fingers as I waited for the prognosis.

After several hours of X-ray scrutinising and specialist heads together in consultation, the most senior of the doctors came in and sat on Dad's bed. His hands were folded on his lap, his shoulders rounded with the news he had to deliver.

'Mr Hancock,' he said, 'you have lung cancer. We can give you chemotherapy which may give you a little more time, but it is inoperable, and terminal.'

The doctor's words faded beneath a cacophony of drumming in my head.

'How long?' I forced out over the noise. Even my own voice sounded muffled to me.

'Twelve, maybe eighteen months at the most.'

Dad took a deep breath, hung his head and nodded. I looked at the specialist pleadingly, but his eyes told me the unbearable truth.

I wanted Dad to fight. I went into a *"We'll beat this"* mode. I bought him books on positive thinking, on how to cure cancer naturally, talked to him about what to eat and what not to. I wanted so much for him to fight, *fight,* but he wouldn't. He'd accepted his sentence.

Within two or three months, he needed oxygen to help him breathe. The chemotherapy took its terrible toll – nausea, hair loss, frailty. He spoke to us about his wishes. Kath would stay on the farm as long as she wanted, but when it was sold, a portion of the proceeds would go to his kids. He spoke to me about his collection of *Australian Motorsport* magazines which were in a tin trunk in his shed. He'd been a subscriber since the magazine's first edition and remembered how interested I'd been in them as a child.

Through the fifties, as each month's book arrived in the post, he'd call me to his side and we'd study the pages together. He'd tell me about new models, better motors, new speeds achieved. He wanted me to have these books. He knew I'd value them.

Dale took Dad fishing in his last months. Kath invited us over for Sunday lunches. We had them in for meals. It was heartbreaking to see my dad grow so prematurely old and weak. He'd been such a fit man – a gymnast in his younger days, a golfer more recently. It was a hard year, nineteen eighty-five.

Carol and John's son, Geoff, had joined the Air Force. He was to holiday with Carol's brother and family in Sydney for a week while on leave, and asked Linc if he'd like to come with him. Linc accepted in a heartbeat. With hay season finished, he was ready for a break. He met Geoff in Geelong. The two of them, with another of Geoff's Air Force mates, went to the movies the night before they were to leave for Sydney. After the film, they were walking down the mall on their way back to Geoff's car when a group of seven or eight roughnecks approached them from behind and began to harass them.

'Run!' said Geoff suddenly.

He and the other lad took off. Linc considered this a drastic step. You don't run from a mad dog, he reasoned to himself, and continued to walk.

'What're ya lookin' at?' one of the gang taunted.

'Nothing mate,' replied Linc, 'I'm not doing you any harm.'

They began to circle Linc and as they walked, one of them put his foot out. Linc tripped over it and as he went down he was kicked in the head. Dazed, he tried to get up, but it was too late. The assailant kicked him again – in the stomach, in the head, stomach, head. He pulled out a large knife and put it to Linc's throat.

'Give us your money,' he screamed.

Linc fumbled for his wallet, threw it onto the footpath. Another kick to his head. He believed he was going to die there. Then one of the pack pulled the deranged one away from him and yelled, '*Run. Run before he kills you.*'

Only fear for his life could have given Linc the strength to run from this drug-crazed madman, who not only wanted his money but to hurt someone. Geoff and his mate were sitting in the car with the motor running as Linc crashed towards them. They helped him into the car and sped off.

When Linc phoned next day to tell us what had happened, Warren wanted to drive to Geelong, buy a baseball bat, find the monster who'd assaulted our son and deal with him in a fitting manner. We phoned the Geelong Police Station and told them what had happened. They told us the victim would have to come in and report it but Linc just wanted to put it behind him. He didn't want to spend his short holiday with police, looking for a madman.

He should have gone to hospital. He must have suffered severe shock. He could have sustained a brain injury. We should have gone to bring him home. Even now, so many years later, the "should haves" haunt me.

After Linc's call to tell us of the assault, I fell into a chair. For days I was so wiped out with a terror that felt as if it had happened to me, that I could barely get out of my chair. My sleep each night was filled with nightmares. How could anyone wilfully hurt such a beautiful person – my kind, loving, sensitive, hardworking son? The questions just kept going round and round in my head. I was beaten, not only by this monstrous act, but also the knowledge that I was about to lose my father. I knew I'd recover, in time, but for now it seemed I'd lost every ounce of physical and mental strength.

Although most of the swelling had gone down by the time Linc returned home two weeks later, his face and eyes were still purple and yellow with subsiding bruises. It was a miracle he didn't die.

'You wouldn't have wanted to see me, Mum,' he said.

I ached even more at these words.

The trauma stayed with him for a long time – especially when in the city with friends at night. He'd start at any movement from behind, mistrusting strangers. He was only sixteen but already I could see the etchings of adult pain in his eyes.

Ben was one of Linc's best mates and cared deeply about what had happened to our son. With him spending quite a bit of time at our place, Marlo began to chum up with him. Ben was a sincere young seventeen year old and although Marlo was still only fifteen, we trusted him to take care of her. However she wasn't his alone. He had to share our daughter with an older man.

Marlo had discovered the music and art of David Bowie. She saved her pocket money to buy his music. Posters of him covered every square inch of her bedroom walls, ceiling, doors. She had scrapbooks of articles about him. Everyone at her school knew of her infatuation and most mornings there'd be students waiting for her at the gate with clippings from papers and magazines. I think they loved her ecstatic reactions. A friend, Rochelle, shared her obsession. One weekend they made a life-sized cardboard mannequin of Bowie – his face cut from a poster. It stood in the corner of Marlo's bedroom for the next two or three years and frightened the living daylights out of me each time I passed the doorway.

Marlo got a part-time job at the local supermarket, after school and on weekends, and so her music collection grew. She and Rochelle heard that Bowie was coming to Australia – part of his Glass Spider Tour, but he wouldn't be coming to Adelaide. Marlo explained to us that they absolutely needed to go to Melbourne to see him. We worked out that this concert would be just a few days before the start of her Year Eleven exams, and so with the best of reasoning we said no. I don't know why we bothered. She had to go. Just as I've had to go to each of Bob Dylan's Adelaide concerts.

'I'll pay for my own ticket and airfare,' she pleaded, 'and I promise I'll have everything ready for my exams before I go.'

Warren and I talked it over and then spoke to Rochelle's mother, Yvonne. Rochelle would be sitting her Year Twelve exams. One of my philosophies as a mother of teenagers was "Kids have to do what kids have to do", and this was one of those things. Yvonne and I would go with the girls and see them safely to the concert. Marlo and Rochelle were at fever pitch. Rochelle had a small car of her own and the two of them drove to Adelaide next day to buy their tickets. When they walked into our kitchen after their trip to the city, the girls looked as cheeky and as happy as a pair of Kewpie dolls.

'Mum, we've bought our tickets,' said Marlo. She paused. Then, 'To all three concerts!'

I shook my head. Marlo looked at me with eyebrows raised and a bottled explosion of excitement building. She caught the hint of a smile on my face and threw herself into my arms. How could we stand in the way of something that was bringing her so much joy? We trusted the obsession would eventually die a natural death. Many people found it hard to believe that we encouraged our daughter through all of this, but to this day, Marlo thanks us for our never-ending support, and for helping her open the necessary doors to her creativity and future.

In May of nineteen eighty-six, we were down at Kiah for seeding. We had some virgin country ready for new pasture, and as it was school holidays we'd have three uninterrupted weeks to get the job done. Before leaving for the farm, we called in to see Dad who was in hospital having more chemo. He looked so ill. Warren and I sat at his bedside. I held his hand, aching with the knowledge that he had only a few months left now. He'd been such a special dad. We all felt loved by him and knew that he was proud of us all. He'd taught us so much – good values and principles – and he'd been so clever. With his patient hands he'd crafted countless interesting things that we'd have in remembrance of his skills – keepsakes for generations. Having left school at the age of thirteen, he'd spent his life educating himself in many fields.

Dad would be sixty-two at the end of May and I'd been trying to think of what to give him for this, his last birthday. A letter, I thought. Over a period of several days at the farm, I wrote about his life and the father he'd been to me. Memories flooded back.

~

In June, nineteen forty-nine, my sister Erica had been born. In those days, maternity confinement usually meant a week in hospital. Dad had to work and so the night after Erica was born, he took me to stay with my Aunty Bet and Uncle Ken – Mum's sister and her husband, in Adelaide. We didn't have a car at the time, so Dad dressed me in my little winter dress and coat, my own soft leather helmet, and placed me securely in the sidecar of his motorbike – a tonneau cover clipped over to keep me safe. I was two and a half. Although I could see that my dad wasn't far away, I remember being a little fearful as we set out into the cold, dark night. Usually by now I was nestled between my parents in front of the fire – listening to their music and nodding off. However, on this night, with the purr of the four-stroke engine for comfort, I soon became preoccupied with the whole star-filled sky that seemed to be moving with us.

When we reached the city, I was handed into the care of my aunt and uncle, and although tucked into bed with their songs and stories, I longed for my parents' brand of loving. A week later, Dad came to collect me.

'Come on,' he said as he lifted me out of the sidecar when we got back home. 'Let's come and see your beautiful little sister.'

Until I was about twelve, I was often at Dad's side. Always interested in what he was assembling or repairing in his shed, I was intrigued with the orderliness of everything – the rows of spark-plug tins, each one labelled and full of small useful things, spanners and wrenches graded neatly from smallest to largest, aesthetically shaped oil cans and the gluggy sound they made as Dad put oil where oil should be.

One day he'd been making fishing sinkers from molten lead and had turned them out of the mould to cool. When I came into the shed he wasn't there. I spotted this row of wonderful silvery white little pyramids. I picked one up. The pain was unbelievable. Dad was distraught when he realised what had happened. The burns to my fingers took weeks to heal. There were lessons for us both.

When the Isle of Man motorcycle races were broadcast to Australia via the BBC, Dad would get me up in the wee hours and with our heads close to the small modern Bakelite radio, volume turned low so as not to disturb the rest of the family, we would strain to hear the wavy distant commentary.

Dad's gift for explaining things precisely made everything he told me seem amazing. He'd been a boilermaker and mechanic – his engineering skills highly sought after and valued by a multitude of motorcycle owners who brought their machines to his shed at home.

One winter's night he brought a motor into the fire-warmed house and placed it on bags on the kitchen floor. It must have been an urgent job and Mum must have deemed it far too cold for him to be working in the shed and suggested bringing the job inside. I squatted down beside him, watching him at work and asking countless questions. His answers had fascinating words in them – bendix, gudgeon, crankshaft. I learned that night, how an engine worked, and as an adult have often found that knowledge useful.

~

Dad had taught me so many life skills. When I'd finished the letter, I felt satisfied it would be the best gift.

A couple of nights later we were sitting around the campfire. The kids had been asleep for ages and it was one of those nights when the four of us had sat, largely in silence, watching the fire die down. We saw headlights at the gate and a car approached. It was Fred, our neighbour. There was no small talk.

'Sue, someone called Kath has phoned and needs you to ring her as soon as possible.'

I wasn't ready for this. Warren and I got into our car and followed Fred back to his farmhouse. With trembling fingers I dialled Dad's home phone number. Kath answered, crying. My head and heart reeled. Through her tears Kath was telling me that Dad had passed away, at home with her. Warren held me as the pain erupted.

Early next morning we drove home. Marlo had been holidaying with Mum on Kangaroo Island. I phoned to tell them but when Mum picked up the phone, she said, 'I know.'

'What?' I asked forlornly.

'It's your Dad. He's gone, hasn't he?'

It wasn't a question. I knew no-one else had phoned her.

'How do you know?'

'I had a dream last night, or was it real? Your father came to me and kissed me and said, "At last I understand".'

He died too young. I still miss him. Whenever I hear a sultry sax, he's there.

# TWENTY-FIVE

For Marlo to pursue her dream of becoming an actress, she'd have to study drama. Nuriootpa High School did not cater for it and so, after a lot of research, we enrolled her at Morialta High, in the city. Our friend, Sue (whose barn Mum had lived in) was now living near this school and offered to have our daughter board with her.

It was time for Marlo to leave the comfort of home, friends and all that was dear and familiar to her, but she was her father's daughter and had courage born of her convictions. She just knew she had to take the next necessary step.

Five or six weeks into her first term, I received a phone call from the school's principal. He asked if he could have a word with me when I came to collect Marlo on the following Friday. As I sat in his office, he told me he'd just realised that Marlo wasn't doing enough subjects. She was doing English, Art, Drama, Dance and History.

'She needs a science subject,' he said.

Marlo was beside me. 'But I'm going to be an actress. I don't need science.'

'I'm afraid you do,' said the principal, 'or you won't get your HSC.'

'Okay, I'll do Maths,' she yielded.

She attended few Maths lessons that year.

In December she flew to Sydney to audition for entry into the National Institute for Dramatic Art – NIDA. Her audition went well but she was told that, at sixteen, she was still a little too young. They asked her to come back in twelve months. She then auditioned for admission into the Centre for the Performing Arts in Adelaide to gain an Advanced Diploma in Acting. Three hundred people had already auditioned and they would accept only fifteen. She panicked.

'What if I don't get in?' she agonised to us that night. 'I may not get my Year Twelve Certificate!'

'Mmm,' I said.

A nail-biting week later she received her letter from the CPA. I was with her when she opened it. She was one of the fifteen.

She and Ben parted. Both families were sad about that. We loved Ben. Marlo was now going out with a young drama teacher – not from CPA. They complemented each other artistically and before long were on stages around the city doing what they loved – acting – albeit unpaid. Marlo has had an incredibly interesting life, which I'm sure she'll write about one day as she's a gifted writer as well as actor.

I was nervous about her going out into the world now. She was no longer boarding with Sue but flatting with a girlfriend, having to look after herself. I was afraid she wouldn't know how to cook, keep house, manage money. She wasn't streetwise. So when she came home on the weekends, I was trying to prepare her for her new independent life. It was a "leaving the nest" disaster of immense proportions. We fought, just as my mum and I had done when I was that age. Marlo had had enough of my concerns and was ready to "set sail". The weekends she came home were fewer. I grieved for her, and for the vitality with which she and her beautiful friends had filled our home.

I consider myself a reasonably intelligent person but it took Warren's "reading me the riot act" before I could see that I had to let my daughter go, make inevitable mistakes and suffer the consequences.

Prior to Linc's leaving school, Warren had believed our son would not be a farmer. 'He's going to be arty like his mother,' he'd say to people.

Now here he was at seventeen, having bought his first tractor, working happily with his father and riding motorbikes with him around the country. Warren couldn't have been more chuffed. But while riding with his mates down at Kiah one weekend, our son had an accident. He'd been riding on the back wheel (front off the ground), doing about sixty kilometres an hour when he lost control and left his bike from the rear, landing on his coccyx. He could barely walk. He'd damaged his spine. Our family GP referred him to a specialist. X-rays were taken.

'There's little we can do for him at this time,' said the officious Mister. 'When he's about forty, he'll have to have a fusion.'

'But what about the pain?' asked Linc desperately.

'There'll be medication to help you with that,' replied the disinterested face.

About this time we were invited by our friends, Darryl (Warren's old surfing mate) and his wife Helen, to join them and three other couples on a four-wheel drive trip to Cape York in far North Queensland. It would be over four weeks in July – a good time for us – after seeding and before hay cutting. Linc said he'd like to come with us. Marlo was still at college. We prepared for another remarkable adventure.

Warren decided to tow nothing as the terrain on the Cape would be difficult enough for cars, let alone trailers. We would tent it.

It's a long way from Tanunda to the top of Australia, and Darryl, our expedition leader, knew exactly how far we needed to travel each day. We'd set camp at around four in the afternoon and pull up stakes at eight each morning. The lead would be taken by a different driver each day so that one day in every five we'd enjoy dust free travelling.

One night we were in wild pig country. We'd seen them from our cars that day – huge, black, hairy things with gleaming white tusks – and as we bedded down that evening, I felt more than a little vulnerable in our flimsy tent. In the wee hours, after the fire had died down to embers, we were jolted awake by the sound of wild grunting and things tumbling – the billy up-ended on the hearth stones, a camp table full of stuff knocked over. Two of the guys rushed out of their tents, yelling and clapping their hands. With squeals of fright, the pigs thudded off into the bush. Disgruntled, they continued to huff and snort around the perimeter of our camp until finally deciding to give up on the place and move on. We carried large eskys full of fruit and vegetables and each night would remove the lids to allow the night air to chill the contents. This was possibly what had attracted them. Had we not had our meat in the car fridges, they might have been more determined to stay.

As we approached Port Douglas, Warren and I told the group what a magnificent spot it was. We were looking forward to revisiting what had been one of our favourite places on our big trip thirteen years earlier. We just couldn't believe our eyes when we saw what had become of the exquisite little town and beach. Tar and cement everywhere, high-rise apartment buildings, the place teeming with holiday-makers. The world had discovered it.

We took the old coast road from there, having prepared ourselves for the challenge of river crossings, crocodiles, and roads washed away by torrential rains. Each of our vehicles had a two-way radio and we remained constantly in touch with each other. One day Warren and I were in the lead. Travelling a section undergoing road works along Cape Tribulation, we rounded a bend to be confronted by a sight I'll never forget. Ahead of us was the steepest, longest road I had ever seen. It went straight up and was so high we couldn't see to the top without leaning forward in our seats. It was covered in loose gravel and large rocks and dropped off drastically at the edges. There were no alternate routes. If we wanted to get to the top of Australia, which was our goal, we had to get up this mountain.

'Oh my God,' I relayed to the group, before dropping the radio and hanging on for the ride of our lives. Adrenalin bristled through my fingertips.

Before we were a third of the way up the hill, we were in first gear – low ratio. Crawling up at snail pace, I stopped breathing each time the car started to slip backwards on loose rocks, but then the tyres would bite in and we'd stay attached to the mountain. Only Warren's skilful driving got us to the top. With all the dirt roads I had negotiated in my life thus far, I would not have tackled this one. We pulled over at the top and got out to watch the other four vehicles crawling up the escarpment – rocking, lurching, slipping. It seemed to take forever and my heart was in my mouth until all had reached us at the safe point. We stood in awe then, each of us looking down at the track we had just conquered. But that was just the beginning. Ahead were roads and river crossings that would have rattled Indiana Jones. From here, rewards for courage were superb – warm and wondrous crystal clear waterholes, running streams and waterfalls where we stopped and swam and washed our clothes.

The banks of the river crossings were steep, slippery and treacherous. At notorious ones, travellers ahead of us would have stopped to watch the sport. On the other side they'd be drinking beer and daring us to come on over. Whenever a vehicle made it across there'd be hearty cheering, and at one crossing even the reverberating bellow of an old brass bugle. On reaching the Wenlock, we stopped to assess it. The river was wide and deep. A couple of our group waded in, trying to find the shallowest way through – testing for holes and boulders. A young lad ahead of us was about to cross when we got there. He told us he'd accepted a dare to drive his two-wheel drive ute to the top of Australia. At first sight of this river, he thought he'd lost the bet, but then with the encouragement of those on the other side, he'd plucked up the courage to give it a go. He'd spent an hour preparing his vehicle before we got there. He'd tied a tarp across the front of his radiator and packed all his gear into the cab and onto the roof. Finally it was time to enter the water. He hadn't gone ten metres when the river lifted his vehicle and began to take it downstream. At this point, six burly spectators jumped into the water and, using all their strength, guided the ute to the other side, albeit off course a little.

We were the last of our group to cross. At midstream we discovered we had a cracked distributor. Our Range Rover stalled. The river flowed through the car up to our seats. We had to get across quickly, so Warren kept turning the key in the ignition to swing the motor over. The car stuttered and laboured, inch by inch, until we reached the other side. We opened the doors and although most of the water rushed out, the carpets were saturated and reeked with growing mould for the rest of the trip.

After seventeen days, we reached our "Everest" – the top of Australia. There'd been flat tyres, broken windows, mechanical problems, vehicles anchored on unforgiving river banks and stuck on sandy beaches. But we had overcome it all and stood now in this most northerly spot, staring out over the Coral Sea to Thursday Island and beyond. There was no ceremony. Most of us were silent, each with our own thoughts, as if farewelling a friend at a funeral. It was over. Done. We returned to our cars and headed for home.

The return trip would be quicker through the inland, but before we left the coast we spent two idyllic rest days in Karumba. The weather was glorious, sand dazzling, sea deep blue and sparkling. We swam, slept, fished and washed our clothes. Around a beach campfire each night, we consumed our fill of freshly caught and cooked barramundi.

While Linc had enjoyed the trip immensely, he'd been in constant pain. Although three of our group were chiropractors, he hadn't wanted to bother them with his predicament. However one of them, Errol, noticed our son's extreme spasm. It was serious, he said, and needed specialist care. He recommended traction as soon as we returned.

It took us another eight days to get home and by then Linc knew that hay baling for that year would be out of the question. Sitting in a bouncing tractor for twelve to eighteen hours a day would be unbearable and impossible.

The day after we got back he began physiotherapy, traction and exercise, but now had to look for work that he could manage through his pain.

One day while driving to Nuriootpa, our neighbouring town, I had an urge to leave the highway and drive down a little no-through road. At the end of this lane was a pottery I didn't know existed. Attached to it was a studio and exquisitely laid out gallery, full of unique and classy pieces. The location and garden were divine. I was surrounded by beauty. A girl came into the gallery from the studio – her hands covered in clay. An earth mother. She introduced herself as Janie. She and her husband

Rob had established the business a couple of years earlier. I felt an instant rapport and asked if they needed help.

'We do actually,' said Janie. 'Why do you ask?'

'My son's looking for work,' I told her.

'Well tell him to come in and we'll have a chat,' she said encouragingly.

It was as if we both knew in that moment that this was predestined. Linc started work there two days later. It was only then that Warren told us that his maternal grandfather had been a potter at Bennetts Magill Pottery for most of his life. I remembered that some of my ancestors too, on my father's side, had been potters in Burslem, Staffordshire in the early eighteen hundreds.

Linc was to have a rich two year association with Rob and Janie Maere at their lovely creative haven. He cycled to work each day, continued his exercises, the traction, and had some Raiki done. Linc felt it was the Raiki more than anything that helped his back which, within twelve months, was almost completely healed.

## TWENTY-SIX

In nineteen eighty-nine we came face to face with an insidious enemy – rising interest rates. The money we'd borrowed at eleven percent to develop Kiah, was now costing us nineteen percent, and as we found it harder and harder to make our payments, the rates went even higher with penalties. Soon we were paying twenty-one percent and our debt started to grow like a cancer. It was impossible to make enough from this farm to cover these costs. We were hanging by our fingernails and losing grip.

Our kids had grown up here, learned amazing skills. We'd loved the years together with our friends, but the bank was beating us down.

The farm sold quickly. I wasn't prepared for the pain. Our machinery was loaded and returned to the Barossa. Sheep that had been so well cared for were sold and some dispersed to other pastures. Kids' possessions were retrieved from beloved cubbies, outdoor cooking utensils packed in boxes, caravans hooked up and the campfire of a thousand stories doused.

With the sale we cleared the debt. I'd found the financial struggle that year debilitating – my first taste of the fear of losing ground. An event that brightened my days though was the arrival of Jerry Hubner in Tanunda. Jerry opened a new and ultra-chic hairdressing salon in town. A descendant of the

Indonesian royal family, he'd spent his childhood in Amsterdam and has had a truly amazing life journey – the truth of it stranger than fiction. Jerry and his older brother came to Australia when they were twelve and fifteen – without their parents. They lived in tough migrant accommodation and it wasn't long before Jerry was at home on the streets, making his way in a hard, racist world. In his words, 'Australia had finished with the "wogs" and "dagoes" and now it was our turn.' He determined to learn to speak English without trace of an accent. I can say he achieved this to perfection. By the time Jerry's parents came to live in Australia two years later, he had been in and out of boys' reformatories and had forged a persona that would keep him safe in the harsh world he'd found himself in. He refused to be a victim. In his words again, 'I marched through enemy lines and have continued all my life to walk through that door of fear.'

He was a person of immense character and we became great friends. He and Warren wind each other up delightfully when they share stories of their boyhoods.

Dreadlocked and well-tattooed, Jerry was taken to heart by all his clients. For a largely conservative community, this said a lot about Jerry. It didn't take us long to realise that he was a man of generous spirit, had more than his share of wisdom, and held a sincere interest in the lives of all those who sat in his chair. He was the single parent with sole custody of three small children, and many were the times he and I sat on his office step after a haircut, talking about our kids and the curiosities and wonders of life.

For the next two years Warren continued his hay baling, ran sheep in the hills and share-farmed. However, he was missing his son as a workmate and had begun to feel he was stuck on a contracting roundabout. The long hours were taxing, leaving little time for his family, and any profit we made just seemed to disappear into machinery replacement, repairs and maintenance. After a particularly long stint in the hayfields he came in one day with a new light in his eyes.

'I've just been talking to Lance (the neighbour whose hills property we had bought in our youth). He tells me there's a good block of land for sale at Eden Valley.'

'Is he buying it?' I asked.

'No, I don't think so. He said it doesn't suit him. Want to come and have a look?'

'Yep,' I replied.

I dropped what I was doing and off we went. Something came over us as we drove through the gate of that property. We recognise that feeling when we get it now. It means "We will be here". It was time to make another move towards Warren's dream.

We drove around and walked some of it. Next day Warren went out on his motorbike to have a better look. The vendor, a farmer from the west coast who was in trouble over drought, needed to sell it quickly. The price was appealing and so we began to think about how we could raise enough money to get into this grazing and cropping block of a thousand acres. Perhaps relinquish some of our hills country. The dream was still very much alive in Warren. We went to see our friends Ian and Nat and asked if they'd be interested in purchasing one of our small blocks. They were. Within three weeks it was theirs. Grant Burge was a neighbour and had been buying property in the hills for a while. Like Warren, he loved sheep work – found it a relaxing diversion from his winemaking. As most of our sheep would be over on this new farm if we bought it, we'd no longer need our shearing shed block, so we offered it to Grant. It would suit his enterprise perfectly, he said. He paid us our asking price. We'd raised fifty percent of the purchase price and the bank lent us the rest.

We settled in May. There'd been good opening rains and we had to move quickly to get crops in that year. Warren began cultivating some of the arable land but the rain was constant and the country was becoming saturated. We'd taken our caravan out there, and at about eight o'clock one night, Warren came back to the van on foot from where he'd been trying to plough – a couple of kilometres away.

'I'm bogged,' he said. 'I need you to come and pull me out.'

We drove back to the shed, fired up the other tractor – the Zetor – and drove out to the paddock. Warren hooked a chain between the two tractors and asked if I would prefer to tow or be towed.

'I'll do the towing,' I said.

He climbed into the tractor that was bogged. I climbed into the Zetor and slowly and carefully managed to pull him out. The ground was becoming a quagmire.

'You'd better stay with me and see how we go,' shouted Warren over the noise of the machinery and the teeming rain.

I climbed into his tractor with him. By now a storm was in full rage. Lightning slashed across the sky. Thunder made speaking and hearing impossible. We soon became bogged again. Warren left me in the Fendt tractor and headed back for the Zetor. I watched him disappearing into the black night, sinking to his ankles in mud. A bolt of lightning lit the area like a football stadium and for a second I saw him again – blurred with rain. I sat in the cab for fifteen minutes, wondering if he'd be able to shift the Zetor from where we'd left it, then I saw his scribbled headlights in the rear mirror and we hooked up again. With my jacket over my head, I squelched through mud and climbed back into the Zetor. As I accelerated, the tractor groaned with the task. It rocked and bounced, and the wheels began to spin and sink. With the heel of my hand bumping the accelerator lever I upped the revs until finally I felt the tractor behind me yield. Like Captain Ahab going after Moby Dick, Warren kept this up for the next few hours, with me at his side, until the paddock was finished.

Once seeding was completed, we had time to explore the place. It was beautiful. Along the three kilometre eastern boundary was an old stone wall, built across the top of a rocky range that looked like a mini Flinders Ranges. Amongst huge moss rocks, she-oaks leaned away from the prevailing winds and wailed like ghosts with the slightest breeze. We walked and climbed to the northern boundary where we looked down in awe on the River Marne – moving like a massive, shining sci-fi serpent along its rocky bed. It took our breath away. We'd seen none of this before we bought it. We clambered down the escarpment and sat down without speaking, on smoothed pebbles underneath an ancient river red gum. Kookaburras laughed. Swallows and large insects darted over the water. A pair of kangaroos and their joey grazed high up on the rock face. Something that felt like contentment wrapped us together for this little while.

As our ears became accustomed to the sounds of the pristine environment, we heard rushing water. We followed the river in what must have looked like a comedic choreography, over stones – some slippery, some jagged. Sometimes fallen trees bridged deeper waters and we negotiated these cautiously. The sound of rushing water got louder. We rounded a bend to see a spectacular gorge and waterfall. Red gums had wedged themselves amongst huge rocks. Banksias, acacias and grasses softened the banks. Magpies shared their place with us. Aborigines had lived and hunted here. My brother Dale, who'd become an archaeologist, would later discover some of their rock art on the property. With the help of colleagues, he organised a dig where they discovered fireplaces and artefacts thousands of years old.

Warren and I have always loved to share our properties with family and friends, and so it was with this one, which we named Birribi. We'd parked our caravan in one of the most accessible and beautiful spots. Our daughter spent an afternoon with us there and left that evening.

>Marlo and Jep dog drove away
>into her still new adulthood
>leaving me showered with her little girl loving
>and the memory of her tired but happy face
>
>I sit here as the day fades
>A crisp breeze teases the back of my neck
>and ruffles my hair
>Stirs the campfire into a friendly rage
>
>The new heat burns my face
>and the smell of smoke
>evokes the days of old farm gatherings
>
>The big old gum tree skeleton
>silhouettes with twilight
>Crows and magpies
>cockatoos
>sit way up high on it and wonder down at me
>
>The hills
>just over there
>are glowing with the setting sun
>and for a breath
>the trunks of big gums white as snow

The beer is wholesome
Bird noise teeming
Without this night song there would only be
a wind hush through the grasses

Soon
simply the hush
and the cracking of the fire

Suddenly a shower of darkened late galahs
screech across the deepest blue
of coming night
and now the mighty hillside rocks
divulge their shapes
The evening light has brought them close
and for a trice I think I hear the ghostly chatter
of the tribe that lived and roamed around here long ago
and I am one of them.

Warren's Uncle Ray – father of his cousin Rob who'd drowned in the Murray – had spent some time with us at Kiah, and now he felt a need to be with us at this farm too. Trying to deal with his grief, he'd kept busy. He enjoyed helping Warren with projects as he'd done for Rob before he died. Tragically, he and Aunty Gwen had become estranged from Rob's wife Wendy and her two daughters. The loss of their adored grandchildren as well as their son, had almost undone them. Their other son, Mostyn, was living in Brazil – working as a teacher. Aunty Gwen and Uncle Ray had visited him there, and from time to time he'd come home to Adelaide. A caring and sensitive man, he wrote to his parents often. They treasured his well-written letters and often shared them with us. He was now the only family they had. One day they received a call from the Australian Embassy in Rio. Mostyn had been murdered. Each year as they came with their broken hearts to our Christmas gatherings, they'd look so utterly alone and overwrought with grief that my heart ached for them.

As Uncle Ray worked with us at Birribi, although he did his best to be cheerful, I knew his soul was shattered.

The purchase of this property had brought a new chapter in our lives. Farming at our beloved Kiah was behind us and although we missed that place, we appreciated the extra time we'd gained in not having to travel there.

Warren had become a member of the Red Wine Club – invited by long-time friend Malcolm who'd bought the first portion of our hills land to plant vineyards. We spent many good times with Malcolm and his wife Jennie. As Warren and I had been in their bridal party, the four of us celebrated their wedding anniversary together each year. Malcolm planned everything well ahead, and at each anniversary dinner he'd talk about his plans for the next one. There'd always be some new posh restaurant on the agenda. They loved to entertain in their grand family homestead. A magnificent single span dining table had been in the house for a hundred years. It could seat twenty, and often did.

Warren and Malcolm went to the monthly Red Wine Club meetings together. After a meal and wine tasting, they'd come back to our place for a coffee and chat. Malcolm was doing well. In partnership with several other businessmen, he'd purchased a prestigious property in the Barossa Ranges – Corryton Park – and was impassioned with ideas for its future. He'd shown us over the estate – magnificent with huge old English trees and manicured gardens. Scattered beyond the hundred year old two-storey mansion were beautiful stone out-buildings – shearing shed and quarters, blacksmith's shop, stables, manager's residence, workmen's cottages.

For Malcolm, everything was poised for success, except that an associate in the syndicate had reneged on an agreement to repay a large sum of money that Malcolm had lent him. It was more than twelve months overdue. Early one morning as Malcolm left his house as exuberant about his day as ever, he asked Jennie to pack him some lunch.

'I'll be back to pick it up around eleven,' he told her.

By mid-afternoon he hadn't been back to collect the lunch and Jennie had became concerned.

Jennie's mother, Miriam, phoned me next day. Her voice was telling me something I couldn't believe. Malcolm had drowned in the property's huge dam.

Trying to deal with the shock of what I was hearing, I already felt an overwhelming sadness. And how was I going to tell Warren that we had lost yet another friend?

With my head reeling, I went down to the shed where Warren was working. As I told him all that Miriam had told me, the colour drained from his face.

Jennie had gone to look for Malcolm and found his car near the dam. She'd called the police who, after searching the estate, arranged for an aqualung squad to come and delve the murky body of water. Within an hour they found his body.

Malcolm couldn't swim and had held a fear of dams since seeing a close friend drown in one years earlier.

Jennie and her three girls were inconsolable. Their loving, energetic, enterprising husband and father was dead. We went to be with them that day. In a state of shock, pain and disbelief, Jennie could barely function and so we just helped make food and drinks for the flow of people who came to either deal with formalities or simply offer love and support.

There was no suicide note, and Warren and I have never believed it was that. Malcolm was too high on life. But whether or not it was truly an accident remains a mystery.

We didn't talk about how these untimely deaths – Dad's, Rob's, Jack's, Mostyn's and now Malcolm's, had affected us. We just knew we had to find courage to deal with it all. But a deep sadness and sense of loss was upon us.

# TWENTY-SEVEN

Lincoln was about to establish his own business. He was almost twenty-one. With exercise, physiotherapy, Raiki and a powerful belief that he would be healed, his spine was almost back to normal and he was champing at the bit to get back into tractors, even though he'd relished his time as a potter. Over a coffee one morning he said to us, 'How do you think Papa would feel if I offered to share-farm the vineyard?'

It took Warren completely by surprise.

'He'd be tickled pink,' he said in a voice I hardly knew.

That Warren himself had not been able to find the passion for growing grapes had troubled him at times, and I knew he believed in family traditions. In a flash we realised it would be our son who would step up to take the vigneron's baton. Warren would have been just as happy to have Linc join us in our business, but from experience he knew how important it was to support our kids in their life choices.

Marlo was excelling at her studies and we were privileged to be treated to a constant flow of quality theatre at the Centre for the Performing Arts in Adelaide. Our daughter was a gifted actor and worked diligently at honing her skills.

During this year, my dad's surviving partner, Kath, decided to sell the farm they'd bought together. When all had settled, I used my inheritance money to buy more sheep for our new property.

In our first year at Birribi, the crops yielded well and so too the wool which was bringing a premium price. Our bank manager said to us, 'If you keep going like this, you'll have a tax problem.'

With our constant mortgages, interest rate increases and business expansion, we'd never had one of those and were delighted at the prospect! We were filled with optimism, until the day we heard a news bulletin on the ABC's Country Hour. The price of wool had crashed. The previous year China had bought no wool from us and with alarming speed Australia's wool had begun to stockpile. It sent prices plummeting by fifty percent. Within twelve months, recovering production costs was difficult. Lamb returns were no better. We'd take a well-finished load of lambs to market and wait anxiously for the agent to phone with the prices.

'Big yarding today,' Gary Nowland would offer. 'Prices were easier.' There'd be a pause. I hated hearing that word "easier". 'Fifty crossbred lambs at ten dollars!'

*Ten dollars? Ten dollars.* It was pathetic. We'd marked, crutched, shorn, drenched, dipped these sheep, fed them, cared for them for almost a year to get ten dollars a head. It was heartbreaking.

Warren decided to grow hay for export. A large fertile flat at Birribi lay waiting for the oats Warren sowed there that year. Good rains pampered the land and a swathe of new green filled us with hope. Farmers love green. At last we'd be able to get our overdraft back in order. At the optimum time, Warren mowed the crop. A few days later, a rep from a hay processing company came to inspect it.

'Top quality hay,' he said. 'You'll be paid a premium. Should be ready to bale in four or five days. It'll go to Japan.'

We were elated.

The next day it began to rain. Not showers. Rain. For three days. By the time the hay dried out, it had lost nutritional value and was no longer of export quality. Our buyer had gone. Potential income from it halved.

We baled it into small squares, but before we could stack them, it rained again. The hay was beginning to blacken – income diminishing daily. After a couple of dry days, we went out to turn the bales – eight thousand of them – by hand. Eventually they dried, but every single one was mouldy. We loaded and stacked them. To sell them then would have been to do so below cost, so Warren began feeding them out to three hundred wethers we'd not been able to sell. There'd been a strike at the docks and the live sheep trade to the Middle East had stalled. Many graziers had insufficient feed to keep their sheep alive while they waited for it to resume, and so the government offered them a dollar a head to shoot and bury their animals. Devastating. We would have found ourselves in the same predicament were it not for this hay, and also about thirty tonnes of lupins we'd harvested that same year. Three times a week I'd drive the ute while Warren trickled out two or three bags of lupins to our stock, who had by now become au fait with the vehicle and would follow us, munching lupins as they ran. Then Warren would throw off twenty or so bales of hay, and we'd leave the flock grazing and growing. It was a gamble. What if we were doing all this and then still unable to sell them?

In October we shore them. Soon afterwards the live sheep trade resumed. It was a huge relief. We sold them for seventeen dollars a head. Still not a lot, but better than shooting them, which would have been soul destroying.

We met our new neighbours John and Maria who lived in a mud brick house they'd built themselves. Daily they planted trees, tended their goats and vegetable garden, made cheese and improved their home. John loved to work. He was Swiss and with a passion for timber, loved building, particularly furniture. He often helped us with jobs, one of which was to convert a large implement shed on our property into a shearing shed with a raised board. A huge project. The raised board would make it easier for the roustabouts to drag the fleeces from waist height rather than having to bend down for each one. The previous year we'd used a neighbour's shed. Roly and Mary Gale, a sociable and generous pair, owned the property across the road from ours and had been happy for us to use their facilities. Warren though, was not completely comfortable with this. Independence has always been vital to him. On the night before our shearing was to begin, the shed was still not finished. Warren, John and I worked till eleven. I went back to the van – two kilometres away, to prepare supper.

'How much longer do you think?' I asked as we later sipped our coffee and admired the wonderful edifice.

'Not long,' said Warren, 'we're nearly there.'

We'd been hanging catching pen doors, pen gates, installing a kitchen and lunch area, and now there were just the two shearing plants to suspend, which was no mean feat. Weighing thirty odd kilos each, they had to be lifted a couple of metres off the floor and held in place while they were bolted onto their posts.

I was ready to call it a day and drove back to the van. Warren came in at three and groaned quietly as he eased his spent body into the bed. He was up again at six, eager for the start of our first shearing at Birribi.

In their early-morning utes, tyres crunching on the newly laid gravel, the shearers slipped quietly into the yard at seven

– ready for another day in yet another shed. Their rowdy late afternoon exits were a different matter.

With wool prices at an all-time low, Warren's dream had stalled. He wasn't obsessed by it or even impatient. There was still time. We were young enough. In our early budgets for this farm we had estimated that our income would knock out our mortgage within a few years. This wasn't looking good now. We have learned over our years of farming, that the predicted rarely matches the reality – either one way or the other.

Through the loss of loved ones and our beloved Kiah, our relationship had grown stronger. And the mettle needed to deal with the disappointments and hardships of farming could only be found in a strong and resilient partnership. I can't say my husband had grown to be calm and patient with day-to-day challenges but I was learning how to handle the squalls.

To test our toughness even further, we inherited a new bank manager who seemed hell bent on our destruction. We'd draw up a budget – as frugal as we could possibly make it, then tell him what overdraft limit we needed to be able to operate for that year. He'd set the limit way below the figure we knew we'd peak at, and predictably we'd reach it two months before our wool was sold. From this point, I'd have to ask the bank teller for cash to buy food each week.

'I'll have to have a word with the manager,' she'd say, as I handed her my cash cheque.

I was deeply humiliated. There were always people I knew in the bank. She'd eventually return to the counter and, as if it was coming from her own purse, she'd hand me the money I needed to feed my family. Forty dollars. I developed debilitating back pain. I couldn't think of anything that might have caused it but then realised it came on each time I walked into that bank.

Eventually we'd be called in to discuss further finance, which was always granted, but only after a line fee of enormous proportions had been charged to extend our overdraft to what we'd told them we needed in the first place.

We'd always worked hard, been as financially careful as one can be in farming, and as we sat in our low chairs opposite this overlord in his high one, he seemed to be attempting to make us feel incompetent and beaten. He didn't know us very well. We were never going to roll over. But I didn't know how to make the stress go away.

An acquaintance of our neighbours, John and Maria, called in to see Warren one afternoon. Warren wasn't at home so Lawry chatted to me for a while. He was in his seventies and had done well for himself. He was interested in our enterprise.

'How much of the vineyard around here is yours?'

'About fifty-five acres,' I told him. 'Grocke family.'

'And how much land do you have at Eden Valley?'

'There's about a thousand out there,' I offered.

'And John tells me you own some land in the ranges too.'

'Yes, we do.'

'How many acres up there?'

'Oh, about two hundred and fifty.'

He was nodding his head with approval, impressed. We were still in our forties.

'Well I'd better be off,' he said then. 'Oh, I see you've got some lemons on your tree. Would you mind if I picked some?'

'Not at all,' I said. 'I'll get you a bag.'

He went to the tree, picked his lemons and came back to the door.

'How much for this bag full?' he asked.

In a flash, I pictured myself in the bank later that day, asking for the money I'd need to buy bread and milk.

'Two dollars,' I said.

He handed me the money and left. The visitor had made me see what we'd achieved, and yet I'd asked for two dollars for something I should have given freely.

Soon after he'd gone, I felt a commotion rising in me – something that was about to disgorge the pain, sadness, injustices and disappointments of a lifetime. I had kept it all in for too long. I leant against the door and expelled the debris with an unholy noise – a weeping – for my father, lost friends, my lost hope.

'God, how has it come to this?' I pleaded through my sobbing.

There was something dreadfully wrong. I didn't care how physically tough farming was. I knew I could meet that, but the financial stress, the lack of understanding and empathy from the bank was so much harder. Being without hope was like being without a soul.

# TWENTY-EIGHT

On a cold night in June we were sitting by the fire watching the news when the phone rang. It was John Welch, the guy who'd joined our grape-picking team back in the seventies, and who'd inspired Warren to do our 'round Oz trip. We hadn't spoken to each other for seventeen years. With one ear on the weather report Warren talked to John, and within sixty seconds had hung up.

'Who was that?' I asked when the bulletin was over.

'John Welch.'

'What did he want?' I asked, curious as to why the conversation had been so short when they hadn't seen each other for so long.

'He's coming over to show me a money-making idea,' said Warren casually, as if it was the most normal thing in the world to offer.

'I bet it's Amway or something like that,' I said disdainfully. 'Phone him back and tell him not to come.'

It was a totally ungrounded conclusion.

'No,' said Warren, nonchalantly. 'It'll be good to catch up with John. See what he's been up to. He just asked if I ever look at ways of making extra money.'

Without doubt, he was talking to the right person. Anything that might create extra income at this time was worth looking at, my husband reasoned. When John arrived, I went into the kitchen to say hello and then returned to my winter fire and television programme. A few minutes into John's presentation, Warren asked him if it was Amway.

'Yes, it is,' said John. 'What do you know about it?'

'Well, Linc was involved a while ago, but it was nothing like this. He was just selling products.'

About four years earlier a mate had approached Linc who, with the open-mindedness of his father, saw it as a way of generating a little more income to support his motorcycle racing.

'This is different,' said Warren, 'I can see it's not about retailing. Do you mind if I ask Linc to sit in?'

'No, not at all,' said John.

Warren came into the lounge.

'Hey Linc, you need to come and have a look at this – it seems interesting. Sue?'

'No,' I said with an inflection, as if to say, "*Are you serious?*"

By the time the presentation was finished, Warren and Linc had seen a concept that had them alight. After John left they tried to explain it to me but my mind was closed. My husband and son were ready to sign up. John and his wife Jenny came back two nights later to do the paperwork. They brought a bottle of champagne. I was furious. This was all going too fast.

'What we need to do next,' said John, 'is have a meeting. Invite as many people as you can and I'll show them the plan. How about Thursday night?'

I sensed Warren was beginning to feel uneasy knowing he had me to contend with, but Linc said, 'Okay. I'll have a few here.'

Warren's competitive nature kicked in and, not to be outdone by his son, he invited a few as well. On that following Thursday night our house was full of people. I went to bed early – angry and upset at the invasion. Next day Warren and I began to argue.

'But you're just being stubborn, Sue. Trust me, this is a great idea. Just listen to this tape. It's by a woman who felt exactly the same as you do, in the beginning, and now she and her husband are highly successful in the business. They're vets.'

'I don't want anything to do with it,' I insisted.

The following Saturday, Linc and Warren went to a function in Adelaide. They left around midday and returned at eleven that night.

'Have you been at that meeting all this time?'

'Yes, there were so many speakers. It was amazing,' said Warren, eyes alight.

I wanted to stop them before they got too involved and one afternoon Warren and I had the mother of all rows. He packed a bag and left.

He didn't come back that night. I guessed he'd be at the farm, but he hadn't taken any food and there wasn't much in the van, so I felt sure he'd be back next day. He wasn't.

Marlo had been home for the weekend and was driving back to town that night in her VW Beetle – first time driving alone on her P plates. It was mid-winter and a storm was raging – thunder, lightning, torrential rain, gale-force winds. I needed to know that my daughter had arrived back in town safely. No mobile phones. At ten the phone rang.

'It was scary, Mum, but I'm home safe and sound.'

I was relieved to hear her voice. One down, one to go. I packed some food and drove out to the farm.

The weather was still violent – the road into our caravan site slippery, boggy and difficult to pick out. There were tracks criss-crossing over the property and before long I couldn't be sure I was on the right one. I was charged with fear – of the storm, but also for Warren's safety. My headlights finally picked up the caravan off in the distance. It looked formidably dark and unoccupied, but as I got closer I could see Warren's ute. As I opened the door of the van, I could see and sense my husband's spent shape in our bed. He was safe. Our daughter was safe. I was safe.

I couldn't switch on the light as there was no electricity without the generator, so I just climbed into bed beside my husband. We held each other without speaking and I knew he had made up his mind to build this business. Nothing I could do or say would stop him.

He began to phone people. Some of the first were Tanunda neighbours, Peter and Wendy. Peter said, 'I don't really understand what you're trying to tell me, Warren, but you're so excited you must be onto something, and we don't want to miss out.'

It was an encouraging start for Warren, and once I'd calmed down and opened my mind, I could see it was a simple and fair concept. The early Amway had earned a bad reputation from people scrambling over each other to make money. This new networking precluded that. In fact, in this system the only way to make money was to help others first. What we were setting out to do was to build a business that would provide us and anyone we introduced with an ongoing, passive income.

There were monthly seminars and, two or three times a year, major events in Melbourne's Tennis Centre. It was in this environment at this time that I conquered an old fear. Through the books I was reading and the encouragement of my peers, I became comfortable with public speaking. I could speak to a room of thousands.

We made some great friends – doctors, winemakers, teachers, builders, students, labourers, farmers in abundance – people from all walks. We learned how to determine exactly what we wanted from life, how to set small goals that led to bigger goals and achieve them. We were encouraged to think about the repercussions of being unable to work for any length of time, the prospects of retirement. How did we picture ours?

We began to dream of world travel which had seemed totally out of reach till now. But our main goals were to earn enough money to never again worry about how we were going to pay our bills, to be able to replace our car when it needed replacing, to maintain our home, have medical and dental costs covered. And we dreamed of helping our family. In reality, Warren wasn't interested in retirement. To have the money to be able to farm the way he wanted to farm was a priority for him. This would include a more organic way of producing lamb, grain and wool.

In the twelve years that we would be actively involved in this multi-level marketing company, we would develop business and communication skills that we could not put a value on.

Mum had gone to Kangaroo Island to live, to try to heal her body of cancer. Always the nurturer, she had, for years, been offering love and support to a raft of friends and acquaintances in various states of crisis. She'd been a shoulder to cry on, a listening ear. It was time now for her to focus on her own healing. She refused chemotherapy, believing that a quiet meditative life by the sea would have an equal or better result. It did.

She project-managed the construction of a beautiful cottage twenty metres from the beach. Sandy, although still working on the mainland, went to the island to help her whenever he could. Together they carted large pre-Cambrian rocks up a steep escarpment in a wheelbarrow – one pushing, the other pulling

– to be used in the building of an open fireplace and chimney. Mum lived there, largely in reclusion, for six years. She allowed only a couple of people into her life and these became close friends. She walked the beaches collecting shells and exquisitely coloured seaweeds and created unique works of art with them. She established garden rooms in the surrounding bush, read, wrote, gathered native herbage for her salads, and caught and ate fresh fish as often as she could. Fairy penguins, echidna, goanna, possums, snakes and sea eagles knew and trusted her. Finally there was no trace of cancer in her body. It was a miracle.

She'd been on the mainland staying with us for a few days and listening to our talk about the new business. She was sixty-four. Linc said, 'I need to book a meeting for tonight but I don't know who to contact.'

Mum said, 'What about me?'

We looked at her in amazement.

'Can I get in?' she said. 'You all seem so excited. I think I'm ready for a new venture.'

She was soon greatly admired and loved by all our friends and associates in the business. It was wonderful to have her with us on the enriching journey it grew to be.

We made some trips to the island to help get her business started, and it kicked off well. But it wasn't long before she was enjoying the functions and fellowship with family and like-minded people so much that she returned to the mainland to live. Mum, at heart, is a social butterfly and had been a hermit long enough.

# TWENTY-NINE

I have always enjoyed meeting new people, and the day I met Sabine Deisen was no exception. As we shook hands she told me the colour I was wearing looked terrible on me. Yellow. She was absolutely right, and we hit it off immediately. Sabine was an artist and a week or two later invited me to her character-filled cottage studio on acreage in the Valley. I loved her unique art – vibrant colours and a naivety reminiscent of the Fauves, Matisse and Dufy, whose work had always inspired me. Her home was full of stunningly beautiful things – pots, bowls, rugs, flowers, and many of her own paintings. She'd painted the flag-stone floor of her studio – an intricate mosaic of something enigmatic she'd been thinking about at the time. It had taken her months. There was not an ordinary thing in her home, or about her. Everything was art.

Among her friends were those of the feathered kind – chickens, ducks, geese – some of whom lived in the cottage with her. It was not unusual for a hen with chicks to be wandering through her house at any time.

It's a wonderful thing to find a kindred spirit with whom your artistic thoughts and ideas can be heard aloud. Sabine loved jazz and played the drums, and one day asked me to come and sing. Another of her friends, Patsy, played the piano – a lovely antique instrument that stood in the studio against an old stone wall with a small casement window. A picture in itself. Before the session began, Sabine brought out a bottle of good Riesling and an aged cheese. I never drank an ordinary wine at Sabine's. In more recent times she's added another string to her bow – planted a vineyard of Shiraz and become an artisan winemaker.

The music became a regular thing, and as we interpreted the jazz standards that we loved, I was in another world. For two or three hours each week I'd sing my heart out. Sometimes another of Sabine's friends, Garth, would sit in and play some melancholy sax. However, after a year or two, we hit a wall. The next step would have been to get with people further along and spend more time with the music. None of us had that time. The sessions became less and less frequent and finally ceased altogether. But it had been another rich jaunt for me into my beloved world of art.

Marlo had completed her studies at the Centre for Performing Arts, graduating in nineteen ninety-one. We'd been highly impressed with the quality of her education there. The lecturers had been brilliant and the courageous productions we'd seen, outstanding. On top of her full-time study, Marlo had always worked weekends. Apart from our paying her rent, she'd been completely self-funded. We were proud of her work ethic, her drive and determination.

Linc's passion for the vineyard was growing and he was eager to develop it further. After establishing a contract with one of the big wineries, he planted ten acres of Chardonnay – a popular variety at the time. Also, there was an eleven acre piece of land adjoining our homestead property which Warren had always used for cropping and grazing. Twelve months after planting the Chardonnay, Linc said to us, 'I'd love to plant Cabernet Sauvignon on that eleven acres. How would you feel about that?'

A vineyard would produce more income for Linc than we could get from grazing it, and we were chuffed at his enthusiasm and ambition. So the planting began. Linc, Warren and Otto – three generations working together now. Although we all guessed that Otto was over the moon, nothing to that effect was imparted.

As Linc's knowledge of new practises grew, there was the odd (civilised) locking of horns as Linc tried to convince his Papa of their virtues. Otto, although he'd been an innovator in his younger days, seemed loath now to adopt changes that seemed radical to him.

Linc spent a good deal of time and money on the vineyard. Grape prices were good. The fruit was still being hand-picked by a lovely and faithful team of locals. It was hard work but the tradition had always been to make it fun with lively chatter, jokes and pranks. The camaraderie throughout vintage was something unique. Teams would pick up conversations and friendships where they'd left off the year before. It had happened this way in the Valley for more than a hundred years.

Sadly, this is now a thing of the treasured past. Where once colourful hats bobbed above the vines by day, now enormous machines, lit up like sci-fi monsters, move through the rows by night. And the teams are machine operators dressed in high-vis work wear, carrying two-way radios instead of snips.

In our own farming enterprise we were having to think creatively to compensate for the current low commodity prices. Our baling plant had done a lot of work and so Warren considered it wise now to sell it, with the business. An associate in the industry had shown an interest and so we offered it to him for a fair price. It didn't take long for the deal to be effected and with the proceeds we bought eighty yearling steers to put on Birribi. The property was now fully stocked, along with the sheep.

After opening rains, it was time to sow our next crops. I had to tow the cultivator from Tanunda to Birribi – a forty kilometre trip. These excursions always worried me because of the width of the implements on the narrow country roads. On this day all was going well until I reached the old wooden bridge that crossed the River Marne, about two kilometres from our farm gate. I pulled up, stepped out the width of the cultivator, then the width of the bridge. There were three or four inches to spare on either side. The railing had long gone, and the river was deep and flowing swiftly. With heart pounding, I inched over the bridge at snail pace, trying to keep the implement dead straight. Any squiggle would have put it over the edge and probably me with it. When I hit solid ground on the other side, I thanked the Lord once more for keeping me safe.

Warren taught me how to cultivate – how to keep the rows straight, to avoid hitting stumps and rocks, and how to handle the corners. He then went off to seed another paddock while, by trial and error, I worked at gaining another skill.

Each autumn or early winter, we'd spend a day or two cutting wood for our two open fires at home. With so much fallen timber on the property, we discussed the prospect of selling some. We began advertising, and before long our dry, solid firewood was in high demand.

It was good for the soul being out in the bush at this time of year. The only interruption to the exquisite silence was the bird-call ringing through the still, damp air. Delicate new grass dressed the landscape in softest green as it pushed through the dry straw of summer. Sometimes we found mushrooms.

Shattering the silence with the chainsaw, Warren would cut logs – some of enormous diameter – into lengths, and then chop each round into pieces. My job was to throw it all onto the ute and trailer.

Instead of selling the hay we grew that year, we fed it to the cattle – value adding as beef prices were heading north. We hoped to sell the steers in twelve months for double the price we'd paid for them. Over that next year we fed and nurtured the herd, brought them in for drenching and tagging. I was very small amongst them, and always ready to jump the fence if any should become cranky. At last they were prime and ready for market. But just then, the price of beef dropped like a stone.

'Ok,' a little voice inside me sang sardonically, 'we'll wait for the market to recover. It's just a glitch.'

But the price continued to fall, and before long our herd was worth no more than we'd paid for it. In fear of further grief, we had to sell them. So in that year, no profit from the cattle, none from the hay (we'd fed it all to them), none from wool and lambs – production costs outstripping proceeds. The only thing making money was our Amway business. We'd shared the plan with our Birribi neighbours, Roly and Mary, whose shearing shed we had used the first year. They had become as excited about the concept as Warren had. They too had a love of the land but in recent times had suffered a tragedy – the loss of Mary's son who, at the age of four, had climbed into a silo of wheat and suffocated. They were still in terrible grief and to cope were throwing themselves relentlessly at work and life. They met Linc and liked him instantly. Mary's daughter, Carmen, was studying jewellery design at uni. After seeing the network marketing plan, she joined Roly and Mary's business, and soon met Linc. Before long the two of them were dating.

The hard work of the business was tempered with wonderful, relaxing weekends away – rewards for particular achievements. Houseboat holidays, cabins on lakes, dinner, bed and breakfasts at five-star hotels.

Sparky and Sarah Marquis were our South Australian leaders and became our close friends. Gifted winemakers, they established Fox Creek Wines with Sarah's parents and went on to create superb award-winning wines. Today their own dynamic enterprise, Mollydooker Wines, is widely known and spoken of with great respect in wine circles. John and Jenny Welch had become good friends too, and a finer group leader than John could not be found. We'd had an inkling of the man's qualities when he'd joined our grape-picking team decades earlier.

With his vineyard work by day and networking at night, Linc gave up motorcycle racing. He'd reached a pinnacle in his sport when he'd won the South Australian Rider of the Year award. He understood his rewards would come later. He and Carmen became a strong team, with a matching, tireless work ethic.

After graduating, Marlo decided to move to Melbourne, believing the city held better prospects for her than Adelaide. She packed up her VW with as much of her stuff as she could fit in, and she and girlfriend, Alex, set out late one Saturday morning. We knew it would be dark before they got there and tried to encourage her to leave early next day, but she was on a mission, and with the confidence and optimism of her father, hugged us tightly, laughed at herself in her tiny driver's space, and drove off.

I had faith in the competence of my kids, and while I felt weak at the knees and shed some tears at the sight of my daughter driving away, I was excited and proud in the knowledge that she was pursuing her dream – the dream that we'd understood and supported from her earliest days.

On a Wednesday in January Warren was reaping the last of our wheat at Birribi. It had been an average crop (which farmers are always grateful for) and with rain on the horizon he needed to get it finished before we left for a weekend function at Melbourne's Tennis Centre, and to visit Marlo. With half a day's reaping to go, a con-rod went through the side of the crank case, and the header motor seized. It was vital for us to be at the function. We'd promoted it passionately to our group and many of them were going. We were due to leave at seven on the Friday morning.

After several phone calls and some suggestions from our competent mechanic, Warren sourced a new motor and went to pick it up – a four hour round trip. Thursday morning we went out to the farm early. Standing high up on the header in the blazing sun, I handed my husband tools, secured bolts while he screwed on nuts, and tried to stay calm while the language of mechanical repairs filled the air. After several hours the job was done. Warren finished reaping just on dark. It started to rain, and we left for Melbourne at seven next morning.

As always, we came away from the seminar with a mountain of information – most important and valued by us, the general business principles. In talking about the function afterwards, Warren and I realised we'd come to the same conclusion regarding our struggling farm enterprise. Sometimes we need to take a step back before we can move forward again. Perhaps it was time to relinquish some of our hills country, to realise some capital until things improved in farming.

Some friends had shown an interest in an eighty acre block. Bill was a dentist, and Penny, his wife, ran a sheep stud. We took them up to the property. Sitting on a log in the shade of an old red gum, we ate the ploughman's lunch I'd prepared and drank a good Eden Valley Riesling. Warren, probably fuelled by a couple of wines, suggested we drive up the Kaiser Stuhl – the highest point in the range. Driving to the top of this peak was a feat that had been achieved by only one person – Warren's dad, in his old Series One Land Rover many years earlier. We got about halfway up before the wheels of our Range Rover started spinning on the loosely formed track. Warren stopped and applied the handbrake. The car was on a serious incline. It began to slip backwards. We all jumped out and threw large rocks behind the wheels. Warren got back in and tried to coax it forwards, but it slipped sideways and backwards a little more. Frantically we piled more rocks behind the wheels. The track dropped away each side of its narrow width. Each time we removed the stones the car would lose traction, and so we had to build a downward track, a little at a time, let the vehicle slip onto it, build some more and so on. It took more than an hour before we had the car back on safe ground. I felt sure we would have scared our friends off buying the property, but afterwards, as we sat drinking another bottle of wine and listening to the crows deriding us, Bill said, 'We'd love to have it.'

At Birribi, we pulled down defunct fences and built new ones. We planted native trees along the waterways in paddocks and around the shearing shed, fenced off groves of red gum seedlings, and established new pasture.

One of the paddocks had some small stone on it and so Warren asked me to roll it. Onto the Zetor tractor he hooked the four metre wide roller that he'd fabricated himself from train wheels welded together. The job took me most of the day and required total focus as there were outcrops of moss rocks and fallen logs to negotiate. When I was finished, I headed for the gate to leave the paddock. I looked back to admire the job and lost concentration. Suddenly the tractor lurched as I hooked a large log with the roller. The tow hitch snapped like a carrot. I was furious with myself.

'It's okay,' Warren said later. 'I'll fix it. You've done a good job.'

I didn't always go out to the farm. There were things to be done at home, including the farm bookwork which had become increasingly involved and time consuming.

Marlo loved living in Melbourne. She'd picked up a few acting gigs but supported herself mainly with waitressing. She was totally independent and worked incredibly hard at trying to establish herself in the acting industry. One weekend she came home for an audition with Adelaide's Magpie Theatre Company. Sitting on our verandah in a welcome burst of winter sunshine, warming our hands around mugs of hot coffee, the two of us were talking. She was spent, from striving for success in the art she loved, and not achieving her goal. She was near quitting her lifelong dream.

'I don't think I'm going to make it, Mum,' she said in despair. 'I can't go on waitressing for the rest of my life.'

'Don't give up dear,' I said. 'I believe you're so close to cracking it.'

She returned to Melbourne. Within a week she'd received word from Magpie, offering her a twelve month contract. Our daughter was coming home.

As she began work in Adelaide, it wasn't long before she was noticed by the State Theatre Company. Work with them followed. The night we went to a production at The Playhouse and saw her name in lights on King William Street for the lead role, the tremor in my voice as I spoke to friends and family members afterwards disclosed a deep pride in the strength and endurance of our daughter. She was now working full-time in acting, well paid, and befriending Australian actors of note.

She rented a beautiful terrace cottage in Adelaide. One evening whilst out with friends, she met a young Air Force pilot. Peter was polished and polite. He pursued Marlo lavishly, showering her with love, attention and exotic gifts. Marlo had some instinctive reservations in the beginning, but when we met Peter, who flashed us his winning smile and impeccable manners, I said to Marlo, 'What's the hold-up?'

'I'm just not sure, Mum,' she said.

However, over the next few weeks, they slipped into a steady relationship.

Feeling settled and secure, Marlo decided to get a dog. She'd heard about a litter of pups for sale and went to have a look. They were kelpie/something crosses. One of the pups sat at her feet.

'I'm your dog,' said the big brown eyes. 'Now let's go home.'

It was nineteen ninety-three. Last month Jeppi turned sixteen and what a dog she has been. What an important part she has played in all our lives. Knowing her temperament now, and the lifestyle she's had, it's hard to imagine her having started life in the city. She hated being left at home each day as Marlo went off to work.

Later that year, Marlo and Peter decided to see Europe together. Marlo asked if we'd have Jeppi stay with us while she was away. Warren said, 'You know Marlo, we only have working dogs on our property.'

'Yes I know, Dad, but she's a kelpie – she'll be alright.'

'She probably will, but she'll have to earn her keep,' he told her, visibly chuffed at the prospect at having another sheep dog to train.

Marlo and Peter were away six weeks. Jeppi fell in love with the farm and displayed a passion for sheep work. Warren became her adored master. If at any time he left the house without her (she being the only sheepdog we've ever had inside), she'd race frantically through all the rooms, checking each door for exit possibilities, climbing couches, chairs, beds, to look out of windows in search of her master. Thankfully she always made me aware of her frenzy with frenetic whining and I'd let her out, short of her hurling herself through a window to join Warren for work.

When Marlo returned, she took her precious dog home, but whenever we visited her in the city, Jeppi would be ecstatic at seeing Warren and not leave his side. When we were leaving, she'd strain on her lead to get into our car, and whimper and whine pitifully as we drove away. One day Marlo phoned and said, 'It's no good, Dad, Jeppi has her bags packed and won't leave the front door.'

So she came to live with us. It was brave and selfless of Marlo. While she missed her pet terribly, it warmed her to see how Jeppi thrived on the farm, and whenever she came to visit, there was always special time spent with her dog.

Lincoln's relationship with Carmen had become serious. I'd had to let our daughter go years earlier and now it was time for our son to leave. They became engaged, and Roly and Mary put on a lavish party for them at their beautiful homestead – Lartunga. Carmen was not keen on commuting from the Barossa to go to uni, so Linc set up house with her in the city. They rented a small flat and Linc would drive to the Barossa and back again daily. I worried about him being tired for the evening trip as he usually worked ten to twelve hours a day, and my fears weren't without grounds. One night he fell asleep at the wheel and miraculously only hit a white post before waking up. There were hundreds of huge red gums lining the road he took.

To follow was a sad year for me, and Warren too I suspect. I think Carmen found the family bond we had overwhelming. Her biological father was living in New Zealand. As a child, Carmen had been with either him or her mother, over several years. She'd attended something like seventeen different schools in twelve years, lost the little brother she'd helped care for when her mother was absent (when he'd suffocated in the wheat silo) and had developed a rigid armour against emotional pain. We didn't see much of Linc that year. It was something we couldn't seem to fix no matter how we tried, and it broke my heart.

Marlo and Peter moved in together and were beginning to talk of marriage. It was a stormy relationship though, and many were the times Marlo would "escape" to her beloved Barossa when things were tough with Peter. One day she phoned us in a desperate state. She wasn't well – physically or emotionally – so we drove to town to be with her. Peter wasn't there. They'd been together a couple of years, but things were going badly and had reached crisis point. There were tears and soul searching, and I think it helped Marlo just to hear her words in the room. She has always had wisdom beyond her years and so we just listened and nodded at her sound reasoning. By the end of that day, they were making plans for Peter to leave the house that Marlo had rented, and a chapter of our precious daughter's life was over.

Soon after this, we were called to a meeting to discuss Linc and Carmen's wedding – with Carmen's parents, Rob and Mary. Sadly, Mary and Roly's marriage had not survived and they had separated. Roly had raised Carmen as his own, accepted Linc warmly as a future son-in-law, but to his sorrow was now out of the picture.

This was to be a wedding of grand proportions and Carmen opened the meeting with instructions on what we'd be financially responsible for. Linc, by now, had accumulated some debt in his vineyard enterprise and we could see his eyes widening at the grandiosity of the wedding plans, as were ours at the thought of the expense. Then Rob proceeded to question Linc about his Amway business, stating that he would in fact have to choose between it and his daughter. We knew Carmen had lost interest in the business and we'd accepted that, but at this ultimatum from her father, we were incredulous. It was so surreal that Warren, Linc and I were speechless.

Next day, Carmen rang to say she needed our deposit for the reception. Linc happened to be in the house and took the call. We hadn't spoken to him about the meeting the night before, but as I listened to him listening, I sensed a death knell. Then, from my son, three words.

'Carmen, it's over.'

He had no tears. An understandable sadness though. We had no doubt that the decisions both our kids made around this time were the right ones.

Over the next couple of weeks, Linc and Carmen packed up their unit and divided their possessions. For the next twelve months they spoke to each other often by phone, but gradually there were fewer calls as their relationship died a natural death. As we talked about it away from the rawness of separation, Linc told us about his dream of finding a partner who would integrate with his family, and never ask him to choose between her and what he deemed prudent in business.

Sometime after his break with Carmen, Linc began to think about world travel. His mate Ben was living and working as a winemaker in Stellenbosch, South Africa.

'Come on over, Linc,' Ben had encouraged. 'It's such a beautiful country.'

Ben's younger brother Anthony was going over.

'Come on, Linc,' said Ant. 'We'll buy a car over there and do a trip.'

So Linc, who'd just finished vintage, agreed. He flew to South Africa. With a plan to travel for six weeks, he and Ant and another young man, Marcus, bought a Kombi van in Johannesburg. The proposed six week holiday turned into a three month odyssey, coloured with a hundred amazing tales.

When Linc first arrived in Stellenbosch, Ben too had just finished a gruelling vintage – his first as a winemaker. Not only was he winemaker, but he'd had to build the winery first. Upon his arrival in the country just three weeks prior to vintage, he'd asked his employers where the winery was.

'Well, we haven't built it yet,' said one of them casually. 'We thought you'd have more idea of what we need. Could you organise it?'

He was in his twenties and aghast. Out of necessity, he undertook the enormous task with courage. It took every ounce of his physical and mental energy as he worked days and nights without sleep. Only slightly restored after a two or three hour nap, he'd power on again, under the stress of trying to integrate into a new country and undertaking the employment of blacks who'd have to be breath-tested for alcohol before they started work each day. The winery was "finished" the night before the first load of grapes came in. Ben took off his project manager's hat to don his winemaker's. So, by the time Linc arrived, he was utterly spent and ready for a break.

After a few days of sightseeing in and around the picturesque city with Ben, Linc was ready to join Ant and Marcus, who'd been surfing in Durban. He was to travel there by bus – an eight hour trip. Ant had arranged to collect him from the station when he arrived. The night before Linc was to leave, Ben had a few mates in – a wind-down after the rigours of vintage. They all had a few drinks, and several of the lads stayed overnight.

Linc was due to catch his bus at seven next morning but it had been four am before they'd called it a night. Linc set his alarm for six and asked a couple of the others to set theirs too as he was afraid of not waking in time. He woke at eight. All had slept through their alarms and Linc had missed the bus.

At eight-thirty he phoned to ask when the next bus was going, explaining that he'd missed the earlier one. There was a prolonged silence from the girl at the coach office. Her voice was grave. 'You missed that bus?'

'Yes, I'm sorry,' said Linc. 'I'll have to book a seat on the next one.'

'We've just had word,' said the girl slowly, 'that the bus you were supposed to be on has collided with a petrol tanker. Everyone on board has been incinerated.'

While travelling along the coast a few hours later, our son phoned to tell us what had happened. As he spoke I could hear he was changed again – another episode etched into his fabric. I could hear bedlam on the bus – adults, children, poultry, dogs. I believe they were oblivious. But Linc wrote to us as he travelled – twelve pages, about his love for his family, his dreams and aspirations.

I begged him to keep in touch and he promised to ring once a week. After he'd been away five weeks, he rang to tell us he'd be staying another three.

'We want to go to Malawi,' he said.

'Just don't go into Mozambique. It's full of land mines,' I warned, grasping at straws and knowing they'd go wherever they pleased.

'We have to go into Mozambique, Mum, to get to Malawi, but don't worry, we'll be careful.'

'Will you call me in a week?'

'I will.'

'Love you.'

'Love you too, Mum.'

He didn't phone in a week. Or two. And we couldn't reach him. Nor could we overcome feelings of terrible anxiety. In the third week I knew that if we hadn't heard from him in a couple of days, there'd be something terribly wrong, as he needed to tell us what flight he was coming home on. He'd asked if we would pick him up from the airport. After three weeks we still hadn't heard and I was wrecked. Warren was trying to be rational but then I read a small paragraph in *The Advertiser*. A bus full of tourists, including some Australians, had gone over a cliff in Malawi. No-one had died but many were seriously injured. I don't know what I would have done had I not heard my son's happy voice within minutes of reading that item.

'Sorry I haven't phoned, Mum, but there's been no service.'

'Where are you?' I tried to sound calm.

'We're in Mozambique. We've been on this amazing island. Just the blacks and us – fishing, singing, dancing, living on the beach, like kings.'

'It's so good to hear from you,' my heart thumping. 'When will you be home?'

'Well, there's still so much to see. We want to go over to Namibia. I think we'll need another four weeks.'

I knew then as we talked, that I'd be okay. It was more than likely he wouldn't have a phone signal for the next four weeks, but suddenly I felt an amazing peace, and all anxiety about his wellbeing left me. I don't think I ever worried about him again. It was the moment I decided it's a futile pastime. I just remembered that the universe is always unfolding as it's meant to, and to trust in the power of that with all my heart.

Linc returned safely after three months away, but for a long time carried a yearning to return to the country he'd fallen in love with.

While Linc had been in Africa, Marlo had thrown herself into the work she loved, and part of that was to go on tour with Magpie Theatre, to the west coast of South Australia. The company was touring a play for schools. Cast and crew were to drive to Port Augusta, then catch a train that would take them to Woomera, Kingoonya, Tarcoola, and ultimately Cook on the Nullarbor Plain. Kids from remote regions would come in from great distances to be treated to this wonderful live performance.

Marlo and her fellow actors and crew, had loaded themselves, props and equipment into a mini bus, and set off from Adelaide early one morning. The tour's production manager, Mark Pennington, had come straight from doing the lighting for a Barossa Music Festival event. He was dead tired and uncommunicative from having worked long hours. Soon after hitting the road, he lay down on the back seat of the bus and fell into a deep sleep. How rude and unsociable, thought the gregarious Marlo.

At six forty-five next morning, Mark knocked on her motel room door to tell her they were ready to leave. Marlo opened it and said, 'You're fifteen minutes early. You'll have to wait!' And she shut her door.

What a prima donna, thought the "no nonsense" Mark. They'd seriously ruffled each other's feathers. There's a wonderful story in how they fell in love, sitting side by side in the van, in mutual awe of Mother Nature as they took to the Outback. At day's end, as they kicked back and allowed the Nullarbor to do its restorative work on them, they began to talk. Mark was in the death throes of a relationship as well, and each evening as they sat on the step of the stationary train, watching breathtaking sunsets, they shared more of their personal lives with each other.

We were totally unaware of this lovely thing that had happened to our daughter in the desert, but after she returned from the tour, I noticed her talking more and more about her friend Mark. One day she brought him to the Barossa, where they spent an hour or two at home with us, sitting by the fire, drinking some wine and chatting. He was a lighting designer with the State Theatre Company, as well as a production and large event manager. We thought he was one of her mates. Next day she rang and asked me what I thought of him.

'Oh he seemed nice dear, but he didn't say much.'

'Well I hope you like him, because he's going to be around for a while,' she said with puppy-like happiness.

There must have been an explosion of joy and love between them then that caused random news-spreading. One day Mum rang and said, 'How about that?'

'How about what?' I asked.

'Marlo getting married.'

'*What?*' I shrieked, in absolute shock.

Within minutes Marlo phoned to tell me. In disbelief, I just listened as she rattled her happiness like a livestock auctioneer. She asked if she could bring Mark up next day and stay for the weekend. I'd been disappointed at hearing this exciting news from my mum instead of my daughter, and so I thought I'd let Marlo tell Warren herself. We sat down for lunch soon after they arrived, and a little later Marlo said, 'Dad, will it be okay if we have the engagement party here in the garden?'

'Sure,' said Warren. 'Who's getting married?'

'We are,' she said. 'Didn't Mum tell you?'

His mouth fell open.

It had happened as quickly for them as it had for us, the two of them soon recognising a life partner in each other. It was wonderful to see the love, respect and utter cherishing between them, and although Mark was reserved in those early days, we sensed that this intelligent, gifted man with kind eyes, would love and protect our daughter all his life.

# THIRTY

When we'd bought Birribi, it had felt like all roads were leading to success, but since the price of wool had halved then halved again, the property was no longer big enough to be viable. It was primarily a grazing block. As much as we loved this beautiful piece of land, we made a business decision to sell it and purchase something with more arable acres. We hoped it would be another step towards Warren's dream.

Because I was the business book-keeper, I could foresee cash flow challenges as they approached. I'd warn Warren but he'd simply reason, 'Well, I'll just need to work harder.'

That had been enough in earlier times, but now we had to work smarter. I was convinced Warren needed to see the figures on paper, and so he became more involved in that side of the business. Together we set up a tight and well-organised accounting system.

We spoke to our real estate agent friend, David Braunack, about putting Birribi on the market. With its Eden Valley location – a noted Riesling growing area – we all reasoned it could attract the interest of vignerons. The auction date was set. We'd had it for ten years and felt sure the value should have doubled in that time, maybe even more, considering the vineyard prospects. We had a few weeks to prepare.

Vintage rolled around and again Warren was helping Linc with the harvest. One night our phone rang in the wee hours. From deep sleep I leapt out of bed, and with heart pounding fumbled with the phone. It was Warren's dad.

'Can Warren come up?' his voice urgent. 'Lin's fallen and hit her head.'

Struggling to be properly awake, we both jumped into the car and drove to their house at the top of the hill. Lin was sitting in a chair with blood oozing from the back of her head. A tendency to low blood pressure had made her prone to fainting. Unable to sleep this night, she'd got up to make herself a cup of tea and had passed out. She looked at us blankly and asked who we were. I phoned for an ambulance which was there in minutes. The paramedics quickly bundled her off to hospital. Otto went with her and we followed. The on-duty doctor examined her and made the necessary head repairs. After an hour or so she recognised us again, and apart from having a headache, seemed her usual self. Even so, the nurse said they'd like to keep her in under observation till morning. Otto wanted to stay with her.

Next morning Warren and Linc left for work early. The team was picking grapes for a neighbouring vigneron. I was preparing to go to the hospital to bring Lin and Otto home but phoned first. The nurse told me the doctor wanted to keep her there until her headache subsided. I went in with essentials – toothbrush, comb, etc. She seemed fine but complained of the headache. I'd been back at home an hour when the phone rang. It was Lin's doctor, telling me her condition had worsened. They were rushing her to Adelaide in an ambulance, with Otto. There was some bleeding on the brain he told me.

'It sounds serious,' I said. 'Where are they taking her?'

'Yes, it is serious,' said the doctor. 'She's on her way to the Royal Adelaide.'

I had to get Warren. But just before I left the house the phone rang again. One of the nurses was telling me that Lin had lost consciousness. They were taking her by ambulance to Gawler, a half an hour away, and from there would airlift her to Adelaide. We'd have to collect Otto from the Gawler hospital, she told me.

Warren and Linc were picking grapes in one of the most inaccessible vineyards in the Valley. This small block of Shiraz was nestled deep in the hills. I drove as far as I could along a rough dirt track. I couldn't see the pickers but knew they were just up this gully and around the bend. I started calling out to Warren as I ran. No answer, so I cupped my hands to my mouth and yelled to the sky. My voice resounded through the small ravine and this time I heard Warren's strong reply.

'Yep.'

'Come quickly,' I yelled, slowly.

'Is it Mum?' he called back.

'Yes,' I shouted.

I spotted him running down the gully towards me, Linc behind him. As we drove home I told them all I knew. They rushed in to change out of their work clothes and we set out for Gawler to pick up Otto.

When the four of us arrived at the Royal Adelaide Hospital, we were ushered into an intimate waiting room and were told that the doctor would speak to us soon. We'd phoned Lin's twin sister on our way, and she and her daughter and son-in-law, and her other sister, Gwen, were waiting for us there. A doctor stepped into the room. His eyes were sad and spoke a thousand words.

'Mrs Grocke has had a brain haemorrhage,' he told us. 'We can operate, but there's more than a ninety percent chance she'll have brain damage and will never be able to talk, walk or do anything for herself again. She's in a coma now, and if we don't operate, she'll die peacefully. The decision is yours but if we are to operate, we'll need to do it soon. I'm sorry I don't have any other options. I'll leave you to discuss it. I'll be back in fifteen minutes.'

We were all in shock. Lin's twin, Phebe, was the first to speak.

She told us that Lin had always said 'If anything serious ever happens to me, don't let them keep me alive if I can't have a quality life.'

We all knew that her wish would be to go peacefully and with dignity, and so our decision was unanimous. She would be eighty next day. And in three weeks she and Otto would have been married sixty years.

Warren's sister, Jenny, was preparing to fly out of London where she and Evan were working, to be with us all for the special wedding anniversary. We'd phoned her earlier to tell her about Lin's fall. Now we had to phone again with this terrible news – that in all probability she would not see her mother again before she died. She booked a flight for that night.

We'd phoned Marlo too, and she arrived at the hospital soon after we'd seen the doctor. We all went to see Lin then – lying as if in tranquil sleep in her hospital bed. Her sisters said their emotional goodbyes, so too her niece with her husband. And then there were just the five of us – Otto, Warren and I, Linc and Marlo – in disbelief that this person who had been so dear to us, would soon die.

Marlo was to be married in four weeks. She startled us out of our deep thoughts as she went purposefully to the foot of the bed, lifted the blanket and stared at her nanna's motionless feet for a minute. Then, 'Nanna, if you can hear me, wriggle your toes.' Our wise girl, in tune with the universe.

The toes wriggled, and with a smile Marlo went to the head of the bed, leant in close and began to describe her wedding gown to her nanna. She told us later that she could sense a peace and a gratitude for this final intimate moment between them.

Marlo had to go to work then. She was in a State Theatre Company production at The Playhouse and had to be there by six for make-up and costume. She planned to come back after the performance.

Jenny's son Jonathan and his family came to say their emotional goodbyes to their nanna, after which Otto, Warren, Linc and I sat for the next three or four hours, just watching Lin breathe easily and evenly, and finding it hard to believe that she wasn't simply enjoying a restful sleep.

We asked a nurse if she had any idea of how much longer she might live.

'It's hard to tell,' she said gently. 'She could go any time in the next twenty-four hours.'

Warren and I spoke about going home for a shower and then coming back. In that moment Lin moved her head purposefully from side to side and groaned as if she was trying to wake up. I said to Warren, 'I don't think she wants us to go.'

So we settled back into our chairs beside the bed, and she became peaceful again. Warren's dad was distraught. Their marriage hadn't been perfect, but in recent years they'd grown close, and in truth Otto had always adored her. We carried on a dreamlike conversation in the room, until something arrested us. Nothing had changed, except that Lin had stopped breathing. And that was it – a beautiful life, of more years than anyone had expected back in the fifties as she'd come through tuberculosis, now over. She'd been a server all her life – never happier than when attending to the needs of others, especially her family. She'd been so loved, by so many. We stayed with her – for half an hour perhaps. Warren and Otto, from either side of the bed, shed their tears and whispered their goodbyes.

Warren went to the theatre to get Marlo who left before her curtain call, which, strangely enough, was written about in a critical way in *The Advertiser* next day. The Theatre Co. phoned the journalist to tell her why Marlo hadn't taken her bow, and a poignant item of apology appeared in the newspaper column next day.

Our dear friend Sparky came to be with us at the hospital that night, supporting us with his unique brand of love and caring. These are the things one remembers.

This had all happened so quickly that we were thrown into an amorphous world in which there was a gaping hole left by Lin's passing. Jenny arrived from London the next day, and while she ached at not having said goodbye to her mother, her deep Christian faith sustained her and gave us all solace. We arranged a fitting funeral at which Linc and Marlo spoke about how much their nanna had meant to them. She'd been like a second mother to them, as they'd so often called in on their way home from school for a dose of nanna pampering.

Marlo considered postponing her wedding, but we assured her that Nanna would not have wanted that, and so, although deeply sad, she and Mark continued with their plans.

Jenny stayed at the house with Otto, who was by now eighty-six and faced with spending the rest of his days without his beloved wife. Lin had nurtured and waited on him all her life, knowing how hard he worked on the land. We reassured him we'd take care of him. I'd do his shopping, cooking, washing, but he'd lost the will to live.

About a week after his wife's death, Otto began to complain of feeling unwell. Jenny took him to the doctor who said he'd like to run some tests. Results came in a few days later. Otto had developed acute myeloid leukaemia and without treatment would live just a few weeks. His prayers had been answered, he told us. He refused treatment. Within two weeks he lay in a coma in the Tanunda Hospital, seemingly in peaceful sleep just as Lin had been three weeks earlier. Jenny stayed with him vigilantly and lovingly, happy in the knowledge that he was ready to meet the Lord. Warren sat at his bedside too, for hours, holding his hand and contemplating the life and the work they had shared. He wept as he said he could feel the love his father had never been able to verbalise.

Some of Otto's close friends came to say their goodbyes, and early on Saturday, the eighteenth of April, nineteen ninety-eight, the day of their sixtieth wedding anniversary, Otto slipped away to be with the love of his life.

In his death he joined the ranks of the men we almost expect to be immortal – the ones we still expect to see walking down the street. These have been men of stamp, of contribution, men of charisma – Barossans, elders of my time in this place, part of the fabric of our community. And the women elders of my time, who have been mothers and nurturers, are those who have given their husbands the support they've needed to be these persons of mark. And in doing so, I'm sure some of them have sacrificed their own deepest dreams and aspirations.

We arranged another funeral, the procedure familiar by now. All the same people were there to pay their respects.

The day after laying Otto to rest, we packed up all we needed for the wedding. Marlo and Mark had booked a beautiful old mansion at Port Elliot for three days. The wedding party and immediate family would stay there. Guests had organised accommodation round about. It would be a miracle if this wedding went to plan, with so much of our focus till then having been on the funerals. In a way it was such a romantic way for those two to have popped off – celebrating their diamond wedding anniversary together after all. And now here was their granddaughter, about to begin a new life with the man she adored and who loved her too with all his heart. Instead of it being stressful, there was an amazing calm as we made the house ready for the wedding. We warmed the rooms with fresh flowers, candlelight, good eating, good wine and random hugs. Marlo was to have one bridesmaid – one of her dearest friends, Ellen – and her brother as bridesman. Linc said he didn't know what his duties were, but Marlo said she just wanted him to be at her side. It was her way of telling him how dear he was to her.

It was an incredibly warm ceremony and celebration. Apart from Marlo and Mark's love for each other, the absence of Lin and Otto seemed to have wrapped us all together in a deep appreciation of family and friends. And strangely, or maybe not so strangely, Linc had met his wife-to-be, Nicole, the night before Otto died. So much was wrapped up in these four weeks of two funerals and a wedding.

Soon after all this we met Nicole, in circumstances similar to those in which we'd met Mark. She and Linc had mutual friends and a few of them had been camping in the hills for the weekend. Again it was high winter and Linc brought her in one Sunday afternoon. We sat by the fire, drank some wine and chatted. She told us later that she'd felt uncomfortable meeting us for the first time after being in camp all weekend, but she didn't know then how much time we ourselves had spent in the bush.

Nicole was an attractive, intelligent and gentle person – a registered nurse working at the Queen Elizabeth Hospital in cardiac procedure.

With Lin and Otto's home now vacant, Linc said he'd like to look after it. The house had been left to Jenny who was more than happy for Linc to rent it, in their absence. Nicole was living in Adelaide.

Linc was twenty-eight, and while he and Nic dated, he slowly and carefully fell in love. After twelve months, all of our family, and Nic's, began to wonder about their intentions. The two of them seemed happy and well-suited, and one day I asked, 'Well what's the story Linc? Are you and Nic getting married or what?'

'I want to be sure, Mum,' he said.

Linc is so much like that. Every important decision must be seriously considered, and I guess his previous failed relationship had coloured his carefulness. Finally, he was sure that Nic was the person he wanted to spend his life with. Nic shared with us later that she too had wondered just when he was going to pop the question. The wedding was planned for November.

Warren inherited the greater part of the vineyard, and Linc the portion he'd developed – about twenty acres. Although Otto had never verbally acknowledged Warren's help for his almost thirty years in the vineyard, Warren had sensed, as he sat with his dying father, that he had appreciated and loved him. And Jenny shared with us that in her final days with him, he had spoken about Warren with love and respect.

In September of 'ninety-nine, Birribi went to auction. We were ready for a new start, to move forward again. Although we'd paid two hundred and fifty thousand for the property ten years earlier, we would have accepted three hundred and fifty at auction. We just wanted to clear our debt and buy something more productive.

The morning before the auction, I woke up with the ridiculous figure of a million dollars in my head. Where did that come from? Just a dream I thought. And yet I was prone to the odd premonition. One morning I had woken with a chilling notion that our sheep were out of water. I'd asked Warren to drive to

Birribi to check, knowing I'd feel silly if they were okay. But someone had been through and shut a gate that was meant to be open, cutting the flock off from their water supply. It was high summer and we would have lost hundreds had Warren not got to them that day or the next.

The day of the auction was surreal. Apart from our dear supportive family and David, our agent, there were only two or three others there, and they were simply onlookers. There was no bid or offer. It completely knocked Warren for six! It hadn't been an easy decision for him to sell Birribi. We loved this farm, but he'd been certain, after much soul searching, that it was the right thing to do. So why this complete failure of an auction? There *was* an answer, but we'd have to wait for that.

For a week or two afterwards, Warren and I felt devastated, outa gas, lost. But, with our inherent fighting spirits, we gradually cast off the destructive demons and as if leaning into a bitter wind, focussed forward – to making Birribi as productive as it could possibly be. And then happily to Linc and Nic's wedding.

Those two had chosen the grand old Barossa home, Kalimna, for their ceremony and reception.

The curveballs that life had been hurling at us had wrapped Warren and me together into a strong package, and on this wedding day we spoke about how important family was to us. To see our kids settled with two fine people was a priceless blessing. The coming together of friends and family who often haven't seen each other for years, the pre-wedding parties, the planning – all are written into the happy section of one's life story. The wedding was a beautiful and joyful two day celebration.

Soon after this was another wedding, the announcement of which had surprised us. We'd lost touch with our friend Roly since his divorce from Mary, but out of the blue came an invitation – to help him celebrate his marriage to Donna. On their wedding day Roly and Donna's emotions could not be closeted. Each had suffered bitter pain in years past – for Roly, the loss of Mary's son in the wheat silo whilst under his watch, and his consequent marriage breakdown. And for Donna, after her own divorce, having one of her two precious daughters choose to stay with her father, far away from where she lived. We loved Donna instantly – a warm, sincere, salt-of-the-earth person, moulded by an incredible adventure of a life beginning in South Africa. The four of us were to become close friends and share many adventures.

# THIRTY-ONE

The bank was becoming nervous after the failure of our land sale. How much more I know of the business world today than I did then. It's so simple. It's largely about security. While all is going well, the person across the manager's desk treats you with respect, pal-ship even, but the tighter the security, even though from uncontrollable circumstances, the higher their chair gets, and respect can turn to arrogance, even contempt, in a short space of time.

Two things happened here to change our lives. I'd always wondered why some people become incredibly successful from a standing start. How do they think, what is it they do, that we too could do if only we knew what? Our Amway business was not going to make us millions. Unfortunately, the majority of people could only see it as I had in my early days, and I understood that. But the business had exposed us to a multitude of inspiring guest speakers from all walks who'd become famous for becoming successful against all odds. We'd learned such valuable life principles from them, and one of them recommended a book – Robert Kiyasaki's *Rich Dad Poor Dad*. As I read it, I had an epiphany. The answer to my questions about success lay, for us, in real estate.

I could see we already had a good base with the land we owned. On turning the last page of this book, I had the feeling of being on a launching pad.

The other thing that happened was that our real estate friend, David, suggested we borrow private money.

'It's the way to go,' he said. 'You'd be surprised at how many successful people do it. A lot of the older Valley folk prefer to lend their money this way, rather than lend it to the bank. They're happy to earn a little more than bank interest, and the borrower benefits by not having to pay business interest rates. Talk to the solicitors. They'll point you in the right direction.'

So we did. This was the start of a productive and professional association with Grant Schuyler, a partner in one of our town's legal firms. We'd done conveyancing with them for generations and had never underestimated the way they conducted business. Where else would one receive a solicitor's bill that said, "For services rendered – $235, but call it $200"?

We've been able to call on Grant at any time, have him answer our questions or look into lines of enquiry that have ultimately helped us with our plans and dreams.

The prospective husband and wife lenders whom Grant sourced for us, wanted to see what we were offering as security, so we arranged a picnic for the four of us at Birribi. We took them to one of our favourite spots, sat on some big old logs, ate the roast chicken and salad lunch I had prepared, drank a bottle of champagne and established the business association we ultimately enjoyed with them for ten years.

One of the best moments of my life was when we paid out that bank. It took the manager completely by surprise and with the lower interest rates and no fees, we could finally get on with building our farming enterprise, unburdened.

Next we found our wonderful accountant, Gerard McQueen, also someone we could call on at any time, and whose informed answers increasingly educated us in the world of finance.

Without really planning to do so, we were gathering an exceptional team of people who were helping us move forwards.

Linc and Nic were now leasing our portion of the vineyard from us, and even though this gave us a little extra income, Warren knew that with our debt level, we needed to have a more versatile farm so we could do more cropping. One day, about two years after Lin and Otto had died, he said to me, 'Do you know what we should do?'

'No, what?' I asked.

'We should sell the vineyard.'

I gasped. 'Don't ever let Linc hear you say that,' I said, knowing how much our son enjoyed his work.

'I just know Linc's been talking about how difficult it is to turn a profit,' he said. 'I wonder if it's something he's ever considered.'

'Just don't say anything,' I said, in my old resistant-to-change way.

About an hour later Linc walked into our house.

'Dad's been thinking of the prospect of selling the vineyard,' I blurted, wondering instantly why I'd done that.

Uncharacteristically Linc responded without pause. 'Oh yeah,' he said, nodding seriously. 'What would you do?'

'Well, we'd probably buy some more arable farming land. What about you?' asked Warren.

'I'd become a contractor,' said Linc without hesitation, causing me to guess he too had considered the option.

Warren talked about his concerns that the wine industry was about to go into decline. He could see signs. There were a lot of new vineyards being planted. Things were booming. Vineyard land was bringing good money. With the improvements Linc had made, the treated water he had piped from the town dams and the fact that these were Valley Floor vines, we dared to consider that it would be a good time to sell. We spoke to Nic about her thoughts. She was as surprised as we all were, but said it was a family decision and she would go with what Linc thought best for them.

Warren phoned Jenny in the UK and talked to her about it. The whole family needed to be considered. The property had been developed over a long period – first by Grandfather Friedrich, then by Otto and Warren, and more recently by Linc. Jenny listened intently, and with all the information Warren could give her, considered it a prudent thing to do. She said she'd have no concerns. The homestead, from whence it had all begun – the hub of four generations, our home now – would be retained.

Warren phoned Marlo and Mark, who were now living and working in Sydney. Like Jenny, Marlo was interested in all the ins and outs, and asked how we'd come to the decision. As long as Warren and Linc were in agreement and we considered it the best thing to do, she too would have no reservations. She thanked us for considering her.

The next day we phoned real estate agent David. Sitting at our kitchen table with him later that day, we put forward the proposition.

'You're joking, right?' he asked.

'No, we're not,' said Warren. 'It's a family decision, and we believe if ever we were to sell, this would be the time.'

David specialised in vineyards and we knew he had his finger on the pulse. A marketing campaign was set up. We would keep six acres with the house to maintain the farmyard, the gardens and a feeling of space. We would still be living in the same environment with the same view, but without the interminable worry of possible frost, hail, disease, supply outweighing demand et al.

Surveyors were employed to realign boundaries. One priority here was to include an easement, so that neighbours who'd also been using the town water would always have access to it. This was done at quite some expense to us, but it was important that no-one be disadvantaged by our restructuring. Even so, there were a few who were upset by our decision. Some people have strong ideas about how they think others should live their lives. There was even one couple who judged us so harshly they ceased to greet us in the street. For someone who loves to say hello to the people of our community, this hurt me considerably.

Within twelve months David had found our buyers – a lovely Barossa family we knew. An unconditional contract was drawn up and settlement date established.

Warren and I began inspecting farms for sale, and Linc started looking at machinery. Ian and Nat's son Kurt had bought a farm at Peake in the Southern Mallee, and Warren had been impressed by it – good value for money, he thought. So over the next several weeks, we visited farms of all qualities, sizes and prices, for sale in this region. One day I was browsing the real estate pages of the *Stock Journal*.

'Have a look at this,' I said to Warren.

It read, "*Parrakie. 1904 acres. 3 titles. Large red brown flats between sandy rises. Renowned strong cropping. Rainfall 375 mm.*" etc.

We rang the agent and asked if we could have a look at it. As we drove into the property Warren and I had one of those moments – it felt right. Stately gum trees lined the driveway. The large cream brick house was comfortable – sixties. There were good sheds, lush pastures, a second older stone home with big rooms, high ceilings. If we were to buy it, the amenities would be a far cry from the basic ones we'd been accustomed to on other farm properties. By the time we left, we were convinced this was the one.

A couple of days later we signed an unconditional contract.

Linc had ordered a grape harvester and was visiting growers in the Barossa, offering his services for the coming vintage. Nic was pregnant with their first child, and we were all blissfully happy and excited about what lay ahead.

Vineyard settlement date came and went, without payment. The contract was unconditional so we were assured it would go through, but bureaucracy, red tape, things we understood were out of the purchasers' control, were causing it to stall. The people from whom we were buying the Parrakie property were patient to a point, but at six weeks past their settlement date, we stood to lose our deposit and forfeit the property. We were communicating daily with their agent and solicitors and appealed to them to hold the farm for us. They agreed, but we'd now have to pay penalty interest and lease it from them until we could settle. We were told we could have passed this on to our purchasers for their delay but we had a strong feeling it wasn't their fault, that it was a bank tactic, and so we refrained.

Linc's grape harvester was on the water from New Zealand and vintage imminent. Without the proceeds of the vineyard sale, he'd have no way of paying for the machine. And not knowing how much longer the bank would take to process settlement, he and Nic feared they would lose their prospective clients, and consequently a huge amount of much needed income. The four of us were beside ourselves with the burden of it all.

Warren and I were in the city one day when we had a phone call from Linc. Warren answered his mobile. He was listening intently and looking at me gravely.

'What's up?' I asked when he'd hung up.

'Linc and Nic are at the Women's and Children's Hospital. Nic has started to leak amniotic fluid.'

'Is that serious?' I asked.

'Yes, apparently,' said Warren. 'The baby's now exposed to the risk of infection and will have to be delivered soon.'

Nic was six months pregnant.

Our precious first grandson, Ethan, was born next day at The Flinders Medical Centre, weighing a mere eight hundred and ninety grams. We rushed to the hospital two hours away, and as we walked into the neonatal unit, I saw my son and his wife sitting beside a crib. Then I caught sight of the tiny babe.

'Please don't cry,' said Nic.

'I think they're tears of happiness,' I said, immediately sensing she needed us to believe he would be okay.

I could see both fear and joy in their eyes as they spoke to us of how they would never allow their faith or their belief for his survival to waver. As Linc spoke softly to his new son, emotion welled in me to see the immense love that had come so instantly to him. With his strong hands he stroked Ethan's head with anomalous gentleness, then put his finger on his wee hand. Ethan clutched it. His tiny hand did not cover from the tip of Linc's index finger to the first joint. We started to learn of the unique care given by a neonatal unit. One of the nurses came over to the crib and said, 'It's okay little fella, don't cry.'

'Is he crying?' I asked.

We couldn't hear a sound. He was on life support and as I watched the monitor, I stopped breathing each time it flatlined.

'Don't worry,' said the nurse. 'It's normal.'

As I watched Linc and Nic's love and recognised my own, I remembered something I had read, something a mother had written to her child – "Before you were conceived, I wanted you. Before you were born, I loved you. Before you were a day old, I would have died for you."

There were days Ethan did well and others not so. At one stage he developed pneumonia. I tried not to be terrified. Linc and Nic's faith grew even stronger and was inspiring. Nic's parents, Nev and Barb, asked their pastor to baptise him, but this little guy already had the strongest will to live.

Warren was in hospital for a kidney stone operation when I received a call to say the bank was ready to settle on the vineyard – *five months* after the due date. The relief was enormous, but on the appointed day, another hitch. The purchasers wanted a clause inserted in the contract to give them first right of refusal, after family, for the purchase of Jenny's house, if ever it should come up for sale. We had to reach Jenny in London. It was night time over there. We needed her signature before settlement at one pm that day. The clock was relentless. Warren was still in hospital, Ethan fighting pneumonia. I had to get it done that day. There were phone calls, faxes, meetings with the conveyancer.

Just before one, at the eleventh hour, I'd finally ticked all the boxes and settlement went through.

Linc started vintage with a huge machine he'd never operated before, and with harvest being a stressful and sleep depriving exercise at the best of times, he now also chose to make four hour round trips to see his wife and son in hospital, daily. For three months there was almost constantly a family member at Ethan's side – talking to him, stroking him, encouraging him towards the time he would be grown enough to come home.

A couple of months before Ethan's arrival, we'd booked a trip to Europe. The plan had been to be back in time for his birth, and for sowing crops in early May. It would be a wrench to leave now. The day before our departure, we went to visit our little Trojan in hospital. He'd recovered from the pneumonia.

'Would you like a cuddle?' asked the nurse.

'Is that possible?' I asked looking at the amount of tubes and wires connecting him to his support.

'We'll have to unplug him and have you completely ready to receive him,' she said. 'He won't be breathing until we hook him up again.'

'If you're sure it's safe, we'd love to,' I said, looking at Warren.

I sat in the chair beside his crib. The nurse put a pillow on my lap and then set about detaching him. She picked him up quickly, placed him on the pillow, and began to plug everything back in. The monitor was flatlining.

'Oh Lord, please keep him safe,' I whispered.

It was wonderful to feel his warmth, his life, and kiss his head gently. The love I felt was enormous. Warren held him then and as he looked at his grandson, I could see something even softer than when he'd first held his own children. Then we said goodbye. We'd be away seven weeks, and although Linc and Nic assured us they'd be fine, I ached as we walked away from the little family of three.

I'd dreamt of this trip since my childhood. The seed had been sown whilst visiting a cousin of my dad's. Her husband had been a cargo ship's captain. As a result of their world travels, Beryl had a cabinet full of souvenirs – miniature replicas of The Eiffel Tower, Big Ben, London Bridge, a gondola. I'd been enthralled as she'd taken them out one by one and told me stories of the cities she'd bought them in. She was theatrical – a singer and elocution teacher. Vibrant, tall, attractive. Sparkling eyes. Similar in appearance and related, as my father was, to singer

Julie Anthony. Her beautiful descriptions made the places seem magical. From then on, I'd had periodic, blissful dreams about being in these places.

Now the dreams were to become reality.

# THIRTY-TWO

Our first stop was Singapore. I was tired, so tired – pummelled from the stress of the past few months – but as we were driven into the city from the airport that night, it dawned on me that we were about to visit some of the most beautiful places in the world.

Our hotel room was huge. I hadn't expected anything so grand. When we opened the curtains next morning, an ink black sky glowered at us from behind two sunlit white skyscrapers. Condensation ran down the outside of the window.

My dreams had never included Asia but instantly I loved the climate, food, gardens, architecture.

After donning our walking shoes, we took to the sweltering streets. The city was so clean it was like something out of a futuristic movie. From loud speakers set high on buildings, a syrupy female voice slid through the streets and alleys, issuing we knew not what. Instructions?

We found Raffles Hotel and had to have a drink there. Warren ordered two beers. The twenty-four Aussie dollars they cost would have bought six of the same at home. We gave the barman thirty. He kept the change.

The hotel was magnificent. Plantation décor. Heavily carved antique furniture against cool white walls. Majestic ceilings. Inveterate palms moving slightly in the drafts of large, slow, man-powered fans. The whole opulent package. As we wandered through the public rooms, my head was spinning with the joy of design, artefacts and architecture.

We wanted to see the old Singapore. A taxi driver took us there – to a marketplace where tourists were scarce. It was raw, unembellished. The people showed little interest in us. They were busy at their industry – plucking poultry, scaling and gutting fish, tossing noodles, cooking, eating. We walked through fish and dish water, weaving our way amongst the mongers, under clotheslines sagging with grey clothes, our nostrils flared with the aromas of Asia – dried fish, mushrooms, ginger, and a mountain of produce we could not begin to recognise. The place buzzed with the sound of work – clattering pans, swift heavy chopping, sloshing of water and the nasal, happy chatter of a social group who'd been at the same daily tasks for generations.

We visited a Hindu temple right next door. Respectfully, we removed our shoes and watched people performing rituals and praying on mats. Business men and women in suits along with the folk of the marketplace. An anarchy of incense burned at the entrance.

Later that day we visited the Singapore Art Museum, and in the evening noticed how beautifully the city lights were softened by its humidity.

Next day we crossed by flying fox to Sentosa Island to see the zoo. We spent hours there. The gardens were divine. Later we walked along Orchard Road. Never before had I seen so many diamonds with such sky-high price tags.

Back to the airport that afternoon where we boarded for the UK.

Jenny and Evan were at Heathrow to meet us. It was so good to see them again and as we drove away from the airport into the countryside, another wave of euphoria came over me. England of all places was the country I'd most dreamed of.

Jenny and Evan lived just outside the enchanting village of Gerrard's Cross in Buckinghamshire. The majority of its population were professionals who commuted to London for work. The large manor-style homes were set on magnificent grounds swathed now in drifts of daffodils beneath huge deciduous trees in bud. The estate that Jenny and Evan lived on, Bulstrode, belonged to WEC (World Evangelisation for Christ). The organisation had once operated from a London premises which, a few years earlier, had been acquired by the City. WEC had not wanted to sell the lovely old building but with their backs to the wall, they had accepted in exchange, this run-down country house on an estate near Gerrard's Cross – Bulstrode.

One of WEC's main purposes is to send missionaries to all corners of the world, and this was their headquarters. Jenny and Evan, from starting out as missionaries themselves, had gone on to become principals of WEC's training college in Tasmania, and were now international leaders of a team of two thousand or more. The entire operation runs solely on the voluntary efforts of the workers (as self-sufficient as they can possibly be), and on monetary gifts from fellow Christians.

The home on Bulstrode had a hundred and fifty rooms. After moving in, the admin team of twenty or so, had set about restoring it. What a huge job it must have been, but its value today, because of their efforts, is phenomenal.

Jenny and Evan showed us through a small portion of the house (perhaps a mere twenty rooms), then took us for a walk on the estate. Deer grazed on new pasture, there were small brooks to be crossed and although it was early spring, the weather was still freezing. We phoned home and were comforted to hear that

Ethan was doing okay. Growing. Our family were never out of our minds on this trip.

We were whacked by the end of our first day in England and so turned in with the chooks. After a wonderful, long sleep we got up next morning to find that Jenny and Evan had packed and were ready for our planned ten day road trip together. We'd be staying mostly in B&B's, with three or four nights in the holiday homes of Jenny and Evan's friends.

The country was in the grip of mad cow disease and tourism had dropped off drastically. I knew it would be a trip to warrant a journal and so each night I'd recall the day's highlights in the lovely little book that Mum had handed me as we left.

We headed south to Torquay. Some of my dad's ancestors had originated from near here. It was all I'd imagined, the sound of it like music to me – soft rolling accents of the south, wintry sea, and gulls, different from our Australian ones. Bigger. Deeper voiced.

Wandering through narrow, hilly, cobble-stoned streets, we passed shops with what must have been decade-old window displays – dusty, faded. Flower boxes of spring bulbs. Washing hanging on poles out of upstairs windows. Pubs whose doorways exuded whispers of warm air. Ancient.

Next day we drove to Looe, a seaside village in Cornwall. Shops and houses all built together, as one. Impenetrably thick walls. Small bright doorways. Low ceilings. It was a grey, cold, drizzly day but cosy inside with open fires and creamy light. We walked along streets with no footpaths, stepping into doorways as cars crept by. Then onto Polperro – another seaside town. From one street, we walked up steep archaic steps to the street above, and then perpendicularly again, to the next one. We chatted to a Cornish man in the doorway of his shop. His tweed jacket had leather at the elbows. A Sherlock Holmes hat gave him dash. Drawing habitually on his hickory pipe, he told us how this bakery had been in his family for three hundred years.

Next day we drove to the city of Bath – tall, stately sandstone. Sitting on a bench in the cricket grounds overlooking the city, we ate our picnic lunch, and I was silent with awe of the age and beauty of the place. We visited the Roman baths that reverberated with the whispers we all found a need to speak in.

The Cotswolds were like fairyland – each village bewitching and unique. Burton-on-the-water was movie-set picturesque. A narrow river divided it with little stone footbridges every so often. And ducks.

We arrived at Stratford-upon-Avon and booked into a cosy B&B. Then out to dinner at Stratford's oldest pub – The White Swan. More than five hundred years of imbibing beneath its undulating roof and chimneys. Our meals were divine – Chicken Roulade with a Stilton and leek sauce and fresh local vegies for me. My generous glass of South African merlot was one of the best I've tasted. We sat in a bay window near the fire, watching the street glistening with rain and old lights, and the Brits scurrying under umbrellas, hats and coats.

Next morning, we indulged in a sumptuous full English breakfast – these a matter of course at most places we stayed in. We visited Ann Hathaway's cottage – fresh and crisp with daffodils in the early morning, sunny coldness. And then to the childhood home of Shakespeare.

In the few hours spent at Warwick Castle, we walked up five hundred and thirty steps, through dark, narrow towers. About halfway up the first one, I had a moment of panic and stopped. I couldn't turn back. The tight staircases were strictly one way. Warren had gone ahead and so with people beginning to mutter, I had to talk to myself sternly to be able to complete the course of steps and then the seemingly interminable length of high rampart walls. My legs felt frightened for hours afterwards.

Driving out of Stratford into the countryside, we could see smoke rising everywhere. Enormous heaps of dead animals were burning. A mass anguish the length and breadth of Britain hung in the air. Newspapers were filled with stories of grief-stricken people trying to keep inspectors at bay. Stud owners were hiding sheep, pigs and cows in their homes. If these animals were destroyed, that genetic line would be wiped out after sometimes generations of breeding.

Heading north through the Lakes District, we felt blessed to have Jenny and Evan's company and their knowledge of the country. Although it was a month into spring, it was still very cold – three to four degrees maximum most days. We were cosy in the car though, and while the sun failed to make its way through the drizzle, we noticed the terrain becoming hillier as we approached Scotland. After booking into a B&B in Windemere, we walked for hours – down to the lake, and around the town.

We passed next day through the village of Troutbeck that looked like it had risen up out of the earth. Cottages were built of local stone, some of which still lay about in small hills where the earth had thrown it up aeons ago. An old lady in bonnet and apron tended turnips in her walled garden. A man in a heavy, patched wool coat, hat pulled down over his ears, passed by in his horse-drawn gig. Rolling hills were dotted with long-woolled sheep, grazing blissfully unaware of their impending fate.

Lockerbie still had a strong air of tragedy about it, even though the aircraft disaster had happened there thirteen years earlier. There were markers and monuments at every turn. As we walked through the main cemetery and memorial park, I tried to imagine what it must have been like to have a passenger jet full of people, fall out of the sky in pieces and hit your town. The inscriptions on the headstones were deeply poignant. We wandered silently.

Glasgow was grim – marred with graffiti, apparently rife with crime. Everything was locked, barred, bolted. We drove through the city quickly, though I'm sure that for the population, there are things to love about it. I've always found a stimulating challenge in discovering beauty one has to search for.

Edinburgh was foreboding for me. Perhaps it was the time of day, the light. By the time we got there, the sun had dropped behind the big hill and the city was gloomy with shadow. With only a couple of business hours left in the day, we poked around the castle.

It had taken us eight days to drive to Scotland, and now we were to drive home in two days.

On our return trip, we stopped at the noble city of York on the River Ouse. I loved the creamy warmth of the sandstone edifices bathed in sunlight. We sat in on part of a Good Friday service in the huge cathedral – the York Minster. The choristers' voices rang to the mighty ceiling.

We spent two more days with Jenny and Evan as they took us to visit special friends in their lovely Buckinghamshire homes, showed us more of Bulstrode, and a few quaint villages round about. They took us into London then, where we were to join a group for a tour of the great cities of Europe. The hotel we had booked for that night was on the Thames, beside The Tower, overlooking London Bridge. We were so grateful to Jenny and Evan whose kindness had made our trip to date so rewarding.

After settling into our hotel, we coated up and set out for a long walk along the river and around the fortress of The Tower and St Katherine's docks. We were to leave for France at five-thirty next morning.

London woke slowly as we rolled through the streets in our luxurious coach. I looked forward to the two days we were to have back here on our return from the continent. I wanted to find the dirty old London of Sherlock Holmes and Dickens. And romantically I wished for gaslights.

We drove to Dover and caught the ferry to Calais from where we drove to Brussels. After booking into our hotel there, we walked the city for several hours.

Next day we drove through country Belgium and into the Netherlands. Farmlands were so low and flat that I had a whole new understanding of the story of the boy with his finger in the dike. The farmhouses were tall and thin with little more than a driveway and border of lanky trees around them, and beyond that, ploughed land – every square inch of fertile soil utilised.

We drove around old Amsterdam, where the white painted window and door frames conquered the gloom of the dark brick structures. From a glass topped boat, we saw the innermost and oldest quarters.

Onto Germany next day where, from Koblenz, we took a river cruise along the Rhine. Vineyards were planted on inclines so extreme I couldn't imagine how it was possible to work them. Whilst on the river we received a phone call from Linc. I gasped at the sight of his number on my phone. We'd had no phone signal for a lot of the time. But there was no need for concern. We were delighted to hear that Ethan was doing well.

That night we stayed in Frankfurt and next day drove through the Black Forest. We stopped on a hill overlooking Heidelberg – one of the most beautiful roof-scapes I have ever seen. It made me think of one of my favourite films as a kid, *The Student Prince*, which had been set in this town. Apart from the buildings and streets, a lot of its charm lay in the whisper of new green buds on trees whose skeletons were still discernible. There was poetry in looking down over the university city through this web. A light snow fell. Fingernails of cold pricked at my face. That night we stayed in Lucerne.

Swiss Alps next day – countryside pretty as a picture. We visited an exquisite church in Innsbruck, decorated in the Rococo style – biblical scenes painted everywhere, in the most glorious pastel hues with lavish gold embellishment. Our hotel in this mountainous snow-covered city was extremely old, and as we dressed for dinner that night, the pealing church bells made me think of home.

Salzburg was on the agenda next day. As the temperature reached twelve degrees, we basked in the sunshine that came with it. For lunch, Warren and I bought mouth-watering wurst and sauerkraut rolls with mustard, and sat on a windowsill in the Mozartplatz Square to eat them. A sweet moment of confluence between us. Without many words, we caught our breath and took stock of how it felt as though we were in a dream. The tour had been exhausting with days beginning typically at five-thirty. We were being driven by our guide to get value for money and to see as much as possible in the three weeks we had. We'd had little opportunity for our own small talk and pleasures, and so relished this one.

We drove for hours then through pristine Austria. Farmhouses as big as hotels accommodated animals as well as people, but the spreads were small. Rainfall is substantial here and the soil so fertile that crops are always abundant. With the help of government subsidies, farms present immaculately – not a thing out of place. I found them visually boring, compared with ours in Australia that are usually dotted with assorted sheds, passé machinery, windmills, yards, weeds, and ruins.

By evening, we'd arrived in Vienna. Much of it quite modern, it could have been Melbourne. Construction workers seemed to be repairing everything at once. The skyline was thick with cranes. After dinner we explored the much more charming old Vienna and eventually found ourselves in a palace where Mozart and Beethoven had performed. An orchestra played the evocative music of the great composers. I had to pinch myself.

Next morning we phoned Linc and Nic to see how Ethan was, and were overjoyed to hear he was breathing without assistance. We lunched that day in a small village of children's shops – Kindburg – where joyously we bought handmade gifts for our dear little grandson. That night we stayed on the island of Lido, with views to Venice.

As we approached Venice by boat next morning, every fibre of my being was alive and singing. I remembered a small wooden gondola with gondolier from Aunty Beryl's souvenir cabinet. What more romantic city was there? We cruised the canals for hours before stepping onto the ancient cobblestones and the square of Saint Marco. The number of people was almost overwhelming. I took photos frenetically. I love my photos. My eyes still delight in the patinas of stone and metal, the proportions and architecture of Europe.

We had coffee in La Laverna tavern where Lord Byron, Oscar Wilde and Ernest Hemingway had plied their craft. A small Latin orchestra of swarthy men in dinner suits played Italian love songs on the street. We looked in at the church where Vivaldi had preached.

Very early next morning we crossed the water to the city again. Shrouded in mist, it breathed with something like the hush of an empty cathedral. Being almost devoid of people, it was even more beautiful. Later, the Murano glass blowers created exquisite works as we watched. We bought Mum a string of handmade etched glass beads for her seventy-fifth birthday, which was that very day. Warren and I poked around the back streets as we love to do. One of the locals took us, by small boat, to the island of Burano where the Venetians live. We had lunch at Al Raspo De Va – five courses of sumptuous Venetian cuisine, all seafood and lovely crisp white wine. The best calamari I'd ever tasted and a magnificent whiting pâté served on small toasts with a squeeze of lemon. Everything so delightfully fresh.

Onwards then to Roma. The Italian countryside was a little more dog-eared. Men were hoeing fields by hand, children playing soccer in their yards. Women with baskets knelt at their tomatoes. There were chooks, small vineyards, fruit trees, ramshackle stucco-clad houses.

Our hotel that night overlooked the Adriatic Sea and as we gazed out at cargo ships lit up like huge hotels, we could hear the sound of waves crashing onto the beach nearby.

Through the rolling hills of Tuscany next day, the farms stole our hearts. My eyes feasted on the quirky houses with their asymmetrical windows – some high, some low, some square, some arched, and their rounded terracotta roof tiles. There were forests of olive trees, Mediterranean pines like our candle pines but almost black, and Italian pines with their tall trunks and huge umbrella-shaped canopies. A few deciduous trees interrupted the evergreen-ness. I loved the architecture of the trees amongst the buildings and ruins, on all sorts of levels. The excitement I felt upon approaching Rome was almost too much to bear.

That evening we walked – just the two of us. We sat in a café and had a beer before dinner, then walked again until we found a restaurant with the kind of atmosphere we always look for – warmth, soft music and lighting, friendly staff. Here, talking intimately across a flicker of candlelight, we put away a delicious smoked salmon pizza with an Italian red wine. We talked about our dreams and goals, and as we did, I felt a deep love for my husband and best friend. With the pressures and stresses of life and work stripped away, I could see and hear the man I'd married. And he was still as handsome.

To be sitting amongst the locals and watching Rome go by was like opening an exquisite gift.

Although the Italian baristas are probably some of the best in the world, I could not enjoy their coffee – short, strong, and never hot.

Next morning, we set out at seven for the Vatican City, but I had woken with a gastric bug. I was afraid of having to spend the day alone near a toilet while everyone else enjoyed one of the places I'd most looked forward to seeing. A voice inside me shouted *"No"*. I prayed for the bug to leave my body and miraculously, within an hour, I had fully recovered.

Genius was everywhere. In the hall of tapestries hung a magnificent work – the resurrection of Christ. Wherever I stood, His eyes seemed to be looking at me. The paintings on the ceiling of this great chamber looked more like sculptures. I could hardly believe they were just paint on a flat surface. It was a circus though. In a crowd of thousands, we were swept along with no chance to linger.

The Sistine Chapel was next. Michelangelo's figures on the walls and ceilings were as if alive, and again, the eyes were upon me, no matter where I stood.

Then onto The Colosseum. The weather was glorious and the ambience and spectacle enough for the crowds to disappear from my mind's eye. That evening we drove around Rome for hours. I found it all stunning and vowed to return.

I was so full to the brim with Rome next day that I had little left for Florence. I took in non-visual things like the lyrical sound of Italian children speaking their language. The sight of magnificent palaces and grand houses went over my head. This day I was content with rooftops. They were uncomplicated, easy to digest. I was saturated, even ready to go home, but Paris was ahead.

We saw the leaning tower of Pisa, Monte Carlo and then Monaco. I loved the Art Deco architecture here – a refreshing change. That night we stayed in Nice on the Italian Riviera in a comfortable hotel on the esplanade. In my nostalgic mood it felt like home – Glenelg perhaps. We spoke to Mum on the phone and she shared the wonderful news that Ethan was almost ready to come home. I longed to hold him.

After a more leisurely breakfast next morning, we drove to St Paul de Vence – an artists' community, ancient and unspoiled. Narrow cobble-stoned streets. Miro, Chagall, Matisse and Picasso had all lived and worked here. One of the most charming villages I had seen so far, with most shop windows alight and alive with stunning works of art.

We arrived at Cannes for lunch. Along the palm tree lined esplanade stood extravagant Art Deco hotels. Thousands of moored yachts bobbed colourfully in sheltered bays. Warren and I walked until we found a cosy café, and at our table for two we laughed as we tried to read the menu. Too hungry to risk words we couldn't interpret, our safe choice was delicate crepes, with coffee. Picasso had painted his "Guernica" near here. The art, the colours –

> Terracotta roofs
> Sea blue muslin curtains feathering out of windows
> on a playful breeze

In the evening
from a garden on a roof
we marvelled at the rain grey sea
brightened by a lighthouse beam
and yachts lit up like villages

With my husband close behind me
his arms around my waist
I closed my eyes and mind
and gave in to my love and senses

Early next morning we left for Grasse – famous for its perfumes. We were now in Provence – vineyards, forests, olive and pine trees, acacia, red poppies. The houses were anomalous, eccentric, many with stepped roof heights – main house two storeys with perhaps a three storey wing at one end. Most were rendered with a cream or pinkish stucco with half round terracotta roof tiles and wooden window shutters painted French Blue or Provence Green. It rained for most of the day but my fire could not be quelled.

We came to Avignon – the ancient walled city where popes had lived. In the town square stood a large and magnificently crafted carousel. Gaudy with age-old colours and lights, it bossed off the gloomy weather. That night we stayed in Lyon.

As we drove through the wine producing regions of Burgundy and the Rhone Valley next day, Paris was foremost in my thoughts. It was just past April and a childhood song was in my heart.

*'April in Paris*
*Chestnuts in blossom*
*Holiday tables under the trees...'*

Despite the traffic being ridiculous, I again somehow managed to block it out and have Paris to myself. Avenues were decorated with the French in their chic clothes and accessories. People sat in outdoor cafes. Trees were indeed in blossom. Artists painted. It was spring after all. We turned a corner and I let out a loud gasp. One foot of the Eiffel Tower appeared at the end of the street just a hundred metres away. Like a full moon coming up over the horizon it was larger than life. Warren wanted to take its lift ride for a view of the city, and while he did that, I walked the streets in awe. I was bathed in a feeling of immense gratitude. The dreams had been blissful, but the reality more so. We went up to Montmartre where the view was good enough for me. As I watched the artists at work, I marvelled at the idea of just how long they had been painting up here. We had a Guinness then in an Irish pub (!) with some of the others from our group, and later descended the 'Martre by funicular. It was time for dinner. We found an inviting restaurant, beautifully lit – a small jewel in a bustling, narrow street. We ate frogs' legs, escargot, and drank a zesty French Riesling. Afterwards, Jeanne Pierre, our driver, drove us around Paris by night, for hours. It was so vibrant. One day I'll have April in Paris, I mused. All of April.

We returned to England where we were met by Jenny and Evan who took us to our hotel. Over dinner, we talked with them about how long it might be before we'd see each other again. They were country people like us but we'd seen how they were valued, and could understand how they'd become international leaders. Jenny has an amazing energy. She's a mover and shaker – one of the most positive, sunny and optimistic people I've known. Against all odds she keeps the physical wheels turning. She knows how to run a house, no matter how large, how to keep people fed, both physically and spiritually, promote what needs to be promoted, and she has an unshakable belief in the power of prayer.

Evan is an academic – historian, scholar, teacher, doctor, and in this job especially, a diplomat. He has had to have a supreme understanding of the politics and cultures of the countries their missionaries are working in, and has had to make sure the leaders and teams are as safe as possible.

As we had this final meal with them we talked about their work, and they shared with us how they missed their family and new grandchildren in Australia. They would soon retire, they told us, and return home to us all.

Our comfortable hotel was near the British Museum, Covent Garden and Leicester Square – all of which we explored over the next two days. On travelling The Underground and realising the depth and magnitude of the construction, I was in awe of its engineering.

As we flew out of Heathrow at midnight, a gossamer-fine net of lights seemed to have been thrown over London – a thousand threads of golden twinkling pin pricks. A fitting way for me to leave as I sat with my elbow on the window's small sill, chin in hand, smiling with delight at one of the loveliest things I had seen.

# THIRTY-THREE

Linc, Nic and Ethan were at the airport to meet us – Ethan's gorgeous little face peeping out of the cloth cocoon against his mother's breast. I took his hand that was warm, plump and newborn baby size. What a difficult time our little champ had been through, but he was now ready for the world. For many months our lives seemed to revolve around him. Although he was asleep most of the time, I could have sat and watched him for hours. He was so beautiful.

We had a seventy-fifth birthday party for Mum a couple of days after we arrived home, with candlelight and champagne and dancing and jazz – a proper party for my Pollyanna Mum. Marlo and Mark came over from Sydney for the celebration and to meet their new little nephew. We'd missed them and looked forward to any time we could sit with them at our table with some simple fresh food, a glass or two of good red and talk a treat about all manner of things.

Marlo had made a decision in Sydney to let acting go. It was a huge resolution for her, based on the soul-destroying highs and lows of "work and no work". She'd seen too many actors spending too much of their lives waiting for the next gig. Marlo is not one to let grass grow under her feet. She entered the film industry at Fox Studios and worked as production assistant, and second and third assistant director on some big films, working with international stars. I couldn't help but recall a parent/teacher interview I'd had with one of her teachers at Nuriootpa High School.

'Marlo spends too much time being an actress,' her teacher had said to me gravely.

Mark was working as lighting designer for The Sydney Theatre Company and production manager for several large outdoor programmes, including The Sydney Arts Festival.

Refreshed after our wonderful holiday, we needed to get back to work on our new farm – Eversden – named in nineteen hundred and six by its original owners. We were the property's second only owners. As we still needed our plant and equipment at Birribi, we enlisted the services of one of our neighbours to break first ground. Ian Farley, one of the Southern Mallee's most successful farmers, had established a huge enterprise. I'd never seen such enormous sheds and so much machinery in one place. Ian was a delight to work with – a unique person with the exuberance and energy of a kelpie pup. Wiry and fit, his deep blue eyes were arresting. He'd call in to our place early some mornings to talk about work in progress or upcoming jobs.

'Would you like a coffee, Ian?' I'd ask.

'Yes please. White,' (during conversation with Warren) 'four sugars,' (more business talk) 'and some toast,' (eyes darting between Warren and me) 'with Vegemite, please.'

Everything happened quickly around Ian. Always so much to do. He'd drive into our yard flat out, pull up and get out of his ute almost before it had stopped – usually leaving the door open. He wasn't going to be in any one place long enough to warrant shutting it. One day his faithful red kelpie, Strawb, had jumped off the ute to fraternise with our dogs while we talked in the yard.

'Alright, must go,' said Ian suddenly. 'Get up, Strawb.'

He hopped into his vehicle and took off. Strawb had been about to jump up but was a fraction of a second too late. He charged after the ute, took a leap, hung onto the tray by his toenails and gradually clawed his way up. As Ian pulled out of our driveway, Strawb turned and gave us one of those dog looks that say so much.

Ian's phone rang incessantly and his two-way radio constantly emitted noise, mostly questions from his workmen. It was hard not to get caught up in his enthusiasm and passion for the region.

The Mallee people were open and generous. Warren had organised a truckie to cart a load of barley to the silos. When fully loaded, the driver had got his semi stuck in a sandy patch. None of our tractors would budge it. Warren phoned a neighbour to see if they had a tractor big enough to do the job. It was Saturday.

'Don's playing tennis down at Parrakie,' said his wife, Lynne. 'Go and have a chat. I'm sure he'll be able to help you.'

Warren went to the courts. Don was playing his singles, and as he changed ends Warren walked with him and asked about a tractor.

'Let me finish my match and I'll come and give you a hand. Won't be long.'

Warren went back to the semi driver and within half an hour Don had arrived with his biggest tractor. He pulled the truck out with ease. This was the first time he and Warren had met. The Mallee people are like that.

We met Pat Larsen – stock agent for Elders. His willingness to help, above and beyond the call of duty, struck an instant chord. Pat is a man of old-school country values, and we liked him instantly. Many are the times he has jumped the rails into our sheep yards to help with drafting, weighing, culling.

I loved our house on this farm – so elegantly sixties that I decided to decorate it in the style of that era. Constant ports of call were several op shops along the way, where I'd buy retro furniture, pictures, lamps, kitchen requisites. Walking into the house was like stepping back in time. Absolutely everything was retro.

Warren's cousin Glen, who'd sold his farm at Western Flat, was preparing to leave his property. Wondering if Glen had any plans for where he was going to live, Warren offered him the use of the second house on our farm. He was delighted with the proposal. Gradually he moved in and it was good to have his company. We'd invite him in for a meal once in a while. Glen knew people in every district of South Australia and had lived a very interesting life. He kept an eye on things when we weren't at the farm, making sure the sheep had enough water, reporting on anything amiss or out of order.

We bought four hundred ewes from an off-shears sale. Warren had read a lot about the Dohne breed – a dual purpose sheep that produced both good wool and meat. He decided to buy one of these rams from a breeder in Western Australia. And Ian Farley lent us three of his Merino rams for breeding that first year.

One of the most difficult things in beginning work on a new property is helping the dogs get used to their new territory. Once they know the run of the place and what's expected of them, it's a wonderful thing to watch them at work. But before ours had got to that stage there were challenges. We'd need to shift sheep to a paddock across the road and railway line. The dogs, of course, weren't sure of where we wanted them to go but were terribly enthusiastic nevertheless. So sometimes the flock would end up on the road to Parrakie, sometimes running along the often-used railway line in both directions, and sometimes disappearing into the bush. Warren would be roaring around on his motorbike, yelling commands at the dogs till his lungs were raw. I'd be on foot, scrambling through the undergrowth, trying to head off and round up small groups of confused and rattled sheep.

It takes a while for dogs to get used to different holding yards too. No two sets are the same. Warren was constantly frustrated with the ones here. He'd built a few in his time. When the sheep baulked at the draft, he'd curse Bill's yards. One day, having listened to his expostulations long enough, I said, 'They're not Bill's yards any more, they're yours. If you can't work with them, fix them.'

So he did. He pulled the whole complex down and built a new set that were a dream to work.

Ian and his team put in several hundred acres of crop for us that first year, and there were good rains. At harvest time two huge headers droned around the paddocks combing and thrashing the plants free of their bounty. Semi-trailers full of grain thundered past the house sending up billowing clouds of dust. The pace was fast and furious – after all it was I.L. Farley's contracting enterprise. We were paid for our grain by cheque, and to deposit these large sums into our small savings account was a fine, fine feeling after years of poor returns.

One day a rep from Elders knocked on our door, in Tanunda. The company knew we'd bought the farm at Parrakie. We'd always dealt with them for merchandise and sold our wool and sheep through them.

'Elders have got into banking,' he told me, 'and we'd really like to have your business. I'm sure you'd find some great benefits.'

I was the only one at home that day, and said to him, 'Thanks for the offer, but we hate banks. We use private money now.'

We had a bit of a chat. He asked a lot of questions about the farm and as he left, he said, 'Well, give it some thought.'

A couple of months later someone else from Elders called. He too propounded the benefits of banking with them.

'We understand the farmer and his needs,' he persisted. 'I'm sure we'd have a product to suit you.'

This time Warren was at home and invited him in. We had realised by now that our small savings account was not going to suit our growing business. But, did we dare to believe he wasn't a wolf in sheep's clothing? He said he could absolutely guarantee that the bank understood farming and the need for flexibility through adverse conditions. And so, from the wonderful feeling of safety we'd had without a bank, we stepped out in faith that this one would be worthy of our trust.

Life was ticking along. We loved the Mallee. At day's end, Warren and I would often sit on the verandah and enjoy a drink together, talk about upcoming jobs, and joke with the dogs who enjoyed this small leisure time as much as we did. There was something soft and gentle about this place. Around the perimeter of the property, a hedge of mallee natives gave us shelter. The huge evening skies would herald coming weather. As we sat, we'd watch our sprawl of sheep grazing in the distance while our small plot on the planet turned slowly away from the sun. At this time of day a cabaret of birdsong tangled the air. Sometimes we could smell the sea.

We inherited a tabby cat.

'What's her name?' we'd asked Bill as we took over the property.

'Don't know, really,' drawled Bill. 'Share-farmer left her here when he finished up. I just call her Kupke – share-farmer's name.'

Kupke was the sweetest cat in all the world. She'd been accustomed to looking after herself any time Bill was away. We'd seen her catch rabbits and any small thing that moved – spiders, moths, mice. She was as healthy as a cat could be. Intelligent. Loving. She'd gallop from wherever she'd been sleeping, to greet us when we arrived, and whenever we were outside she'd follow us all over the place, having a lot to say along the way. When Warren was working sheep, she'd be in the yards with him, amongst the mob. She knew when we were packing to return to the Barossa. As we drove away, she'd sit at the front of the house with sad eyes blinking. Glen would feed her then, but we were spending an average of four days a week there by now.

We had five years with Kupke. One day she wasn't there to greet us. I had a sinking feeling. Later that day, Warren found her lifeless body under the pine trees, the remains of a baby brown snake beside her. It was in her absence that we realised how large her presence had been.

# THIRTY-FOUR

We often called in to Birribi on our way to Eversden. Life was hectic. The farms were more than two hundred kilometres apart. We had our three thousand acres but not in one parcel. On the trip between farms one day, I said to Warren, 'Do you think it would make sense to sell Birribi and buy some more land in the Mallee?'

'Well. Yes. It probably would,' he said after some thought.

While Birribi was spectacularly beautiful, it wasn't as productive as Eversden. We talked about asking Roly to sell it for us. He'd become a real estate agent after having to sell his farm when he and Mary split up. He'd be the perfect agent having lived and farmed in that district for so long. Even though we didn't have high hopes for what we might get for it, considering what had happened at the auction three years earlier, we gave Roly a call. On looking over the certificate of title he said, 'You've got nine sections here.'

'Yes?' said Warren.

'You could create nine titles and sell them off as hobby farms. No building restrictions out here.'

'I wouldn't want to do that,' said Warren. 'It'd be a shame to break up this big parcel of land.'

'Know what?' said Roly. 'If you don't do it, the next chap will.'

The region was already being broken up into smaller allotments. In fact, this was one of the reasons we'd considered selling. Putting hobby farmers and dyed-in-the-wool farmers in a mix together can be like detergent on a barbecue.

We knew that one of our neighbours had spent time in prison. His small holding was pretty well hidden in the hills amongst huge rocks and bush. Even so, the police had found him there when they needed to search his property.

I was in the caravan by myself one day when I spotted him walking across the paddock towards our camp. Built like Rictus Erectus from *Mad Max*, he was as scary as a bachelor's kitchen. Warren and this guy had had a nasty altercation a week earlier. He knocked on my caravan door.

Be brave. Nowhere to go. Can't always judge a book by its cover – the monologue running through my mind. I stayed in the van with the door locked and talked to him through the flywire screen.

He was looking for Warren. Our cattle had been on his property and eaten his crop, he fumed.

In fact, it hadn't been our cattle. Warren had seen this guy's own cattle on the crop and knowing the personality of the bloke, had taken a photo of them. I told him this, politely. He mumbled something and left. Personally, we had nothing more to do with him, but we did hear stories from time to time of his continuing associations with the police.

'Okay,' said Warren to Roly, after some deep thought. 'I hear what you're saying. What would we have to do?'

'Well, it won't be cheap,' said Roly. 'The property will need to be surveyed. I know a good man. We'll have a walk around, look at fence lines, topography, water sites, proportions. It could cost twenty thousand. Then you'll have to do quite a bit of fencing.'

It sounded risky. What if the blocks still didn't sell?

'They'll sell,' said Roly. 'It may take a while but there's a demand for this type of property. They'll attract people looking for a tree change. You've got so many features here – the river, stone wall, views, moss rocks, native bush, red gums, gorge.'

So Roly brought his surveyor up and, with Warren, they walked the property, marking out suitable allotments. It took many months of fencing and dealing with bureaucracy before we were issued our nine new certificates of title.

'Now, we'd better work out some prices,' said Roly over a coffee, when all was ready.

'What do you think?' said Warren. 'Three or four hundred dollars an acre?'

That would have given us three or four hundred thousand total – our optimistic estimation.

'No, no,' said Roly. 'People pay for trees and beauty with these blocks. We could probably put a hundred and twenty thousand on this lot,' pointing at the map, 'maybe a hundred and fifty on the gorge, say a hundred and forty-five on the shearing shed block, a hundred thousand on this ten acres near the electricity pole.'

Warren and I had our mouths open.

'That looks like over a million dollars,' I said when he'd finished.

The premonition. The flash that had seemed so preposterous the night before the auction three years earlier. A million dollars! So this is what had been in store for us.

With Roly's glossy advertising campaign, blocks began to sell.

As a result of reading Robert Kiyasaki's books, I was beginning to understand the power of capital growth. Bill Gravestocks had offered some vendor finance when we purchased Eversden in the Mallee. Ten years' worth in fact, and we'd taken him up on that. It was a retirement income for them. Now, with proceeds coming in from the sale of our Birribi blocks, we could have paid this money back. But, if we bought another property instead, both that and the farm would be gaining in capital value. We considered it wise to begin diversifying and so began looking for rental properties to purchase. I didn't want to spend too much on our first one. It would be prudent to start slowly and carefully. After going to three or four auctions and several more open inspections, I saw a house advertised in our local paper.

'This one sounds good,' I said to Warren. 'It's open this afternoon. Let's go and have a look.'

When we got there, the agent was standing outside. He handed us a brochure.

'I apologise for being out here but the smell inside is unbearable.'

When we stepped through the front door, we were almost knocked over. The house reeked of years of cigarette smoke, and non-housetrained pets. We had a quick look through, breathing shallowly.

'Let's get out of here,' said Warren.

'Wait a minute. I think it's got potential.'

I liked its situation. It was on the edge of town overlooking vineyards. The thousand square metre block had some nice trees and a garden that would respond to care. Some magnificent trees graced nearby properties. I visualised small rooms doubling in size with the removal of a couple of walls. Despite it being a humble pre-fabricated cottage, it had a large stone-walled bathroom with spa. We offered a little less than asking price, cash unconditional, and within three weeks the property was ours.

We set to work immediately. An old friend came to help us. Warren had met John Brennand through motorcycling. John was an outstanding moto-cross rider. When we'd first met him he was working for GMH on the assembly line, but latent within him was an amazing artist. He won a scholarship, left the factory and went to university. By the time he came to help us with this project he'd become a man of letters, an accomplished visual artist and performer.

Any spare time we could find, we spent there at the house with John – removing walls, painting all the rooms a warm white, installing a new (pre-loved) kitchen, cleaning up the garden, hanging new curtains, laying new carpet and having the place rewired. Within four months the place had been transformed. We advertised it for rent. The first couple who came through were young, vibrant, sharp.

'Wow,' said the young lady. 'This is so nice.'

They became our first tenants. It had been a rewarding exercise. We asked the agent to come back and give us a new appraisal. He was amazed. We'd spent fifteen thousand dollars on renovations and raised the value by forty thousand.

We had to be wise with the money that was rolling in from the sale of our blocks. Although we were pleased with the quality and results of Ian Farley's contract work at the farm, the cost of it had subtracted a lot from our bottom line and so we began purchasing necessary plant and equipment from clearing sales in and around the district.

I enjoyed these sales despite the fact that I was usually one of only a handful of women there. We'd arrive ahead of selling and walk up and down the rows of tractors, trucks, ploughs, field bins. Warren would examine the items he intended bidding for while I'd take in the visuals – stored away in my head for future poems or stories. Young farmers dressed in jeans, checked shirts, Blundstone boots, peaked caps with farm machinery logos. Old farmers in more sensible broadbrimmed hats, plainer shirts, work pants with braces – shaking hands with neighbours and old acquaintances, talking about the weather, sheep prices, and bargains bought at last week's clearing sale.

'Sale-o, Sale-o,' an agent would call as the crowd headed for the tray-top truck piled haphazardly with boxes of nuts, bolts, irrigation fittings, welding rods, ropes, grease guns, etc. When these sundries had been sold, the mob would sweep along the rows as, one by one, items were bid for and knocked down. Beneath his ample hat, the ruddy-faced auctioneer sometimes came to a piece of machinery that had some age behind it – needed work. He'd make a joke or a light sarcastic remark and a rolling deep-voiced chuckle would go up. The farm implement shed usually contained the household effects, and lunch – put on by the local school or sporting club.

Usually held through summer when the money from crops was in the bank, or not, the sales in the Mallee were most often hot and dusty affairs. And then there were the excursions afterwards – farmers towing their purchased treasures home along rough bush tracks. I was asked to tow a field bin (about thirty tonne capacity and as wide as the road) after one sale. Warren drove the Leyland Hippo truck he'd bought. The track was so corrugated that one of the wheels fell off my bin. The noise and shuddering brought me to an instant halt. Not surprisingly, Warren was able to repair it with the tools he always carries, and we arrived home just after dark.

One of my roles on the farm has always been to be "on hand". There are a multitude of things to do. It may be to run into Lameroo thirty kilometres away to pick up some chemical, machinery parts or a thousand litres of diesel fuel that I fill myself. I may be called on to help with fencing, bleeding brakes on a tractor, shifting plant, drafting sheep, tailing and castrating lambs, loading hay.

A ewe had stepped into a short off-cut of steel pipe left behind by a windmill mechanic. It was so tight on her leg that her hoof had become inflamed and swollen. It would take an angle grinder to get it off. We put a bag over her to protect her from the sparks and for twenty minutes I held her upright while Warren worked with the care and precision of a surgeon to cut the pipe from her leg. We dressed the wound and sensed her gratitude as she walked away to join the flock.

John Brennand was often with us in these first years at Parrakie. Although he is quite a bit younger than Warren and often silent and thoughtful, the two have worked together happily on our properties for sometimes weeks on end. To leave the cities for a while and work with us in the bush, recharges him creatively, especially when we're fencing. He says he loves the way the wires hum in the wind. After tea at night he'd sometimes say, 'I think I'll go and have a sing.'

He'd climb into an empty grain silo down by the sheds. Great acoustics. He has an amazing gift for harmonic chanting and as he'd warm up, the dogs would go crazy at this canticle from a container. We have been privileged to receive a couple of CD's of his hauntingly beautiful music.

He and Warren and Wayne, my sister's ex-husband, extended our shearing shed together. The shed had become inadequate for the amount of sheep we were now shearing and hadn't been upgraded since its primitive beginnings. Again, we had a goal to complete the build before shearing, and long hours were put in to achieve it. I'd be down in the shed with the men till nine or ten at night, handing them tools, painting woodwork, sweeping up off-cuts and attending to aesthetics. A shearing shed is a wondrous thing.

Wool stencils and hand-forged bale hooks hung on big nails rusted into old timbers. Wooden shelves sagged with shearing sundries – combs and cutters, hand-pieces, oil cans, fly strike powder, emery papers. A splash of brightness was the bundle of new white wool packs in a corner. Two presses, side by side, waited for their fill of soft rolling fleeces. Stainless steel urn on the old wooden cupboard. Bar fridge next to it. Feng shui of the shed. The red Formica and chrome table and chairs from Birribi came with us – all clean and ready for the constant meals ahead. We were to meet and befriend a whole new shearing team.

Warren had heard about a wool-classer who lived in Parrakie. He visited her. Andrea was our age and had worked in sheds Australia-wide for years. A tough task master for her rousies, she was soft to the core in spite of it. She agreed to do our classing and told Warren she had a daughter who was a roustabout.

For two or three years an assortment of shearers passed through our shed. These workers are in short supply and like to know all their needs will be met before they agree to anything long term. It's a tough job. We appreciate that and have always done our best to provide conditions that will make their job as tolerable as possible. In return we've ended up with a well-oiled machine – salt-of-the-earth Mallee people, many of whom are from farming stock if not farmers themselves. Andy Dyer, our shearing contractor, is reliable and efficient. An amazingly skilful shearer himself, he often graces our board. I think he likes our sheep – plain, free-combing Dohnes. And I enjoy cooking for them all. It's rewarding to hear the sounds of satisfaction as they eat, and to have them thank me heartily for the meals.

After the day's last run we enjoy a beer and a chat together in the shed – again stories of people of the district, best farming practices, and sometimes worst. Stuff that shearers learn as they go from farm to farm. As good as a rural newspaper really.

Warren seemed happy with the way his life was going. He was now able to farm the way he'd always wanted to. The dream that he'd worked so passionately towards for so long, was coming to fruition. We didn't have the three thousand acre holding yet but were always vigilant for land sales nearby. Warren switched to organic fertiliser in favour of the harsh phosphates. In all his reading he'd been attracted to ideas of low chemical farming. It was wonderful to see the way our pastures responded, to discover earth worms at work, to see our sheep thriving. To lean towards the organic way was a noble idea and would have worked had it not been for the drought to follow.

We loved our farm and our enthusiasm rubbed off on friends and family who sometimes came to stay for weekends. The house was more than adequate to accommodate everyone. Mum often came down and did what she'd done with me for years – pottered in the garden, watered, weeded, planted. She's left a lot of gardens to be remembered by. The two of us would sometimes go for an evening walk in the bush, catching our breath at rare birds, native trees and flowers. We came across manmade treasures too – old jars, bottles, crockery, saucepans – discarded by farmers gone. Things to take home and put on shelves.

Marlo and Mark came home from Sydney for Christmas each year and if there were important family functions, they'd fly back for those too. I missed my daughter and friend and spoke to her often on the phone. We'd been to visit them in Sydney during the Olympics. The city had been so dressed up and alive. Marlo and Mark's little rented house in Leichhardt was warm and enchanting – eclectic, full of books, artwork, interesting pieces. There was a five page spread of their home in a prominent fashion magazine. They worked hard and were doing well.

Linc and Nic's business was growing. They had established a good clientele. Linc was growing his "stable" of machinery and broadening the range of services he could offer. We were now able to help our kids a little, financially – something we hadn't been able to do when they were younger. As sad as that had made me at the time, I realised now that it helped them become the hardworking, resourceful people they are.

I was content with my life. Although living in a man's world was challenging, it was enriching and never boring. From time to time however I'd long for female company. There just didn't seem to be time for it. In our three days a week at home in the Barossa I'd have to tend my house and garden, deal with mail and bills, replenish food supplies, and I loved to catch up with family. Any time I could care for our beautiful grandson was a happy time for me.

Association with girlfriends was so lacking in my life that I resolved to do something about it. I put on a girls' lunch. We had such a great time that we decided to do it regularly. Once every couple of months, five of us still get together – each of us taking a turn at hosting. Over a sumptuous meal and wine to match, we catch up with our news, talk about what we've read, what we've seen on the screen or heard on ABC radio. And sometimes, after a few wines, we get silly and tell stories that bring on laughter to the point of tears.

I soon realised how important these feasts of discourse were, in bringing some balance to my scales so heavily weighted on the male side.

Donna was another friend. Her dreams and goals were nearly indistinguishable from my own and we had a passion for houses in common. She and Roly owned a lovely home in the Adelaide hills overlooking a golf course. Roly was still selling real estate and Donna working as a psychiatric nurse. We'd dreamed of holidays together on the beaches of the world, and now the four of us were planning to go to a Global Wealth Conference in Pattaya, Thailand. There would be speakers from around the world talking on various investment strategies – share trading, real estate, gold, cattle, olives, etc.

We arrived in Bangkok at midnight. A man held up a board displaying our names and we followed him out of the coolness of the airport into the hot damp night. Climbing into a small urban van we searched for non-existent seat belts and before long were travelling at a hundred and forty kilometres an hour through heavy traffic. It was two-thirty when we arrived at our opulent hotel. Warren and I fell into our bed that was big enough for a party and slept without waking. Next morning, we stepped from our room into a huge foyer wrapped in a curve of floor to ceiling glass overlooking a glorious bay of sparkling blue. The view stopped us in our tracks. Large yachts, small boats and sail boards rocked in rippling wakes. The gleaming beach was alive with holiday-makers and enterprising Thai – basket weavers, hat-makers, toenail painters, masseuses – all offering their wares.

The floor of this foyer was covered in the most exquisite mosaic of handmade tiles – smooth-edged turquoise blues, oranges, wine reds, laid in stunning design. The feel of it beneath my bare feet bordered on erotic. A young man dressed in traditional Thai uniform stood with his hands behind his back – his only job to greet people, show them to the lift and keep this magnificent floor clean.

The conference, held in the hotel, was to begin next morning and run for five days. The information we'd come away with would be invaluable, especially that from real estate guru Dolf de Roos who told us how important it was to invest in what you are passionate about. Think back to your childhood, he said, and recall your favourite pastimes. I was on track.

~

Through my childhood, spring had always been time for hut building. I can't remember an activity I enjoyed more. Dad had given us a large piece of weldmesh with spiky ends. In a shady spot on the lawn, we'd drive it into the ground to create a half cylinder shape, then clad it with hessian. The little house was made homely then with wooden crates, flowers, curtains and tablecloths. On hot days we'd hose it down so any breeze would lower the temperature inside to deliciously cool. I'd be blissfully happy to have created our own little haven where we could play mums and dads of every ilk – dramas in which we lived every kind of social dilemma imaginable.

~

Now it was time to learn how to buy, build and furnish real homes.

By four pm speakers would have finished for the day and we'd go out to play. An affable Thai man named Eddie appointed himself our driver. We rode on elephants, saw traditional dancing, spectacular temples, and he delivered us into the hands of the best masseuses. In the evenings we wandered the streets, shopped, ate, drank and tried to elude the prostitutes who wanted everyone – men or women. The heat was oppressive but bearable as we returned each evening to swim in our hotel's sparkling pool.

In Bangkok we cruised the Chao Phraya River for half a day in a small wooden vessel. The indigenes who lived along the river had little privacy as we motored past their shanties that hung over the water.

> Children swung from suspended tyres
> Swam and splashed
> their laughter ringing round the dwellings
> Washed clothes hung on ropes
> and women sat at seasoned tables
> readying their daily fish and rice.

We left the country then, refreshed and enriched, and returned to exciting times at home.

# THIRTY-FIVE

It had been years since we'd made any improvements to our home. It was looking sad. Roof and gutters were beginning to rust, paint on the outside timbers peeling. The old detached original kitchen was fretting with salt damp, and our dining room still had its original rammed earth floor which was breaking up beneath the carpet. It was time to give the old girl a spruce up.

'I think we need to re-roof the place,' I said to Warren.

'And I really need an office,' said he.

We were on a roll.

'We could enclose the back verandah to create a family room. And what about a guest wing?'

We'd always assured Mum that if she was ever unable to care for herself, she could come to live with us. The offer had always comforted her.

'Okay,' said Warren. 'Let's do it.'

The home had been built in eighteen eighty-nine by Warren's paternal grandparents. Lin and Otto had extended and renovated it in the fifties, and now it was our turn.

I'd dreamed of this for so long. This was our shot at it and I wanted to give it all it deserved. It would be a quality build – worthy of past and future generations.

We approached local builder Roger Kruger, whose work we admired, and then Jamie Gladigau – practiced architect and old school friend of both Linc and Marlo. The day we began discussing our ideas with them, it felt like a dream. Building began in January. September was the end goal.

For a long time Warren and I had talked about exploring the Kimberley – a region we hadn't spent much time in during our big trip of the seventies. We decided to do it that year, while our house was in disarray.

We'd built lane-ways through the farm so that each paddock and trough could be checked without opening gates. It would be easy for Glen to keep an eye on things while we were away. Crops were in. We'd had good opening rains. Our friends, Reg and Judy – parents of Marlo and Linc's friend, Ben – were to come with us. We'd be away five weeks and would camp.

We bought a rooftop sleeper and mounted it to our Range Rover. Into the back of the vehicle Warren fitted all we'd need for the trip – sink, stove, fridge, storage containers, spare fuel, water. All slid in and out on rails. We had a soft case each for our clothes, two deck chairs and a table. It was the most compact unit I had seen.

Three or four years earlier we'd been camping with Roly and Donna at Coongee Lakes and had lived from the back of our ute which, in the end, looked like a shoe clearance. Warren swore then that when we went camping next, it would be five-star.

So on this trip to the Kimberley, on setting camp each afternoon, we'd simply open the back of the Rover, lift out our chairs and table, grab a beer from the car fridge, and sit back to enjoy the scenery.

First stop was Coober Pedy. We began to relax and contemplate the five weeks ahead of us. However, after tea and bedding down this first night, a wild wind whipped up. Although I knew our comfy bedroom on top of the car was strongly built and that the car weighed two and a half tonnes (I'd woken Warren to ask him), I thought at any moment we'd be tipped over. Reg and Judy were in a tent. In howling winds, all through the night, we could hear the muffled thud of Reg's rubber mallet as he tried to keep their shelter anchored.

Next morning we couldn't sit down for breakfast. In a wind that felt like it was coming off the South Pole, we had to keep moving to keep warm. I wondered if the desert nights would always be this cold.

Continuing northwards that day, I was filled to the brim with the joy of travelling. To hit the road and have the demands of business peel off, layer by layer, is life restoring for me. By now I think we'd resolved that we needed to have a break from work once a year – to refresh our souls, recharge the batteries.

From the cosiness and comfort of the car, we were helped along that day by a raging south-westerly. Despite the wind, the Outback did its job on me. Acacias, wedge-tailed eagles, the soft colours of the low roadside flora, red dirt and big sky sucked out any remnants of business matters left in my head. That night we pulled up about twenty-five kilometres north of Kulgera. Routinely we'd start looking for a spot around four pm – ideally something with a few trees or at least some reasonably sized bushes for shelter, and dry firewood. This spot was perfect although we did notice a bore pump nearby. We set camp – not a big job for us but quite time consuming for Reg and Judy. They'd just finished setting up when a bloke came roaring up in his four-wheel drive and started the single cylinder diesel engine that pumped water to the station stock troughs.

'It'll run out of fuel about midnight,' he called to us as he sped off.

We stayed up, knowing that in all probability we wouldn't get to sleep until the thing had stopped. The Outback began to freeze again and so we stoked our campfire, donned our warmest clothes and drank a bottle or two of good red wine. Reg and Judy's sons, Ben and Nick, were now making some superb reds. At about ten-thirty we turned in but lay awake as the motor knocked away apologetically. At *four* it spluttered, then shattered the night with silence. At seven we raked the coals and stirred the fire back to life. The kettles were soon hissing and, standing on frost crunching grass, each behind our own bush, we carried out our morning ablutions. We sat then on our rugged-up chairs, warming our hands around mugs of hot coffee and staring wearily into the friendly flames. I was happy.

In Alice we stocked up on supplies enough for the journey through the Tanami Desert, and dry foods enough to sustain us in case of a breakdown. After a wander about town, we headed for Yuendumu – the Aboriginal settlement where we'd spent our enriching three months in the seventies. The road was bitumen now, although still only one car's width. It took us three and a half hours to get there, compared with the eleven hours last time. Our friends, Tony and Helen, were still living and working there, and welcomed us in their usual loving way. They'd invited some mates to join us around a drum fire and barbecue in their backyard that night – folk who'd lived and worked in Papua New Guinea for some time and were now doing a stint here for this community. Yuendumu was sadly run down – administered now by the Aboriginals themselves.

After a leisurely talk-filled breakfast next morning, we hugged Tony and Helen goodbye and headed into the back country. At Rabbit Flat we refuelled and filled spare jerry cans – last fuel for several hundred kilometres. Camp that night was near the Tanami mine – barren, desolate, big land.

Next morning we drove for twenty or thirty kilometres through an enormous herd of Brahmin cattle. They seemed peaceful, but it was hard to imagine what they were eating. It was so dry.

We came upon Wolfe Creek meteorite crater – second largest in the world and millions of years old. Standing on its rim we turned to take in the three hundred and sixty degree view to the horizon.

> Dead flat stony landscape
> Not a structure
> Not a tree
> A place for sand-coloured scuttling creatures
> Silence was a sound
> that made my heart beat faster

That afternoon we reached Hall's Creek and were thankful for hot showers. The warm night loosened us in our camp chairs.

At Fitzroy Crossing next day we had lunch on the town lawns. Populated largely by Aborigines who were also enjoying the well-kept gardens, the town looked taken care of now. I began to realise just how many Indigenous people live in the top end. We arrived in Broome at about six. The city was enormous now – no longer the quaint, sleepy town of the seventies.

Night had fallen and we were trying to find the caravan park. A local must have been on the same two-way channel as we were and kindly directed us to the Cable Beach Park.

'What's your booking number?' asked the receptionist when we got there.

'We haven't booked.'

She looked up from her desk in amazement. 'We're booked out twelve months ahead at this time of year,' she said, as if speaking to someone from another planet.

We drove to the Broome Caravan Park – about four kilometres out of town and away from the beach. They had two un-powered sites left on the outer reaches of the park – against the bush and a long walk from the amenities. We didn't care. Kangaroos grazed near us as we enjoyed our barbecue by moonlight.

For three beautiful days we wandered Broome like kids at a fairground. It still had a uniqueness with its big old weatherboard and corrugated iron houses shaded under vast verandahs.

During our time away we phoned our builder, Roger, once a week, to see how renovations were coming along. We'd been basking in glorious weather while his team had been suffering days of five degrees maximum. Apart from that, everything was going smoothly he told us. Another of our blocks at Eden Valley had sold and so there were no concerns about having enough money to keep paying the builders.

While we'd had Cable Beach to ourselves in nineteen seventy-four, we shared it this time with thousands. A resort stood here now, and at day's end, people lined up along the concrete sea wall to take photos of the sunset which was no more beautiful than those we saw regularly from our farm. But we joined the crowd in their enjoyment of the place.

After Broome we headed for Derby where we lunched at the Wharf Café. Not your swanky, up-market café, but your old-style fish and chip shop, with an eclectic modernity that, in a twist, actually did make it stylish. Fresh barramundi with chips and a Greek salad was my choice. Fish and chips were wrapped in paper. One of my life's most memorable meals, the barra' had been caught that morning. Heavenly. We had a beer then in The Boab Inn – the locals' pub. A no-nonsense Irish girl with a Mohawk haircut was in charge, while Aborigines and station hands swapped lies at the bar.

Later we drove to Windjana Gorge where we "staked our claim" for the night. Other travellers were rolling in, and there were only a handful of trees. We'd be grateful for shade in the morning as the days were quite hot by now. After setting camp, we drove out to Tunnel Creek – a grand and towering site where, in the early nineteen-hundreds, an Aboriginal named Pigeon, who'd been hunted by police for three years, had finally been apprehended, and tragically shot. The rock formations were enormous, with a creek disappearing into the blackness beneath them.

On returning to camp we pulled the tops from our icy beers – five o'clock protocol – and walked into the magnificent gorge. Freshwater crocodiles basked on the sandy beaches or floated motionlessly on the mirror of water. The sinking sun set the massive rocks ablaze with top end colours – salmon pink, purple, orange, white.

Next night we broke camping rules and set up in the dry bed of the May River. With the wet season still at least three months away, we figured it should be safe. We chose a high spot that looked like it would be an island in all but a raging torrent. It was quiet – not another soul in sight – possibly something to do with the sign that said, "Beware of Crocs". We went to bed with strange night sounds batting at the air. Just before daybreak and from deep sleep, I sat bolt upright, heart pounding at the sound of something enormous approaching. A road train full of cattle thundered past within ten metres of our camp. The driver hardly slowed for the creek crossing that he'd probably done a hundred times.

We camped next to running creeks crowded with trees, palms and huge ferns. The music of small waterfalls and birds rang through the bush. We swam, lit fires against the sometimes still cold nights and went to bed early. Reg and Judy are wonderful travelling companions. Reg has a sense of humour that never rests. We can sit around a campfire recalling hilarious life events, after which Judy and I can laugh ourselves to sleep. Or on other nights we might fall into deep philosophical discourse.

Reg is someone you can rely on to have brought everything you could possibly need on an outback trip, and often multiples of the same which can sometimes give rise to teasing, and at other times thankfulness.

At King Edward River, a volunteer ranger directed us to what had once been an important site for the Aboriginals – the Kwini mob. Set beside the river it had a profoundly spiritual energy. There was a hush and an etherealness about the place. Soft grasses and shady native trees spread over a park-like area of two or three acres. On the walls of a natural amphitheatre under a craggy outcrop were age-worn paintings of Wandjanas, Bradshaws – the Bradshaws so ancient that even the Indigenous can no longer read them. They believe they were painted by the spirits before people were created.

In small niches in the rocks lay human skeletons. As I stood in awe there, a gentle wind of ghostly voices sighed through the place. I felt like praying, in thanks for this experience. But I felt a deep sadness too. Why had these people had to leave this incredibly beautiful place?

We needed permits to visit Kalumburu – an Aboriginal reserve on the north-east coast. Giant mango trees and coconut palms shaded us where we camped and although it was only August, storm clouds and humidity were building. Some of the local lads were playing football in bare feet, on a concrete basketball court covered in broken glass. Their "football" was a two litre plastic Coke bottle a third full of water.

We spent a night on the beach at McGowan Island. At sunset, a black girl stood fishing from a large rock – her only means, a simple line and hook. With a clear, uncluttered mind I could see the entire beauty in it. I must remember to do this more often, I mused – to see between the lines of life.

El Questro was five-star camping. Where the Pentecost and Chamberlain Rivers meet, the camp grounds were thick with tropical trees and enormous spreading eucalypts. The increasing heat and humidity couldn't touch us here. The slow-flowing river and small waterfalls were constantly in shade and we swam several times a day. A classy open-air restaurant tempted us in with icy drinks, sumptuous food and mellow jazz– an absolute anomaly out here.

Then on to Zebedee Springs. A fifty minute strenuous walk through dense bush, over rocks and fallen logs took us to Emma Gorge. The reward was worth the trial. Exquisite sparkling water fell a hundred metres into a crystal clear rock pool about fifty metres across, and although the water was freezing, we swam again.

Wyndham was our next port of call. At the Five Rivers lookout we watched the sun drop onto a vast shimmer of shallow water as far as the eye could see. Next to us stood a solitary, pensive woman. In the middle of our small talk, she told us she had terminal cancer.

'I come up here every night for this,' she said, as she dragged on her cigarette and sipped from her stubby of beer. 'I should have been dead long ago, but watching the day end from up here, just seems to go on saving me.'

At Kununurra we boarded a light plane to see the Bungle Bungles. This vast, towering and foreboding rock formation had always looked so mysterious in documentaries and I was so looking forward to seeing them from above, but in our small aircraft, the day's abnormal air pockets and thermals had us faltering through the air like paper in a whirlwind. There were eight of us on board. A girl behind us threw up. There was an ugly chain reaction. For the entire two hour flight, whether flying high or flying low, the pilot could not make us comfortable. Death would have been kinder.

We were so relieved to return to our camp. With feet like lead, we laboured to climb the ladder to our bed on top of the car where we slept for hours, till the terrible nausea passed.

Our last stint would be in Darwin – two days in modern side-by-side self-contained apartments overlooking Cullen Bay. We absolutely loved this place again – vastly different though from the hippy city of the seventies. It was cultured now, with fabulous markets, restaurants and galleries. We imbibed it all for two full days, then headed south to the Alice and home.

# THIRTY-SIX

Linc and Nic were expecting their second child and ready to buy their own home. After a few weeks of searching, they found one they loved in the Barossa – a beautifully appointed, solid old house on a big block that came with magnificent views over rural countryside. They moved in just a few days before the birth of Jacinte Claire – a gorgeous baby with dark hair and big eyes. Double the love now with two delightful grandchildren.

September had come and gone and our renovations and extension were nearing completion. We'd continued to live in the house while the work went on around us, and couldn't have asked for a more skilled, meticulous and unobtrusive team. Throughout this joyful time, Warren's input astounded me. I'd had no idea he had such strong and contemporary concepts about home design. Thankfully we rarely disagreed.

We'd planned to have Christmas at our place that year – eighteen of us. On the twenty-third of December we were in organised chaos. There were ten tradesmen finishing off. Warren was helping all of them. I was shopping, cooking, wrapping presents and answering countless questions about small details. It was crazy and euphoric. The magnificent extension was finished just in time.

Christmas was a joy. There's a different element to it when there are twinkle-eyed children to watch.

In the new year I began browsing op shops for the treasures that are part of our home today – unique pottery, mid-century stuff and anything with a Scandinavian or Indigenous history.

What a far cry our home, garden and lifestyle was from my humble beginnings in the wee stone cottage of my early childhood.

~

I'm sure my parents had been thankful for their four small rooms. The kitchen had a wood stove that kept us warm in winter, and on summer days of searing heat, we'd go down into the cellar for some respite. My bedroom was austere – in it my bed and a wardrobe. My parents' room doubled as our lounge. In it was their bed, a dressing table, my sister's cot and the three-seater club lounge. Although this little house could only be described as lowly, it had my mother's stamp of elegance about it. Crystal glittered on white doilies on the dressing table. Curtains and bedspread were of fine cream lace. There might not have been quantity, but my mum has never compromised on quality.

Although gardens were not the recreational, landscaped living spaces they are today, Mum always grew flowers. Rectangular raised garden beds flourished spectacularly throughout the seasons. With a bunch of stocks in hand I'd close my eyes and draw in long draughts of the divine perfume. To this day, the smell of these flowers takes me back to this sunny, cheerful garden of my first home – a living canvas of colour. To be allowed to water the fragrant assortment with a bronze rose screwed to the end of a hose, and to see the wet brilliant blooms nodding and sparkling in the sunlight, delighted me down to my toes.

There was a patch of buffalo grass off the back verandah. Dad's shed was nearby, and a large rainwater tank – our only water supply. Behind the shed was a perpetual wood heap – to fuel the stove that sang constantly with kettles. Our loo, like everyone's, was down the back – emptied once a week by the man with the night cart.

At the end of the war, Dad had bought a wrecked Airspeed Oxford aircraft that sat spectacularly in our yard. A source of great entertainment for me and several other kids of the town, this aeroplane was full of switches and instruments that stimulated our healthy imaginations. Of course, Dad had explained to me how they had been flown, and that they had been a training aircraft.

Our tiny stone cottage was built right up to the footpath, European style, and on the street grew an enormous Moreton Bay fig tree. The tree is still there, albeit old and feeble now. From the corner of the house to the neighbour's property, ran a picket fence – two or three pales of which were missing. I'd sit on the rail in this gap to watch the townsfolk come and go.

Neighbours on one side, the Staricks lived in the house behind their grocery store. On their way home from market, farmers would park their small trucks, often raucous with livestock, in the shade of our big tree, and call in to the shop for their weekly supplies. I loved to have them speak to me, and have never failed to appreciate the value of that country town familiarity.

The store was wonderfully aromatic, with the smell of spices and apples, onions and soaps, cheeses and aniseed balls, sugar in hessian and flour in calico. The door squeaked as you entered and a small bell tinkled. The floorboards creaked, and so too the cellar door as it was opened. The young and cheerful grocer would clomp down the wooden steps into the dark and dank unknown, and re-emerge with butter or cheese, and sometimes lemonade. There were no fridges, so most houses had cellars.

Built onto our cottage at the front was a small lean-to sleep-out. When my uncles and aunts came to stay, Mum would make up the large single bed in this room with crisp white linen. The only other item in the room was a chair – and fresh flowers she'd picked from the garden and placed in a fine china vase on the window sill.

'All ready now,' she'd say with sunny satisfaction.

~

I must have inherited the love of homemaking from my mum.

Now with our renovations complete, I was thankful for the beautiful environment that we too had created. We were in a fortunate phase of our lives now and I dared to hope it would last.

We had a call from the agent who'd sold us our rental property – to tell us the house beside it was now for sale.

'It'd be good for you,' he said. 'Another big block. You'd have half an acre on a corner. Could be useful down the track.'

We went to have a look. The pre-fab cottage was in the same state as the other one had been at purchase, and we bought it for little more than land value. Soon after starting renovations however, we found it too far gone. A bulldozer would make the scuttling quick. We'd subdivide the block and build two new homes. But before we had a chance to start, we had a call from an Elders real estate agent. A farm known as The Ranch, not far from Eversden, had come up for sale. Nine hundred acres. It hadn't registered for me but Warren must have done some quick sums. Adding this to Eversden and our Barossa hills country, his magic number would click over – *three thousand acres of good productive farming land,* and almost all of it in one parcel. There was little discussion. We had the money and signed an unconditional contract. A lifelong dream was about to become reality. I remembered my husband's words from forty years earlier when, although I'd been in love with someone else, *he* knew we'd spend our lives together.

'*I believe if you want something badly enough you'll get it.*'

When a goal is set "in concrete" there seems to be a force that tracks it down. Warren always believed that this amount of land would give us a good living. With a growing and self-replacing flock of sheep, we watched our Dohnes reliably achieving a lambing rate of a hundred percent plus, and naively and briefly we basked in a feeling of having reached our zenith.

One day I was reading *The Trading Post* newspaper when I spotted a small ad on the back page, "*For Sale - House in Crystal Brook on 2,000 sq.m. Three bedrooms. Two bathrooms. Large living area. Three car garage. Established trees and garden. Nothing to do. Unused church hall included. Price - $122,000*".

We phoned the agent next day and made an appointment to see it. The house was fifteen years old – well-appointed, neutral colours, modern, immaculate. The hall was about fifty years old – corrugated iron, one huge room with a garage/workshop attached, and an interesting little foyer in the front. It was full of junk and dark with small windows, but the draw-card for us was its magnificent jarrah floor. We could picture a very modern house in it while, considering the price, the vendors could only have seen a shed.

We'd just sold another block at Eden Valley and so bought this property for a little less than asking price. We appointed a rental manager and had the house tenanted within three weeks of settlement.

A young builder from nearby Gladstone had been recommended to help us with the conversion of the hall, but as it turned out, it would be a while before we would start that.

We were still farmers first and, farmers or not, three thousand acres or not, life would *not* always be golden.

## THIRTY-SEVEN

About nine-thirty one night we were home in Tanunda when the phone rang. At that hour it could only be Glen.

'Got some trouble here,' he said.

'What's wrong?' I heard Warren say.

'Sheep at The Ranch are out of water.'

'How long have they been out?' Warren's voice urgent.

'I checked the day before yesterday. Everything seemed alright then.'

Warren grabbed the keys to his ute, two dogs, kissed me and rushed off. It would be near midnight before he got there and there'd be little he could do that night, but he'd be on the job at first light.

At dawn he discovered the windmill rod had broken. The holding tank was empty. Being high summer, the sheep were drinking large amounts in a day. Pacing restlessly Warren waited for the water from our rainwater tank at Eversden to fill the portable one he'd loaded onto a trailer. When it was full, he raced it over to The Ranch, four kilometres away. As he filled the trough, the sheep were nearly knocking him over to get to it. He knew they shouldn't drink too much but couldn't keep them away. We learned later that putting electrolytes in the water may have helped. As the thirstiest had their fill and walked away, they went down like flies. Seventy young ewes died that day.

When Warren phoned to tell me what had happened I could sense there had been little in his lifetime that had come near to the heartbreak he was feeling at this moment. The tragedy threw him into deep despair, then anger, then resolve. Windmills don't often break and as long as they're working, there's water filling the tank, but this tank had proven too small. With the mill malfunction it had emptied quickly. We'd have to install a bigger one. We were rarely away from the farm for more than a few days and the new tank would hold enough water for at least a week. This would never happen again. Warren dug a long pit with his front-end loader and buried the dead. As an animal lover he was distraught.

Then another blow. Our crops had been promising good yields when there'd been a frost in the district, at flowering time. We thought we'd been unaffected. Everything looked okay but a few weeks later, when it was time to reap, Warren found large areas where the heads that looked plump were in fact empty – shamming, like a carcass powdering with a kick. So much time and effort in the planting and tending. Now these vacant, heartbreaking crops. We were in the pits. But we had to let it go and believe in better times. If we couldn't do that, we couldn't farm.

We had to re-establish a bank overdraft, but next year would be a better one. Our flock would increase. We'd have rain, good crops, and the overdraft would be knocked out. We believed, as we're meant to.

We had an average yield the following year and we're always happy with that, but prices suddenly dropped by fifty percent. The northern hemisphere had enjoyed an exceptional harvest, resulting in a world-wide glut of grain. We were not to make any headway that year.

I found myself thinking constantly about diversifying. Farming is such a gamble, but people will always need houses, I'd muse.

The last of our blocks had been sold, and we'd bought The Ranch with the proceeds. We'd hoped to convert the church hall in Crystal Brook into a home with money from harvest. But there wasn't enough for that now, so we decided to borrow against that property to do the conversion. The rent from the two houses would be more than enough to cover the mortgage.

Again we engaged our architect, Jamie, and between us designed something urban and elegant. Tim Zander was the perfect builder for us. In his late thirties, he too was passionate about property. He'd been buying old cottages in his town, doing them up, and renting them out.

We went to "The Brook", two hours away, for short stints to see the work in progress and to do some ourselves. At first, we'd stay in the pub which was like having a short holiday, but when the house got to lock up, we'd stay in that. Our trusty helper, John, was with us again on this project. He and Warren did a lot of the early interior gutting. I knocked hundreds of nails back into the huge expanse of jarrah flooring and was on hand for the countless "would-you-just…" jobs. Finally, we'd created a unique and modern home from the bones of a hall. It was time to have a celebratory family get-together there.

Everyone came. We spent the afternoon preparing and tasting food and wine for the evening repast – talking, laughing and listening to good music. As night fell, we lit dozens of candles, tried out the new mood lighting, and enjoyed the sumptuous meal we'd created with love and passion. We all slept on the floor.

It was crutching time at the farm. Sheep backsides were dirty from the soft spring pastures and blowflies would soon be about, so Warren and I went out to muster The Ranch. We took three dogs with us. Robert was the happiest dog in all the world and brilliant in the paddock. Terry was faithful and nurturing to everyone and, with the courage of Attila the Hun, excellent in the yards, and Flo, our youngest was still learning. Jeppi, retired now, stayed back at the farmhouse. Warren was on the quadbike and I was driving the ute. It was hot.

We'd mustered the sheep into one big mob and the task now was to travel them the four kilometres from The Ranch back to Eversden.

'I'll start with Terry and Flo,' said Warren. 'Robert can stay on the ute for a while then I'll let him off and rest the other two.'

Before we got back out to Ranch gate however, Robert, nearly mad with the need to be working, managed to climb the metre and a half high hurdles of the ute and drop from the top of them while I was driving slowly. We'd spent a huge sum of money having a torn cruciate ligament in his hind leg operated on, but the procedure had been unsuccessful and he'd lost the use of that leg. After dropping onto his three good legs, he raced for the sheep, but within minutes was sitting in the shade. This was unusual. He must have winded himself, I thought, and so we gave him a drink and put him back on the vehicle. He carried on about not being able to help. At the end of the four kilometre drive, as we were nearing the shearing shed, he started yelping. Again I thought it was a "let me off, I want to help," performance, but when I looked in the rear vision mirror I was alarmed to see him extremely distressed. His tongue was hanging out, his eyes wide. I jumped out of the ute and yelled to Warren.

'Robbie's in trouble.' He hurried over and by now Robert was on his side, panting furiously. 'He could have heat stroke,' I suggested.

I ran up to the house and phoned the nearest vet, more than an hour's drive away. 'I think we may have a dog with heat stroke,' I said. 'What can we do for him?'

'Bring him straight in,' she said.

'I don't think we have time. What can I do for him now?'

'Get his head cool. Wet towels.'

I grabbed a bucket of water and a towel and ran down to the ute.

'I don't think he's going to make it,' said Warren. 'He stopped breathing. I gave him CPR.'

I put the wet towel over Robbie's head. He was gasping for life, then silence, a terrible stillness. Warren pumped his chest again.

'Come on Robbie,' I said in a voice high-pitched with fear. 'We've got sheep for you. It's crutching time.'

He opened his eyes and tried again to live. Then Warren said, 'I think it's going to rain. I've got to get these sheep shedded. Do you think you can do this if he stops breathing again?'

'Yes, I can.'

He stopped breathing another three times. 'No Robbie,' I cried. 'Come on, mate. Don't die.'

I kept up the cardiac pressure – each time for a little longer before he'd respond. Finally, he lay peacefully, breathing, and looked up at me with his beautiful brown eyes. He'd made it. It was a miracle. We carried him to his bed and he slept.

At seven next morning the shearers rolled in and the pace was fast and furious as usual. Warren had made a bed for Robbie near the shed and every half hour or so went out to check on him. He'd begun to behave strangely and we thought he may have suffered brain damage. Then he became abnormally thirsty and couldn't stop drinking. Warren came up to me in the house where I was cooking.

'I think you'd better come and say goodbye to Robbie,' he said.

My heart sank. His happiness had always rubbed off on us. He'd made us laugh. We'd loved him so much.

We both went down to him and, stroking his head gently, said our goodbyes and thanked him for his willing work and faithfulness. He lifted his head, gave a little sigh and died. We buried him there at the farm but felt him around for months – running in the wind on his three legs beside the others, at the work he'd loved so much.

Soon after this we had a happy phone call from Marlo with the news that she was pregnant. Life can be like that. Darkness and light. Joy and sorrow. She asked if I'd like to be with her for the birth of their baby. I thought about it but influenced by my own experience and therefore my only real knowledge of childbirth, I thought it should be a private and special time between her and Mark alone.

We'd just finished seeding when Otto Patrick Pennington was born after a thirty-six hour labour. We went to Sydney a few days later. As I held another beautiful bundle of new life, I felt a love every bit as big as for Ethan and Jacinte. Marlo and Mark were wrung out from days of nurses' conflicting information over Otto's jaundice. Some were saying it was common and nothing to worry about. Others were saying it could be life threatening. Marlo's anxiety had reduced her to tears when, with a sudden burst of conviction, Mark said, 'We're taking him home. We're only five minutes from the hospital and we can bring him back any time if we need to.'

Marlo, still terrified that something could go wrong, was gently consoled by her decisive and caring husband. I could see he believed in their ability to take care of this darling little boy, as scary as it was for them at the time.

Coming back to the Barossa to live was on their agenda. They wanted Otto and any future children to have the kind of country upbringing they themselves had enjoyed. But I couldn't imagine them giving up their work in Sydney.

Difficult as it was, I had to leave my daughter then to return to work on the farm. I phoned her often. She struggled with new motherhood and my heart ached for her, and at not being there to help her.

A few months later Marlo asked if we'd like to come over and look after Otto for three weeks while she worked as production assistant on a big television commercial. Mark, as usual, had several jobs on the go.

Warren isn't fond of Sydney and a week there was all he could take. Being cooped up all day in a small flat, sent him stir crazy. And he can't handle the lack of eye contact in the streets, the indifference. He'd be out and about in Rose Bay feeling alienated, isolated. One day, in defiance of the anonymity, he piped cheerfully to a passer-by, 'G'day, mate.'

The bloke nearly jumped out of his skin. Probably thought he was about to be accosted.

Warren went home and I stayed for another two weeks. Before I left Sydney, Marlo and Mark told me they'd be househunting in the Barossa at Christmas time. Being near their family was that important to them. They were coming home. It was the best news I could imagine.

## THIRTY-EIGHT

Our friend Roly was still selling real estate. We were at the farm when he phoned to say he was in the area and would like to pop in to say hello. He walked into our kitchen twenty minutes later with excitement written all over his face. I made a coffee, and when the three of us were sitting down, he reached into the inside pocket of his jacket and pulled out a piece of paper which he unfolded, smoothed and slid across the table towards Warren and me.

'What's this?' asked Warren, grinning at Roly's exuberance.

'Read it,' sparkled Roly.

It was an offer from one of our neighbours – to buy Eversden. The amount on the piece of paper was double the price we'd paid for it four years earlier. It seemed unbelievable. One thing I'd learned from being the mother of teenagers is how to remain poker-faced at startling news. Warren did a pretty good job too on this occasion. I don't think it was the reaction Roly was expecting. While it was a huge sum of money, I knew Warren was happier at work than he'd been in his whole life, and would be hard pressed to give up his farm at this stage. His dreams and goals for it hadn't been reached, and he was only halfway through his breeding programme to have a flock of pure Dohne ewes.

We told Roly we'd think about it, and after he left we talked about the offer. Warren said he couldn't think of anything he'd rather do than farm, even if we did have the money.

'I'm not ready to retire,' he said. 'What would I do?'

I nodded. I knew how my husband's passions ran. He was not about to give up the farm he'd dreamed of for so long.

He phoned Roly next day with his answer. Roly too has farming in his blood, and while he probably believed we'd made the wrong decision, he said he understood. Warren phoned and thanked the neighbour for his offer and explained why we would decline it. As I sit here now, I can only imagine how different our lives would have been, had our answer been yes that day.

Roly and Donna invited us to spend a few days with them in a friend's shack near Marion Bay. Set among sandhills and dense coastal flora, it was a peeling-green corrugated iron hut whose patina described its age. When I walked into it, I closed my eyes and sighed with delight. Firstly, it smelled right – the smell of heating water, of condiments in the cupboard, of seaweed, salty sand, collected shells. I love a shack, each one unique – the armchairs that don't match, the shabby lino floors, the retro dresser full of miss-matched coffee mugs and crockery, candlewick bedspreads, the cupboard full of games.

A set of louvre windows was atilt, giving vent to a salty breeze and frame to a sparkling blue sea surging softly onto pristine sand. Not another building was in sight. As evening fell we took a table and assorted deck chairs to the sandy clifftop just outside. With lanterns lit, we opened a bottle of crisp, cold Riesling. Inevitably fresh fish was the fare, and as we ate and drank, talked and laughed, we watched the night come in and colour the small tree trunks black, and the hut disappear

– all but the lantern-lit window. A shack takes me back to my beginnings and reminds me that life can be led very simply.

~

Some of my happiest times as a child were spent in humble dwellings. My dad's brother, Lindsay, and his wife lived in an old limestone cottage on their dairy farm at Port Wakefield in South Australia. From time to time we'd visit them there.

Aunty Zena loved her cows. As she'd summon them for the evening milking, my sister and I would stand on the fence to watch the distant string of them respond to her high-pitched calls. *'C'mon Daisy. Bella. Clara. C'mon.'*

Leaders those. With udders swinging, they'd all eventually amble through the gate beside us, offering sideways glances with pretty eyes. Every one had a name, a unique personality, and a very wet nose. In the dairy, I revelled in the atmosphere of happy industry. Milk, rhythmically and mechanically extracted from the soft sensuous udders, travelled unseen through shuddering hoses then swirled through little glass domes at the end where large clanking cans were rolled into place to receive the creamy bounty. My aunt's shrill voice cut through the noise of the motor. Uncle Lin was a taciturn man whose answers were minimal.

'Yep.'

'Over there.'

'Nope.'

'Almost.'

The routine was the same morning and night, but we were rarely there for the pre-dawn milking.

After playing all day in haystacks, with pups, or collecting eggs, we'd be dead tired by teatime. Once the herd had been milked and were filing back to the freedom of their paddock, the dairy would be cleaned from top to bottom. Aunty Zena would return to the house then to cook us all a remarkable meal. In summer we'd eat in the dining room. Dark and cool, the room smelled of soot from the large open fireplace. There was no electricity and so kerosene lamps would be lit and placed on the long cedar table. Meals were hearty – usually a roast of lamb or beef with roast vegetables, followed by generous servings of trifle or pudding with custard *and* homemade ice cream. In wintertime we'd eat in the kitchen where there was always a fire in the wood stove. With tummies full and tired as a chain gang, we'd be tucked in then – all three of us in a double bed in the candlelit spare room. We'd drift towards sleep with the old-house sound of the grandfather clock ticking away as Mum sang us the song she always sang there.

> *'My grandfather's clock was too large for the shelf*
> *So it stood ninety years on the floor*
> *It was taller by half than the old man himself*
> *Though it weighed not a penny weight more*
> *It was bought on the morn of the day that he was born*
> *And was always his treasure and pride*
> *But it stopped short never to go again*
> *When the old man died...'*

~

Marlo and Mark bought their house in the Barossa. While they'd been home for Christmas we'd driven them around as they looked at properties for sale. As they were returning to Sydney next day, there'd been a sense of urgency as we drove from place to place. About to throw it in without results on this stifling hot day, they were prompted by something unknown to look at just one more. The agent was still preparing this one for the papers. We drove in to the property. The house was old, eclectic, junk everywhere. Warren did a U-turn and was driving out through the gate when Marlo said, 'Dad, can we go back in. I've always pictured pepper trees.'

There were several of those. The main house had been Stockwell Winery, converted a couple of years earlier into a two-storey, unique dwelling which was now vacant. We looked in through the windows. There were solid timber roof beams, pine tongue-and-groove walls, quirky windows and doors. Behind it and adjoining stood a stone building that had once belonged to the pub next door. Cobb and Co. had passed through here regularly in the eighteen hundreds and rested their horses overnight in this beautiful stable. It had been converted by the vendors into a B&B. Joining these two buildings together were a couple of raw and roughly made rooms with potential – a welcome challenge for Mark, born renovator. The yard held no trace of a garden, which opened a world of possibilities for our green-thumbed Marlo. Down the back beside a creek, stood a self-contained cabin ready for letting. The thriving pub next door had a young entrepreneurial couple at the helm – the ambience they'd created and their menu so appealing that people were coming from the city to dine there. An old stone flour mill could be seen through tall gum trees a hundred metres away. All this on three quarters of an acre on the edge of the Valley. This would be their home.

State Theatre Co. knew of Mark's imminent return and re-instated him as lighting designer. Soon after, he was also offered an executive position with the Adelaide Festival of Arts, which he accepted. His work as outdoor events manager for the Sydney Festival continued.

Because much of Mark's work could be done from home, Marlo was able to say yes to a job as second assistant director on an S A Film Corp. film, as well as some part-time work with Maggie Beer, and voice-overs for radio and television.

Linc's wife Nic had returned to part-time work as a district nurse, and her name was synonymous with outstanding expertise, and a calm and lovely manner. She also developed a work-from-home business – designing and creating kids' nightwear.

Two thousand and six brought good opening rains. Again we sowed our crops. July's follow-up showers were encouraging. I was to have my sixtieth birthday in November and so, preferring the idea of a holiday to having a party, I booked a trip to Bali. We had enough frequent flyer points for our airfares, and knew the cost of living over there would be no more than at home.

In August it stopped raining. From then we watched our crops struggle through the growing season trying to find any dampness left in the soil. By October we dared to hope they may still come to something if it stayed reasonably cool, but out of the blue, a heat wave. An anomalous hell-fire blast of nature savaged the land for four long days of above forty-five degrees. The plants withered as the last remnants of moisture were drawn from them.

When the heat had passed we walked through the crops – in the silence of knowing there was nothing we could do. There was little left. The disappointment was oppressive. A physical gravity settled on me so that my legs felt like lead. I was drained of hope and the belief that I could rise above it. Mother Earth herself took on a surreal, even alien guise, and ceased to feel like the friend I'd always loved.

We didn't talk about it – words were useless – but I knew Warren was whipped too. After a few days, with the will we've always found to hurl off soul-destroying emotions, we began to think of those who had lost so much more in the Black Saturday bushfires and so, re-summoning our strength, we prepared for another year.

Thankfully our flock was growing and we'd get something from the wool and lambs. We had income too from our rentals, and we'd invested money with our friends, Sarah and Sparky – into their new winemaking business. No documents – just a gentleman's handshake. A wonderful feeling to trust friends to that extent. We knew they were people of integrity.

The only job I hated, and that with a passion, was shifting sheep from The Ranch down the Mallee Highway one kilometre, along Gravestocks Road another three, to Eversden. And back again. The highway teems with semis and B-doubles, all ripping along at more than a hundred kilometres an hour. I park our ute on a bend at one end of this stretch, and Glen parks his at the other. Even with our high visibility signs, flashing lights, hazard lights and flags, the semis often fail to slow.

On one occasion a truckie must have been half asleep. I was standing on the edge of the road near all my signage, waving my flag furiously with the realisation he wasn't slowing down. Warren was on his quadbike in the middle of the road with his back to the looming semi. Driving a large mob of sheep with the help of the dogs, he was trusting me to stop the traffic. With the fear that something terrible was about to happen, the scene before me went into slow motion. They're all going to be killed, I thought – Warren, dogs, sheep. This guy's not stopping. Suddenly he hit the brakes. Warren turned to see him just metres away. The sheep scattered in all directions.

My husband switched his UHF radio to the truckies' channel and offered some lurid advice to the "cowboy" truckie, while I tried to make sense of my ragdoll legs.

There have been numerous close shaves like that, and although we've had to do this drive countless times, I still tremble for the hour or so it takes to complete the job.

By now we were running a thousand ewes. The new shearing shed and yards were a dream to work. Andrea, our wool-classer, and Trish, her roustabout daughter, were hardworking, salt-of-the-earth people, and we valued their expertise and mateship.

Trish is another of those people who sees the humorous side of everything, and we've had our share of laughs – so uplifting after a hard day's work. Andrea has helped with more than classing. She's a vegetable grower extraordinaire and we have been fortunate over the years to receive baskets full of the freshest organic food and preserves, all lovingly produced from her garden and chook house. She bought the derelict Parrakie pub many years ago, and over the years has converted this rambling old stone building into a comfortable home. She herself has been plumber, electrician, mason, landscaper, painter. In her younger years Andrea classed wool in some of the big sheds of Western Queensland. As we've enjoyed "happy hours" together at my farmhouse kitchen table, she has spun some entertaining yarns about her life on these stations.

October was time for our holiday in Bali – the country still reeling from the Sari club bombings. After a couple of days on the island we learned how to handle the intense pressure to buy and how to have fun with the good-natured Balinese. It was a joyful time for us – sitting in their restaurants, drinking *Bintang*, eating traditional food and being forever fascinated with the industry of the people.

We wanted to see as much of Bali as possible and thanks to our competent driver, Wayan, we achieved that. At a place off the beaten track, near Singaraja on the north coast, our accommodation was a hut set in beautiful gardens on the beach. Only a handful of people were staying there and that night we ate in. The staff set a table for us at the water's edge – white cloth, silver service, candles. Scent of frangipani wafted through the air. Padding through the sand in bare feet, the cheerful, attentive waiters brought us numerous courses and quality wine to compliment the food. All this for a *total* of twelve Australian dollars.

We returned home from Bali refreshed and steeled, we thought, for the heartache of a non-existent harvest.

Again we had to increase our overdraft limit as it had cost us more to grow the crops than we yielded from them.

The next year, two thousand and seven, some things had to change. We could no longer employ John as we'd done for several weeks each year. To save money on crutching, Warren decided to hire an automatic handler and do it himself. The huge contraption that grabbed the sheep and turned them over in a cradle was so noisy that the animals were terrified of going up the ramp to meet their fate, which was only a clean bottom, not Armageddon, and by evening Warren had popped his cork over the inadequacy of the "monster" to hold the young sheep securely. He'd spent most of the day expending more energy trying to re-position sheep than he would have if he'd crutched them all on the board in the shed. My job had been to push them up the ramp and it hadn't taken long before I was having to lift each one from a stubborn sitting position. The job took nine hours and I had never been so physically exhausted. Our spirits were dashed by the end of that day, but in the morning, as our boots impressed the soft, loamy earth of the Southern Mallee, we were restored for work again.

In September, Claudia Frances, Linc and Nic's third child, was born – in the same room of the Tanunda Hospital that Linc had been born in thirty-eight years earlier. Picture-book pretty with an abundance of dark hair, she has been almost constantly happy. Her eyes twinkle with joie de vivre as she runs to us for a cuddle whenever she sees us. Our family was growing and we loved that.

By October of that year we could again see disaster looming. Again our crops were failing. The country was now in the grips of the worst drought in Australian history – a behemoth drought that disfigured the landscape, and the souls of men and women. We were now in danger of losing everything we'd worked for. Our energy, faith, and joy in work was almost depleted. Retirement was large on my mind and so too our neighbour's earlier offer to buy the farm.

'There are other things I want to do with my life now,' I said to Warren.

'But you're writing your book,' he said. 'What else would you want to do?'

Over three years, I'd found time for a page a week.

'I want to see more of our family and friends, write *more*, paint again, learn to play the piano, travel, go to the theatre.' I took a deep breath. 'What would you do?'

'I don't know,' he said.

Warren has always known what he wants to do, and in that moment it was still only to farm. I knew he would not leave the land on this note.

The success of our enterprise relied on our unity, and although I knew I could dip my toe into retirement if I wanted to, in reality there was something in me too that was hunting down the prize of one last bumper harvest.

My old school pal Rosemary was about to turn sixty. She'd been living in Sydney since the early seventies. Knowing she was coming back to the Barossa around this time, I organised a surprise birthday lunch for her. As close as she, Jill and I had been as kids, she and Jill hadn't seen each other for almost forty years. When Rosemary caught sight of Jill in my house, she gathered us both into her arms as the three of us cried, laughed and hugged. Marion came too – the girlfriend with whom we'd shared so much of the rawness of youth. It had been at least forty years since we two had seen or spoken to each other, but as she walked up the steps to my house, I saw only the seventeen year old girl of all those years before.

Over a long lunch, the four of us rekindled the love that had never died, and we sky-larked like school girls through our rich reminiscences. For two or three hours our poignant adolescence was re-lived. I longed to do this more often, but in my heart I knew that the wonderfulness of that day could never be had again. Even so, meeting up with old friends became a category in my retirement plan.

Although it had been decided that we'd continue to farm, Warren did decide to put The Ranch on the market. We needed to reduce our overdraft, and gearing down might be the way to go, he said.

We'd been happy with Elders Rural Bank. Our manager had sat with us in our home once or twice a year while we discussed plans for the coming cropping seasons and worked through our budgets – for what they were worth. How could anyone have predicted the three successive years of continuing drought that lay ahead?

We'd established a relationship of mutual respect with our regional manager and felt he was acting in our interest more than any previous manager had done. In January, two thousand and eight, after yet another dismal harvest, we phoned him to arrange a meeting. We needed to know if the bank was prepared to continue its support. He rarely answered his phone, and the protocol with him was to leave a message, which Warren did. He hadn't phoned back in a week and so Warren rang again. After constant calls and messages from us, it was *ten weeks* before he got back. It was like waiting for an old dog to get to his destination. By then I was at my wits' end – lacking sleep and overwrought with wondering what was in store for us. Finally, the meeting we'd been waiting for was arranged. We sat with the manager in our home. He apologised profusely for the length of time he'd taken to respond. Apart from his utter lack of professionalism, he was a nice bloke, and after ten weeks of my wanting to throttle him, I was surprised at the sense of forgiveness I had towards him, even though he'd offered no excuse. I was amazed too at Warren's calm as he said, 'Now, are you guys happy to continue supporting us? How are Elders sailing? We've heard rumours of some financial challenges with the company.'

'Look, we're fine,' he said. 'We understand what the farmers are going through, and you need to put those crops in.'

*Yes we do,* I thought emotionally, *and we've been waiting for ten bloody weeks to know if we can.*

'You're not nervous about us?' asked Warren.

'No, we're not,' he said.

It was an enormous relief. Although it was late to do so, Warren ordered fertiliser. It was now in short supply, and the price had gone through the roof.

Early in May, we had a phone call from our Elders real estate agent. 'We've had an offer on The Ranch,' he said.

'Oh?' I said, 'What's the story?'

He told me what the prospective buyer had offered and said, 'He's a local guy and would like immediate possession.'

I relayed the information to Warren who was driving. We had five hundred ewes on the property who'd just begun to drop lambs and couldn't be moved. We'd ordered enough fertiliser to crop several hundred acres of it and besides, it wasn't enough money.

'The offer's a bit short,' I said to the agent, after a quick pow-wow between my husband and me.

Later that day Warren phoned our bank manager and told him.

'No, not enough. You don't want to give it away,' he said.

We didn't hear anything more from the agent. Later we wondered why he hadn't sat down with us to see if we could come to an arrangement to suit both parties – work it through to the end.

In May it rained, a little. The farmers fired up their tractors, hooked up their ploughs but the land was parched. We were going to need long, soaking rains before subsoil moisture could be restored.

Wayne, Erica's ex-husband, was having a quiet time at work and came to help with seeding. With two tractors going, he and Warren got the crops sown in good time.

Because of the hard years behind us, there was now little grass for the sheep and no hay, so we had to sell some of our ewe lambs, which under normal circumstances we would have kept for breeding. This gave us some much needed income.

In June we had a call from our bank manager. He needed to speak to us. As he walked through our door, his eyes told me that something dreadful was about to unfold.

*Oh my God what?* I thought.

There were no overtures.

'The bank wants its money back,' he said.

We both sat down. He kept standing.

'It doesn't make sense,' he said emotionally. 'There's no logic to it.' We gestured to him to sit down. 'Head office don't know you. They don't know your fighting spirit.'

His platitudes had no effect.

'When?' asked Warren, despair written on his face.

'By December.'

Christmas. This meant either finding another bank to finance us, which was highly unlikely, or selling all or part of the farm by the end of the year. We received a standard letter about how failure to repay the loan would result in foreclosure, and in that case the farm would go up for auction. A fire sale. As long as there was a bid to cover our debt to the bank, it would be sold, even if the bid was way below market value. The courting words of the bank rep who'd visited us six years earlier were ringing in my ears – '*We understand the farmer and his needs.*'

Our last remnant of trust in banks, that had been tenuous anyway, had gone. I felt empty. Gutted.

We went back to the person who'd made the offer on The Ranch but it seemed he'd spent his money on new machinery and was out of the picture. My sense of panic rose.

We had equity in other properties. I would set to work to see if we could gain some respite using that. Warren was relieved to have me handle this while he continued to work the farm, which could not and would not be ignored. His mind raged daily against the prospect of being beaten at this stage of his life.

I phoned a local solicitor. One of his clients was a private lender with whom we had a small mortgage against one of our houses.

'We're looking to borrow some more money against the house,' I said.

'How much are you looking for?'

I told him.

'I'm sure that'll be okay. I'll speak to my client and get back to you.'

We had the loan within three weeks at an interest rate much lower than the bank's. How deeply we appreciated having lived in this community all our lives and having gained the trust and respect that a business transaction like this requires. We paid off our overdraft with Elders.

Each month we held our breath for rain. We prayed as clouds swelled, blackened, then disappeared. The pathetic spits of rain just teased us, and although constantly thirsty with lack of any moisture deeper than the surface, the Australia-hardened crops grew, albeit sparsely. In October we drove around them. The heads of grain were again beginning to dry, too early. Warren would snap one off here and there, rub it between his palms, and mostly chaff would blow away in the wind. Terrifying. How could we handle another year without income? In this drought we sensed that even some people outside the farming industry were aware of the farmers' plight and were trying to imagine what it would be like to manage their mortgages without an income. There were daily stories in the newspapers.

The neighbour who'd made the generous offer four years earlier was in the same drought and no longer in buying mode. He asked if he could lease our farm with the view to buying it in two years' time, but we needed more income than that would provide – to pay our interest and live. So we had to keep working, and trust.

Two thousand and two and 'three had been good years in the Southern Mallee. What restitution it would be for us to experience one last bountiful harvest. Yet I noticed a shift in Warren's passions. I could see him preparing mentally to leave the land he'd loved for so long. He began to intersperse reading four-wheel drive and caravan magazines with his farmers' bible – *The Stock Journal*. He talked of trips he'd like to take, of restoring old Land Rovers.

We spoke to Roly and put Eversden up for sale. We knew it wasn't a good time. There was no money about, but it would be a good way to test the market. There were locals interested but everyone was in the same boat – there was debt to be dealt with before more land could be purchased.

These last few years had taken their toll on me. Fear, insomnia, withdrawal were unwelcome demons. Being with our beautiful family was one of my only respites, but there seemed to be too little time even for that. I had to throw off this debilitating sadness. I needed to be as mentally strong and fit as Warren was, for us to survive. I prayed for it, and one morning woke up with a new and healing peace – an absolute knowledge that there was a plan for our good.

# THIRTY-NINE

Lifelines often arrive when we need them most. I was shopping one day and bumped into Phyl Friend, mother of my teenage sweetheart, Leon. I hadn't seen her for years. We chatted a while and I asked her how old she was.

'Sue, I'm going to be ninety in a couple of weeks. Can you believe it?'

'What a milestone,' I said. 'I should come and have a coffee with you.'

'That would be lovely, Sue,' she said in the vivacious young voice I remembered.

I rang her on the day of her birthday and she told me that Leon and Chris had organised a birthday lunch for her, with her nearest and dearest.

'Come and have a coffee tomorrow,' she said.

I was surprised by the emotion I felt at the thought of Leon being there. It would be great to see him again. It had been forty-four years. I wondered how he'd feel about it. Would he be aloof, or warm? Would he be fat, bald?

Next morning, I forced my way through consuming nervousness and went to Phyl's home. Leon opened the door, and his arms. He was taller than I remembered and was still slim, strong and fit. I wasn't surprised to see his grey hair, but he'd lost none of it.

The house was buzzing with the excitement of celebration. Phyl looked amazing – beautifully dressed, slim, petite, attractive – more like seventy than ninety.

Although there was still the same quiescence about Leon, we chatted comfortably, trying to fit the happenings of the best part of our lives into two wee hours. He told me he'd married fourteen years after we parted, had two sons, and then separated from his wife after twenty years. He was now with Suzanne – petite, vivacious, fifteen years or so younger than Leon. Chris was there with his wife of forty years. He too greeted me warmly. He'd had a medical practice in Esperance for decades. Leon had owned a dive shop and boat charter business in Wollongong for as long. He was a professional diver. I asked him if he'd suffered any ill effects from the accident he'd had whilst in the Air Force.

'No, I've been really well,' he said. 'Suzanne loves to cook. She keeps me healthy.'

He seemed happy. He showed me photos of his two handsome sons and told me he was to be a grandfather for the first time in a few months. That so many years had gone by was hard to imagine. One day we'd been teenagers in love, and now here we were talking about our grandchildren. The time flew and it was time for me to go. As we hugged each other goodbye, it felt like part of the timeless hug we'd left each other with forty-four years earlier. Only happier.

It's said as we get older the past becomes larger. It's almost intoxicating to revisit the days when we were so young and carefree.

Harvest was heartbreaking. With no rain, the lupins had all died. Warren turned the sheep onto them. The header scraped around other paddocks reaping more dust than anything. Again, our income did not cover costs. Was this climate change? Was this what we were to expect of the future? The average rainfall here was supposed to be sixteen inches. We'd had nowhere near that for years.

That Christmas, Warren's gift to me was a set of CD's he'd found in an op shop. They were of famous tenors singing the songs of perhaps my mother's childhood, but also of a time lodged in my psyche from somewhere not quite known – something primordial – perhaps from the grandfather I never knew. I'd been told he loved this music. Richard Tauber's *We'll Gather Lilacs*, Joseph Schmidt's *Tiritomba*, John McCormack's *Roses of Piccardy* – a far cry from Dylan, jazz, and even the classical music I'd been listening to for years, but they struck a deep chord. It was the first time a gift had moved me to tears. After absolutely all, I realised how much I meant to Warren, and that Christmas was his time to buy me something special – to show, apart from his appreciation, his deep love for me. What moved me most was how well he knew that this gift would touch me. No-one else could have known it.

Warren was the first true grazier in the Grocke lineage. There'd been vignerons before who'd done a little farming on the side and run a few sheep, but Warren had taken a lifetime to build to this point where he had a farm and a flock big enough to provide a good living for us – if only we weren't suffering the worst drought in Australia's recorded history.

In all my years, I had never seen the Barossa, with its reliable twenty-two inch rainfall, looking so forlorn. With drastic water restrictions there was a death knell about the gardens – a dryness, a brownness I could hardly bear to look at. Trees were dying by the hundreds. The Barossa is scattered with vineyards that, no matter what, are green for more than half the year. Now, even the vignerons were struggling, with not only water restrictions but a world glut of wine that had caused prices to plummet. With the pall of the global economic meltdown on top of all this, the ethos of our community was at an all-time low.

Earlier this year, a dear friend, Sue (Mum had lived in her barn and Marlo had boarded with her), had asked me to undertake Power of Attorney in her affairs as she succumbed to the spectre of dementia. With my lunch-friend Marion (not school buddy), who'd been a legal secretary for years, as co-POA, we set to work. Once or twice a week we'd meet at Sue's home and help her sort through years of accumulated papers and documents. The mere paying of bills was beyond her now and we undertook to set up direct transfers, deal with banking and investments, cancel subscriptions to countless mail order companies, organise home help and tie up a hundred loose ends. While Sue was still largely unaware of the seriousness of her condition, her sense of humour was thankfully unaffected, and we had a lot of laughs, but as time went on, she began to lose the confidence she'd once had as a fiercely independent woman. Having spent her childhood in England, she'd seen much of the war and The Depression before being sent to Australia where she'd attended Clyde School for Girls in Woodend, Victoria. After the war, she'd married an English agronomist, David, who took her to live on a tea plantation in Uganda. In a primitive environment, she'd lived with the blacks whilst raising her young daughter.

Now she was almost totally dependent on us. In despair, she knew it was time to leave her beautiful home. We took her to visit the best aged-care facilities in the region, several times, while she gradually got used to the idea of living in an environment she never could have imagined for herself. Sue had come from a family of old English money, and now a lifetime of collected antiques and treasures had to be sorted and packed. Although it couldn't have been easy to relinquish them, the trauma was lessened by the fact that Sue's daughter, who'd come from interstate to help clear the house, was happy to take most of them. Sue's son and his partner who lived nearby, spent some time helping too. Now it was time for Sue to wage the brave fight to let go of all that had been her life, in exchange for a bed-sitter within a complex for people in the final stages of their lives.

It took Marion and me another several weeks with the time we had available, to empty the house of all that was left, and present the property for sale. The whole affair took us nearly two years. I'd had to become super-efficient at finding time to undertake this while running our home, our rental properties, helping with the farm and our little ones. I absolutely ached at not having enough time with them.

It was a taxing two years for Marion too, who was and still is grieving for her daughter and granddaughter who died in a tragic road accident. Sometimes there can be enough pain for a lifetime in one moment. The mother of all suffering must be to lose a child. We give our children their names and expect them to be using them long after we have passed on. I can't imagine what it must be like to cope with such a loss.

Through and despite these tough economic times, Linc's vineyard contracting business was growing, but he empathised deeply with his clients who were now struggling to cover their costs. The grape glut that Warren had predicted was now upon the Valley. At vintage time, Linc ran two teams who worked around the clock – weather permitting. As was normal though, as business owner and responsible for all logistics, he had little time for sleep, and by the end of vintage was almost robotic.

So routinely, just prior to this "silly season" each year, he and his family would take two weeks' holiday at Wallaroo Beach. Marlo, Mark and Otto, and Warren and I sometimes spent a few days with them there – a precious family time of fun, talking, swimming, games, sleeping, reading, the stuff childhood memories are made of. And for us this year a sea-coloured distraction from the brownness of drought.

In December, two thousand and eight, the skies opened. The dust of years that had settled on the trees, streets and buildings, began to spatter and speckle away with the first blessed drops of rain. Rain. People were euphoric. From the telegraph wires in our back paddock, a string of sulphur-crested cockatoos hung upside down like fluttering flags – ecstatic too about the deluge. We dared to hope the demon drought had broken.

Marlo was pregnant, and again asked if I'd like to be with her for the birth. Still I had my reservations, but this time realised it was more about my doubting whether I had the courage for it. She blossomed through her pregnancy, and it was wonderful to have her so near this time, and to bond with the little one in her belly. On April the first, we had a phone call just before midnight.

'It's on,' lowed Marlo from the car.

I leapt out of bed.

'Are you coming?' I said to Warren.

'Yep,' he said as he clambered out of bed and began to put on his clothes. This surprised me. We hadn't even spoken about being there together.

I thought we'd just mill in the corridor but Marlo was doing well and wanted us in their room. We crept in. Mark's lovely mother, Joan, was there too. The attending nurse's eyes widened.

'Marlo and Mark, are you okay with your family in here?' she asked.

'Yes, we are,' said Marlo happily. 'Mum, have you got the camera ready?'

A close friend of Marlo's, another midwife, had been invited to help. We'd become a crowd in the small room. Watching Mark's powerful love and caring, and Marlo working so bravely and peacefully to bring this gorgeous little girl into the world, was a privilege beyond words. Within two and a half hours the babe's head presented – deep blue with the umbilical cord wrapped around her neck. The midwives handled the emergency calmly and competently. I took an amazing series of photographs that Marlo and Mark were delighted to have later. A far cry this birth, from her thirty-six hour labour with Otto four years earlier. After little Sylvie's first ravenous feed, we all had a cuddle. One of the few regrets I have is not being with Marlo for Otto's birth. This had been such a joyful experience.

Now we had five beautiful grandchildren.

Ethan at eight is a highly creative child. At the age of three he developed an exceptional interest in piano – an obsession almost. The moment he'd walk into our home he'd head for my old cassette tapes and put on his favourite – *Honky-Tonk Man*. One day we made a make-believe piano together, out of cardboard, and as the honky-tonk music filled the room, he pretended he was the pianist – for an hour. He was four. Encouraged by my applause, I could see him imagining himself as performer extraordinaire. The energy of it was powerful. Just recently he discovered the joy of writing. Inspired by my industry, he's written his own short biography and is now writing stories.

'Grandma,' he said to me recently, 'the time just flies when I'm writing, and I hate it when I'm interrupted. I just have to get it down.'

I understand it well.

Jacinte loves to paint with me. Although she's a social butterfly, she enjoys her own company and gets lost in creating beautiful works of art. When she started school, she could write her name and no more. Within months she was writing prolifically. I read one of her essays – two pages (albeit with spelling errors) about her annual beach holiday. Her teacher had been amazed at how quickly she'd learned the power of language.

Otto is four and has been profoundly articulate since the age of two. I can sit with him and discuss anything – from the habits of ants to the planets. With the wisdom of Solomon, he seems to have an understanding of everything under the sun. We took him to the farm with us for shearing while Marlo and Mark were overseas. Five of our shearing team had come in for lunch and as they ate they were talking about their farms. Burly blokes all of them, they filled the room. Otto at two and a half and still tiny, was standing against the wall, listening with great intent. There was a lull in the conversation. He put his hands behind his back, one foot up against the wall and said in the deepest voice he could find, 'You boys got tractors?'

At this stage his interests lie in machinery – cars, trucks, tractors, anything with wheels and engines – a boy after his grandfather's heart.

Claudia at two is a bundle of sunshine. She lights up a room with her smile and loves to be with all the kids, deeply interested in what they're doing – watching, learning, having a go.

Sylvie is nine months old now and a happy one as well. I could look at her angelic face all day. Already fiercely interested in everything going on around her, she'll be in on all the chatter as she gets older. I love them all deeply and dream of being able to help with the nurturing of their gifts as they grow and we retire.

In April it rained again – a substantial opening for the farmers. I offered to help with seeding. Warren had planned to put in another seven hundred acres but because we were down on sheep numbers, and consequently potential income, he decided to put in a thousand. Scaring ourselves, we'd asked, 'What are the odds of another year of drought?'

But we had to take the risk.

We bought some cereal rye from one of our neighbours. It was expensive at four hundred dollars a tonne but would do well in drought conditions. The crops went in without a hitch. In the one hundred and eighty horsepower Belarus tractor, I cultivated and harrowed for several weeks, while Warren followed with tractor and seed drill. As the last of the barley went in, it rained again – a good, soaking rain. In July another inch and a half, and in August the same. Our relief and gratitude was huge and healing.

Water catchments in our state began to fill. The dead trees and gardens were removed. Replanting began. By September our Barossa looked as beautiful as I'd ever seen it. Nature is so forgiving.

The Mallee, normally tough as old Land Rovers, had been tested to its limits, but it too burst into new life. Birds that had disappeared from the region returned. It seemed we would get the good yields we'd worked for and dreamed of for so long. The crops and pastures grew well. We drove around them weekly, taking pleasure in the wonderful sight. The land was stroking us now. Our sheep looked magnificent. Lamb prices were good. We'd had a fantastic lambing percentage – a hundred and fifty percent from the Dohnes. One Monday early in November we drove around the lambs at The Ranch. They were six months old.

'A lot of these look almost ready for market,' I said to Warren.

He'd dreamed of producing hundred dollar lambs and said, 'Yes, they're not far off. Another two weeks, I reckon. We'll draft off a hundred or so and get some cash in before harvest.'

A sheep sale is held every Tuesday at Dublin – three hours from our farm. When we've got a mob ready to go, we bring them in on the Sunday evening to empty out. The carrier picks them up Monday and delivers them to the sale-yards, ready for the start of selling first thing Tuesday.

The night after we had been around these sheep, we saw a weather report. The presenter was warning of an abnormal heat wave expected to arrive later that week. Within four days we were into the longest, hottest November heat event on record – eight straight days of between thirty-eight and forty-five degrees. A savage, blasting, hell-fire heat. Within days, our prime lambs had lost their bloom from heat stress.

Then it rained.

We brought the lambs in and went through them. Standing in the damp yards amongst them, we could see that it would be many weeks now before they'd be ready for sale. The Mallee was quiet – sorry, empathetic. We walked amongst our sheep – quiet too. We felt their backs for condition.

'What about this one?' I'd say, hopefully, of a big-framed lamb.

'No, too backy. Feel him, he's lost it.'

It was like a storm had been through – a heat storm – and we were surveying the aftermath. We were inert with disappointment and discouragement. The sheep milled and murmured. They'd been through hell but it was over now.

Two weeks later we drafted off the best of them, eighty or so, and sent them to market. We needed the money. They made nowhere near the hundred dollars we would have got. We put the rest back on a paddock of lucerne that had come to life after the rain, but it would take a long time to get them back to prime condition.

When crops are flowering, over a period of three or four weeks, farmers listen to weather reports obsessively. They fear frost. We'd had only three or four through that winter. It seemed unlikely there'd be any more now in November, but still at flowering time we held our breath.

At six one morning, soon after Warren had got up, he came in to me and said, 'Come and have a look at this.'

I got up and followed him outside. Like a billion tiny white crabs, a hoarfrost had our land in its grips. Again the draining energy, the sadness, the silence.

It was difficult to gauge the damage. We decided to mow the cereal we'd planned to reap and bale it for hay instead. Then we mowed the oats we'd sown specifically for hay, and while we waited for it to season on the ground, it rained again.

'It's going to spoil,' I said to Warren, bracing myself for more carnage.

'No, it's okay. It's only light rain and the days are warm. We've cut it high enough. The breeze'll get underneath it.'

It did dry, and seasoned well, and our contractor baled it. Early next morning we drove out to inspect the job. Looking across the proud paddock of quality hay, I drew in a long thankful draught of the fragrant fodder air.

The patches of oats that hadn't been frosted were ripe, but it was too hot to reap them. It's illegal for farmers to reap on days of extreme fire danger. The huge metal header combs can hit rocks and create sparks. So we waited. Finally the heat passed, normal late spring weather returned, and the headers cranked up. As Warren began to reap, he realised that the recent heat wave had affected the grain and our yield would be down. He reaped for three days, then it began to rain. This is the one time of year on the land that farmers don't want rain. With too much of it, the grain will begin to sprout in the heads and rot. The rain was torrential. In November. More than we'd had for any other month of winter, or the year! Harvesting stopped. We could hardly believe what was happening to the remainder of our crops.

One day I was at the silos getting some wheat and barley tested. While the girl in the office was rigorously scrutinising our grain under magnification, I was talking to a couple of other farmers. There was something in their eyes – probably mine too. These years of hope followed by gut-wrenching disappointment had taxed us all to the nth degree. There was a melancholy about us all, a slowness of step, a drooping of shoulders, an effort to be philosophical that bordered on cynicism.

On top of the devastation, because of a world glut, this year's prices were thirty to forty percent lower than the previous year's. And as we stood in the silo office, we were being told that our grain was low grade with the rain, frost and heat damage. Our prices would be slashed even more.

It will take more than a good year with poor prices for the overdrafts to be reduced. It will take more than a good year with good prices to recover. It needs at least two of the best years imaginable. What keeps a farmer on the land is

> Waking up each morning to the sounds of crows and magpies
> wattle birds that call 'Wake-up! Wake-up!'
> It's being out the back
> delighting in a mob of well-proportioned ewes
> nuzzling into life a brand new drop of snow white lambs
> The smell of new mown hay
> The peace of mind in seeing it to the shed

It's the sigh of gentle breezes through the mallee
Noticing the earth change colour
with the passage of the plough across it after rain
the smell of that
It's the sight of big white fleeces
rolling off the backs of sheep
The tight full bales clanking out of presses

It's the beer with the team at the end of the day
and watching a sky that envisions tomorrow
as we talk of the good seasons
rarely the bad
It's the smells – of lanolin and sheep manure
The earthy smell through summer rain
Gum trees sweating oil in the savage heat
Exhaust of diesel power
that does the work of horses
it's sending in a load of finished lambs
to bring the best price ever
It's the distant drone and lights of tractors in the night.
These are the things we will miss.

~

We'll soon pack our bags and go. The dogs will miss it too. We've still got Jeppi. She'll be seventeen soon. She gets up early every morning and takes her exercise – a good walk round the farmyard. Not too far. Her eyesight's failing. At the sound of sheep in the yards, she'll come down for a look but knows better than to volunteer for work. She's no longer a match for the protective ewes, but what a worker she has been. Terry too is getting old – almost time for her to hang up her bark. When will it be?

There'll be a lot of work in getting the farm ready for sale – preparing and presenting plant and machinery, packing up.

The farmers around here call me "Mate". They know I'm Warren's help-mate.

Marlo said to us not long ago, 'I'm so proud of you guys. You've spent the best part of your lives farming, and against all odds you've never given up. It's a great achievement.'

It warmed me to hear these words. I'm married to a good, strong man. Marlo's right. He has never given up, and miraculously, and most importantly, we've become the best of friends.

We'll go back home to our Barossa, the Grocke homestead. We still have our land in the ranges and Warren will run a few sheep. He has projects on the desk and we'll travel. He wants to drive around the world. Who am I to doubt it will happen? We'll build a hut in the hills – a studio and family retreat. I'll be Grandma extraordinaire and take the children to see and hear the things they love.

My head is filled with the embryos of books, and paintings. My garden will become an outdoor art space, and we'll grow vegies. We'll have our friends come in for lunch and I'll prepare fine food. We'll drink good wine and talk the talk of farmers, artists, readers, friends. I'll retrieve my old vinyl from the cedar cupboard, hook up the turntable and listen to Dylan, Cat Stevens et al. Sitting on the beaches of Kakadu, we'll fish for bream and barramundi. I'll write. There'll be novels and another memoir in the life we still have planned.

Christmas will be at our place again this year. We'll leave the disappointments of harvest behind as we enjoy the rewards of being a family blessed. Erica's Mark, who loves to cook, will bring the turkey – succulent beyond compare. Her daughter, Amy, highly accomplished and awarded chef, will bring in something of exquisite flavour and presentation, and place it without fuss on our country table. Nic will make her special cheesecake. Something vegetarian and delicious will come out of Marlo and Mark's country kitchen. Our friend Sue will be with us as she's been for more Christmases than I can remember, and we'll talk about the days she can recall – those in England and Uganda. Mum will be there of course – adored Gigi of all the little ones. At eighty-three she'll bring songs, love and laughter, champagne and chocolates.

The beautiful children will be as excited as we always were when we were young. I used to read Dylan Thomas's *Memories of Christmas* to Linc and Marlo when they were kids. Linc was forty last week.

As we've loved our farms, we love the Barossa. It will be home as it always has been. It's where our ancestors settled in the early eighteen hundreds after leaving their homeland in search of religious freedom – to live the lives they chose. With their sepia faces they look out at us from old photographs on the walls and we are better able to imagine their lives now that we have lived so much of ours.

Soon, from our beautiful, rambling home, we'll remember to watch the vines all around us turn red and gold as autumn steps up. We'll have leisurely breakfasts on the terrace and watch the morning brush her colours onto the cliffs down by the river. Like a stage-set, the trunks of young gums down there look alight in the dawning sun as the neighbours' cows and goats come out. We have good neighbours – the Diers. We'll be able to say hello to them more often. They've been there as long as we have – generations. Perhaps we'll walk the three kilometres into town, do a little shopping, have a coffee. We'll touch our hats to Lin and Otto as we pass the cemetery just down the road. Perhaps there'll be water in Bethany Creek and we'll remember the rafts of our childhood. As we pass the carob trees near Gomersal Bridge we'll remember the kissing and cuddling in cars as we listened to Paul Anka and Bobby Rydell. We'll pass the grand old house that used to be the doctors' surgery, where I had two stitches put in my chin the day I fell off my bike. Past the churchyard where we used to play in the hedges and amongst the headstones. Past my first home with my giant fig tree. Past the bakery where we bought our lunch on Mondays – a pie and a sugar bun for one and fourpence. We had our wedding reception where Stan Arnold's bike shop used to be. The shop had been an eyesore to some of the townsfolk.

'Disgusting really,' they used to mutter.

Each morning he'd wheel all the bicycles waiting for repair out into the street and lean them against the wall so he had room inside to work. There were never less than twenty out there – dusty, rusty, cob-webby things.

We'll think we've seen Jack Traeger (Rosemary's father) walking down the street – a tall straight man in smart wool cardigan. Tweed cap. One hand behind his back, the other holding his pipe to his mouth – a little puff of smoke leaving him every now and then. But it can't be Jack. He died a while ago. It's just a tourist who looks like him. We'll come to Rosemary's old house and stop, remembering the night we danced and found each other there.

~

I dreamt it was shearing time. Dawn was breaking. I was standing near our sheds amongst implements and discarded bits of machinery. There was a sound like horses approaching, but it was our team, all those we'd employed over the years – shearers, tractor drivers, mechanics, fencers, roustabouts, contractors. They'd all come to pick up something from this heap in our yard, with our permission. Each was dressed in black, and I wished I had a camera to take a photo of all those who had played such an important part in our lives. Just one girl. After each had found their reward, we all just stood there silently in the growing light. Then the girl kicked the grassless, dusty soil.

'I can feel the promise of another year's pasture beneath my feet,' she said.

# Acknowledgments

**The team at Aurora**. Warren and I were in the car on one of our beloved outback trips when I received Linda Lycett's first email response to my submission: "I think you have an excellent story to tell … held me from beginning to end … full of action, love, pain and learning."

Encouraging words, but I was waiting for the 'however'. Then her next line: "Aurora House is interested in publishing 'So Big The Land'." From that moment to final production, the accomplished team at Aurora House has been professional, warm and delightful to work with. Thank you to Linda – founder/publisher; Ryan Waters – editor; Debbie Watson – proofreader; Sarah Vogler – publisher; Simon Critchell – cover designer. Relationships have been forged.

**Evan Davies**. When I first started this story, my computer skills were minimal. At my calls for help, my academic brother-in-law would walk down the hill to our house and acquaint me with Word's wonderful tools, get me out of some of the tangles I'd got myself into, and in his gentle manner, convince me that the computer was my friend. It is.

**Mark Pennington**. My son-in-law of amazing IT skills. There were terrifying moments of having lost a whole day's work – for example, the day my entire manuscript turned to 'z's. With amazing sleight of hand, he would restore the lost or scrambled. In his busy schedule he would make time, without hesitation, to help me.

**Renee Hancock**. My dear mum, who has bound our beautiful family together with her love and laughter. She has wanted to read every draft. I would delight in her sounds of amusement, her murmurings, her gasps as she read. I am so grateful for her encouragement every step of the way.

**Ethan, Jacinte, Otto, Claudia and Sylvie**. My precious grandkids. They have kept me on task, constantly asking: "How's your book going, Grandma? Are you an author yet?"

"No, still a writer," would be my answer. "When I'm published, I will be an author." I love them all dearly and want them to know how much their unfailing belief in me has meant.

**Lincoln Grocke**. My beautiful son – another of my willing helpers. I needed help with compiling the photos. He had just lost one of his mates in a tragic farm accident. In the middle of his shock, grief and assisting the bereaved family with funeral arrangements, he offered me his time to teach me the skills I needed to complete this task. In his extremely busy life he too has always been happy to come to my rescue, and, over a coffee and chat afterwards, has given me his special brand of encouragement and love.

**Marlo Grocke**. My precious daughter, who has helped me with her amazing literary knowledge. When I thought my manuscript was ready, I submitted it to a literary agent who told me she would like to work with me. Her first suggestion was that chronologically is not necessarily the best way to write an autobiography. While I wasn't sure how to go about it, I was completely open to the idea. The agent was not yet available to help me, and I was in a hurry.

Marlo knew what she meant. Often, at the end of her busy work days and over a glass of red wine or an ambrosial cup of organic tea, she would teach me how to interweave the past with the present. "Forget chronological," she said. "This is the story of your life with Dad. There'll be many opportunities to return to your childhood throughout the story." And so she taught me how to segue smoothly from one period of my life to another. As someone who likes everything in order, this took some getting my head around, but finally I got it. Thank you, my beautiful daughter, for all of this; for your help with social media going forward, and for your unfailing love and friendship.

**Warren**. My husband and best friend, who has encouraged me from the beginning of this work, interested each day to hear what I had written. There were times, through the drought years, I couldn't read aloud as it was all too raw and painful. I'd hand the manuscript to him to read, and when he too stalled with emotion, we'd take deep breaths and know that together we would overcome the trials that were battering us. I thank him for taking me on the amazing journey that has made me the woman I am today, and for his uncommon love, which warms me and makes me feel safe. Without him, it would not have been *this* story.

# About the Author

Sue Grocke lives in the Barossa Valley – a wine growing region of South Australia. For most of her life, she has farmed with her husband, but interspersed with this has been overseas travel and the outback wayfaring that delights and inspires her. Her two children and their families are a shining light in her life. She began writing poetry and short stories at an early age. Some of her awards include:

*FAWQ Toowoomba Literary Awards 2014* – Highly Commended Poem: 'Waiting Watching Listening'. Included in Anthology 'Northern Light'.

*Rolf Boldrewood Literary Awards 2016* – Highly Commended Poem: 'Beneath the Stars of Mother Country'.

*Poetica Christi Press Annual Poetry Competition 2017* – Special Mention Poem: 'Sleeping in Sturt's Stony Desert'. Included in Anthology 'Wonderment'.

www.ingramcontent.com/pod-product-compliance
Lightning Source LLC
Chambersburg PA
CBHW042248240426

43672CB00020BA/2987